Other Books and Series by Jeff Bowen

Applications for Enrollment of Chickasaw Newborn Act of 1905
Volumes I thru VII

Cherokee Intermarried White 1906 Volume I thru X

Applications for Enrollment of Creek Newborn Act of 1905
Volumes I, II, III, IV, V, VI, VII, VIII & IX

Visit our website at **www.nativestudy.com** to learn more about these and other books and series by Jeff Bowen

APPLICATIONS FOR ENROLLMENT OF CREEK NEWBORN ACT OF 1905

VOLUME IX

TRANSCRIBED BY
JEFF BOWEN

NATIVE STUDY
Gallipolis, Ohio
USA

Other Books and Series by Jeff Bowen

1901-1907 Native American Census Seneca, Eastern Shawnee, Miami, Modoc, Ottawa, Peoria, Quapaw, and Wyandotte Indians (Under Seneca School, Indian Territory)

1932 Census of The Standing Rock Sioux Reservation with Births And Deaths 1924-1932

Census of The Blackfeet, Montana, 1897- 1901 Expanded Edition

Eastern Cherokee by Blood, 1906-1910, Volumes I thru XIII

Choctaw of Mississippi Indian Census 1929-1932 with Births and Deaths 1924-1931   Volume I
Choctaw of Mississippi Indian Census 1933, 1934 & 1937, Supplemental Rolls to 1934 & 1935 with Births and Deaths 1932-1938, and Marriages 1936-1938 Volume II

Eastern Cherokee Census Cherokee, North Carolina 1930-1939 Census 1930-1931 with Births And Deaths 1924-1931 Taken By Agent L. W. Page Volume I
Eastern Cherokee Census Cherokee, North Carolina 1930-1939 Census 1932-1933 with Births And Deaths 1930-1932 Taken By Agent R. L. Spalsbury   Volume II
Eastern Cherokee Census Cherokee, North Carolina 1930-1939 Census 1934-1937 with Births and Deaths 1925-1938 and Marriages 1936 & 1938 Taken by Agents R. L. Spalsbury And Harold W. Foght Volume III

Seminole of Florida Indian Census, 1930-1940 with Birth and Death Records, 1930-1938

Texas Cherokees 1820-1839 A Document For Litigation 1921

Choctaw By Blood Enrollment Cards 1898-1914 Volumes I thru XVII

Starr Roll 1894   (Cherokee Payment Rolls) Districts: Canadian, Cooweescoowee, and Delaware Volume One
Starr Roll 1894 (Cherokee Payment Rolls) Districts: Flint, Going Snake, and Illinois   Volume Two
Starr Roll 1894 (Cherokee Payment Rolls) Districts: Saline, Sequoyah, and Tahlequah; Including Orphan Roll   Volume Three

Cherokee Intruder Cases Dockets of Hearings 1901-1909 Volumes I & II

Indian Wills, 1911-1921 Records of the Bureau of Indian Affairs Books One thru Seven;
 Native American Wills & Probate Records 1911-1921

Other Books and Series by Jeff Bowen

Turtle Mountain Reservation Chippewa Indians 1932 Census with Births & Deaths, 1924-1932

Chickasaw By Blood Enrollment Cards 1898-1914 Volume I thru V

Cherokee Descendants East An Index to the Guion Miller Applications Volume I
Cherokee Descendants West An Index to the Guion Miller Applications Volume II (A-M)
Cherokee Descendants West An Index to the Guion Miller Applications Volume III (N-Z)

Applications for Enrollment of Seminole Newborn Freedmen, Act of 1905

Eastern Cherokee Census, Cherokee, North Carolina, 1915-1922, Taken by Agent James E. Henderson   *Volume I (1915-1916)*
             Volume II (1917-1918)
             Volume III (1919-1920)
             Volume IV (1921-1922)

Complete Delaware Roll of 1898

Eastern Cherokee Census, Cherokee, North Carolina, 1923-1929, Taken by Agent James E. Henderson   *Volume I (1923-1924)*
             Volume II (1925-1926)
             Volume III (1927-1929)

Applications for Enrollment of Seminole Newborn Act of 1905 Volumes I & II

North Carolina Eastern Cherokee Indian Census 1898-1899, 1904, 1906, 1909-1912, 1914 Revised and Expanded Edition

1932 Hopi and Navajo Native American Census with Birth & Death Rolls (1925-1931) Volume 1 - Hopi
1932 Hopi and Navajo Native American Census with Birth & Death Rolls (1930-1932) Volume 2 - Navajo

Western Navajo Reservation Navajo, Hopi and Paiute 1933 Census with Birth & Death Rolls 1925-1933

Cherokee Citizenship Commission Dockets 1880-1884 and 1887-1889 Volumes I thru V

Copyright © 2012
by Jeff Bowen

ALL RIGHTS RESERVED
No part of this publication may be reproduced
or used in any form or manner whatsoever
without previous written permission from the
copyright holder or publisher.

Originally published:
Baltimore, Maryland
2012

Reprinted by:

Native Study LLC
Gallipolis, OH
www.nativestudy.com
2020

Library of Congress Control Number: 2020917992

ISBN: 978-1-64968-089-1

Made in the United States of America.

This series is dedicated to the descendants of the Creek newborn listed in these applications.

DEPARTMENT OF THE INTERIOR.

Commissioner to the Five Civilized Tribes.

NOTICE.

Opening of Land Office at Wewoka,
IN THE SEMINOLE NATION, INDIAN TERRITORY.

Notice is hereby given that on Monday, September 4, 1905, the Commissioner to the Five Civilized Tribes will establish a land office at Wewoka, in the Seminole Nation, Indian Territory, for the purpose of allowing citizens and freedmen of the Seminole Nation to select allotments of land for their minor children enrolled under the Act of Congress approved March 3, 1905 (33 Stat. L 1060), and for the further purpose of allowing citizens and freedmen of the Seminole Nation, whose allotments are incomplete, to select additional land in order to bring the value of their allotments up to the standard of $309.09, as nearly as may be practicable.

Each child whose enrollment in accordance with the Act of March 3, 1905, has been duly approved by the Secretary of the Interior, is entitled to receive an alllotment of forty acres without regard to the character or value of the land selected.

Selection of allotments for minor children must be made by their citizen or freedmen parents or by a duly appointed guardian, or curator, or by a duly appointed administrator.

TAMS BIXBY,
Commissioner.

Muskogee, Indian Territory,
July 29, 1905.

This particular notice makes mention of the Act of 1905. The Creek and Seminole were closely related tribes. Both tribes' notices were like similar in nature.

DEPARTMENT OF THE INTERIOR,

Commission to the Five Civilized Tribes.

Closing of Citizenship Rolls

OF THE MUSKOGEE OR CREEK NATION.

WHEREAS, on June 13, 1904, the Secretary of the Interior, under the authority in him vested by the provisions of the act of Congress approved March 3, 1901, (31 Stat., 1058) ordered that September 1, 1904, be and the same is hereby fixed as the time when the rolls of the Muskogee or Creek Nation shall be closed:

Notice is hereby given that the Commission to the Five Civilized Tribes will, at its office in Muskogee, Indian Territory, up to and inclusive of September 1, 1904, receive applications for the enrollment of citizens and freedmen of the Muskogee or Creek Nation, and that after that date the application of no person whomsoever for enrollment as a citizen or freedman of said nation will be received by the Commission.

Commission to the Five Civilized Tribes,
TAMS BIXBY, Chairman,
T. B. NEEDLES,
C. R. BRECKINRIDGE,
Commissioners.

Muskogee, Indian Territory,
June 25, 1904.

A notice like this was printed in newspapers and posted throughout Indian Territory.

INTRODUCTION

This series concerns Applications for Enrollment of Creek Newborn, National Archive film M-1301 (Act of 1905), as described in the National Archives publication *American Indians*. It falls under the heading Applications for Enrollment of the Commission to the Five Civilized Tribes, 1898-1914, M-1301 and is transcribed from microfilm rolls 414-419. This shows the application forms filled out by individuals applying for enrollment in the Five Civilized Tribes under the Dawes Commission. These applications contain additional information that wasn't abstracted to the census cards that you find in series M-1186. This particular roll (Creek by Birth) contains its own series of numbers separate from M-1186. To find each party's roll number you would have to reference M-1186. On July 25, 1898, there was an Indian Territory Division created in the Office of the Department of Interior. This division was created because of the increased work caused by what was called the Curtis Act, named after Senator Charles Curtis. Basically, this law stated that the tribal rolls needed to be descriptive and pointed out that each tribal roll was without description and had to be redone. At this point there was such a struggle among the Creeks to accept that the Government was going to change their way of life, again, that their leaders were refusing to cooperate in handing over their census information. The Commission had found that enrolling the Creeks was a difficult task not only because the Creek feared what was coming but also because their tribal structure was consistent with being a confederacy with forty-four different bands whose tribesmen lived in different towns of which each had a king that was supposed to keep track of their citizenry. The Commission reported that there was very little evidence of any census that existed and what there was had been kept carelessly. There were attempts and tribal conflicts along the way, but the Curtis Act would make it so they had to do it again no matter what effort from the past. In 1899, Agent Wesley Smith educated Washington to the fact that it was difficult to verify Creek eligibility. The acts passed by the Creeks themselves concerning enrollment since 1893 had been strewn amongst the archives of the Creek Council in Muskogee, I.T., and there was no provision ever approved for the printing of the those enrollments. There was confusion and difficulty let alone the fact that surnames were practically unknown among the Creek. But there was no confusion on March 9, 1905, when the Commission stated they would come to seven towns in the Creek Nation and accept applications that had to be made on a standardized blank form and contain a notarized affidavit from the mother and the attending doctor or midwife. A few by mail, but most of them were offered to a field party led by Commissioner Needles. The Commission took in applications for 2,410 children by the deadline of midnight, May 2, 1905.

This series contains applications and correspondence from 1,171 of those claimants. Realizing there were over 2,400 applicants originally, it is understood that not all were accepted. Also included are names of doctors, lawyers, mid-wives, and others who attended to the Creek Nation before and during this time in history.

Jeff Bowen
Gallipolis, Ohio
NativeStudy.com

Applications for Enrollment of Creek Newborn
Act of 1905   Volume X

NC-763.

Muskogee, Indian Territory, October 18, 1905.

Carrie Fisher,
    c/o Sam Fisher,
        Cathay, Indian Territory.

Dear Madam:

    In the matter of the application for the enrollment of your minor child Aubrey Fisher, born October 2, 1903, as a citizen by blood of the Creek Nation. You are advised that it will be necessary for you to furnish this office with the evidence of your marriage to Sam Fisher, the father of said child. Such evidence my[sic] consist of either the original or a certified copy of the marriage license and certificate.

                      Respectfully,

                                    Commissioner.

N.C. 763

Muskogee, Indian Territory, October 25, 1905.

Mrs. S. W. Fisher,
    Cathay, Indian Territory.

Dear Madam:

    Receipt is acknowledged of your letter of October 21, 1905, enclosing certificate of your marriage to Samuel W. Fisher. You state that you desire same to be returned to you after copy has been made and complain that you do not understand why same was demanded.

    In reply you are advised that in cases of this character where the mother is a non citizen, this office demands such proof of marriage or other evidence that the citizen parent is really the father of the child; no exception has been made in your case to the general rule.

    Said certificate is herewith returned.

                      Respectfully,

                                    Commissioner.

AG-10

Applications for Enrollment of Creek Newborn
Act of 1905   Volume X

THIS CERTIFIES THAT

Mr. Samuel W. Fisher of
Indian Territory
and Miss Carrie Rescom of Slater Saline County, State of Missouri

Were United in

Holy Matrimony

At Slater Mo. on the fourth day of November A.D. 1902 by authority of a License bearing date the fourth day of November A.D. 1902 and issued by the Recorder of Deeds of Saline County Missouri.

Witness my signature

William O. McGuire

Justice of the Peace

Witnesses

John W. Rollins

Miss Marha[sic] Gibbons

I, Anna Garrigues, on oath state that the above is a true and correct copy of the original.

Anna Garrigues

Subscribed and sworn to before me this 25 day of October 1905

J McDermott
Notary Public.

BIRTH AFFIDAVIT.

DEPARTMENT OF THE INTERIOR.
COMMISSION TO THE FIVE CIVILIZED TRIBES.

IN RE APPLICATION FOR ENROLLMENT, as a citizen of the Creek Nation, of Aubrey Fisher, born on the 2 day of October, 1903

Name of Father: Sam Fisher   a citizen of the   Creek   Nation.
   Tuskegee Town
Name of Mother: Carrie Fisher   a citizen of the United States Nation.

Applications for Enrollment of Creek Newborn
Act of 1905   Volume X

Postoffice   Cathay, Ind. Terr.

Child present
AFFIDAVIT OF MOTHER.

UNITED STATES OF AMERICA, Indian Territory,
Western   DISTRICT.

I, Carrie Fisher , on oath state that I am 19 years of age and a citizen ~~by (blank)~~ , of the United States ~~Nation~~; that I am the lawful wife of Sam Fisher , who is a citizen, by blood of the Creek Nation; that a male child was born to me on 2 day of October , 1903 , that said child has been named Aubrey Fisher , and was living March 4, 1905.

Carrie Fisher

Witnesses To Mark:
{

Subscribed and sworn to before me this 4 day of April , 1905.

Drennan C Skaggs
Notary Public.

AFFIDAVIT OF ATTENDING PHYSICIAN OR MID-WIFE.

UNITED STATES OF AMERICA, Indian Territory,
Western   DISTRICT.

I, Sarah C. Fisher , a Midwife , on oath state that I attended on Mrs. Carrie Fisher , wife of Sam Fisher on the 2^d day of October , 1903 ; that there was born to her on said date a male child; that said child was living March 4, 1905, and is said to have been named Aubrey Fisher

Sarah C. Fisher

Witnesses To Mark:
{

Subscribed and sworn to before me 17th day of April, 1905.

JB Morrow

My Commission Expires July 1, 1905.   Notary Public.

Applications for Enrollment of Creek Newborn
Act of 1905   Volume X

C 764

DEPARTMENT OF THE INTERIOR,
COMMISSION TO THE FIVE CIVILIZED TRIBES.
Eufaula, Indian Territory I. T., April 6, 1905.

In the matter of the application for the enrollment of Yancy McFarland as a citizen by blood of the Creek Nation.

MARY SMITH, being duly sworn, testified as follows:

Through Alex Posey Official Interpreter:

By Commission:
Q What is your name? A Mary Smith.
Q How old are you? A About twenty-three.
Q What is your post office address? A Eufaula.
Q Are you a citizen of the Creek Nation? A Yes, sir.
Q To what town do you belong? A Okfuske Canadian.
Q Do you make application for the enrollment of your minor child, Yancy McFarland, as a citizen by blood of the Creek Nation? A Yes, sir.
Q Who is the father of the child? A James McFarland
Q Is he a citizen of the Creek Nation? A He is a citizen of the United States.
Q Is he living? A He is dead.
Q Was he your lawful husband? A No, sir.
Q Were you ever married to him? A No, sir.
Q Did he ever recognize this child as his? A Yes, sir.
Q Did he contribute anything towards the support of the child? A Yes, sir.

---oooOOOooo---

I, D. C. Skaggs, on oath state that the above and foregoing is a full and true transcript of my stenographic notes as taken in said cause on said date.

DC Skaggs

Subscribed and sworn to before me this 22 day of July, 1905.

J McDermott
Notary Public.

Applications for Enrollment of Creek Newborn
Act of 1905   Volume X

NC-764.

Muskogee, Indian Territory, October 18, 1905.

Mary Smith,
   Eufaula, Indian Territory.

Dear Madam:

In the matter of the application for the enrollment of your minor child, Yancy McFarland, as a citizen by blood of the Creek Nation it will be necessary for you to furnish the affidavits of two disinterested witnesses as to the birth of said child. Said affidavits must set forth said child's name, the date of his birth, the names of his parents, and whether or not he was living on March 4, 1905.

You are requested to inform this office of the name under which you are finally enrolled, the names of your parents and other members of your family, the Creek Indian town to which you belong and your final roll number as the same appears upon your allotment certificate and deeds.

Respectfully,

Commissioner.

BIRTH AFFIDAVIT.

DEPARTMENT OF THE INTERIOR.
COMMISSION TO THE FIVE CIVILIZED TRIBES.

IN RE APPLICATION FOR ENROLLMENT, as a citizen of the Creek Nation, of Yancy McFarland, born on the 9 day of Sept , 1901

Name of Father: Jim Mcfarland[sic]   a citizen of the none[sic] citizen Nation.
Name of Mother: Mary Smith   a citizen of the   Creek   Nation.

Postoffice   Eufaula I.T.

AFFIDAVIT OF MOTHER.

UNITED STATES OF AMERICA, Indian Territory, }
   Western   DISTRICT.

I, Mary Smith , on oath state that I am 24 years of age and a citizen by blood , of the Creek Nation; that I am the lawful wife of   Josiff Smith *(illegible)*, who is a citizen, by blood of the Creek Nation; that a male child was born to me on 9 day of September, 1901 , that said child has been named Yancy McFarland , and was living March 4, 1905.

Mary Smith

Applications for Enrollment of Creek Newborn
Act of 1905   Volume X

Witnesses To Mark:
{

    Subscribed and sworn to before me this 13 day of November , 1905.

    My Commission expires   L. G. McIntosh
    Apr 10, 1907   Notary Public.

~~AFFIDAVIT OF ATTENDING PHYSICIAN OR MID-WIFE.~~

UNITED STATES OF AMERICA, Indian Territory, }   Affidavit of two witnesses
    Western   DISTRICT.

~~I~~, We Lewis McGilbra , and W. T. Fears , that we are acquainted Mary Smith on the 9 day of September , 1901 ; that there was born to her on said date a male child; that said child was living March 4, 1905, and is said to have been named Yancy McFarland

                               Lewis McGilbra
Witnesses To Mark: W. T. Fears
{

    Subscribed and sworn to before me this 13 day of November , 1905.

    My Commission expires   L. G. McIntosh
    Apr 10, 1907   Notary Public.

BIRTH AFFIDAVIT.

DEPARTMENT OF THE INTERIOR.
COMMISSION TO THE FIVE CIVILIZED TRIBES.

    IN RE APPLICATION FOR ENROLLMENT, as a citizen of the Creek Nation, of Yancy McFarland, born on the 9 day of Sept. , 1902

Name of Father: James McFarland (dec'd)   a citizen of the United States ~~Nation~~.
Name of Mother: Mary Smith (nee Asburey)   a citizen of the Creek Nation.
Okfusky[sic] Canadian Town
                        Postoffice   Eufaula Ind. Ter.

Applications for Enrollment of Creek Newborn
Act of 1905 Volume X

AFFIDAVIT OF MOTHER.

UNITED STATES OF AMERICA, Indian Territory, Western DISTRICT. } Child is present

I, Mary Smith , on oath state that I am about 23 years of age and a citizen by blood , of the Creek Nation; that I am not the lawful wife of James McFarland, who is a citizen, ~~by~~ *(blank)* of the United States ~~Nation~~; that a male child was born to me on 9 day of September, 1902 , that said child has been named Yancy McFarland , and was living March 4, 1905. That the midwife that attended on me at the birth of the child is now dead.

Mary Smith

Witnesses To Mark:
{

Subscribed and sworn to before me this 6 day of April , 1905.

Drennan C Skaggs
Notary Public.

NC-765.

Muskogee, Indian Territory, October 18, 1905.

Bedia Doyle,
    Eufaula, Indian Territory.

Dear Madam:

In the matter of the application for the enrollment of your minor child Leo Doyle as a citizen by blood of the Creek Nation You are advised that it will be necessary for you to furnish this office with proof of your marriage to Sam Doyle, the father of said child. Such proof may consist of either the original or a certified copy of your marriage license and certificate.

For the purpose of identifying Sam Doyle, the father of said child, upon the final roll of citizens by blood of the Creek Nation you are requested to inform this office of the name under which he is finally enrolled, the names of his parents and other members of his family, the Creek Indian town to which he belongs and his final roll number as the same appears upon his allotment certificate and deeds.

Respectfully,
Commissioner.

Applications for Enrollment of Creek Newborn
Act of 1905   Volume X

(The letter below typed as given)

COPY

Nov 13 1905

To the Comishion Of the Five Civilized Tribes

    Sir you have my marriage certificate I sent it in 1902 for the enrolment of Mabel Doyle sister to Leo Doyle. My husband name is sam H. Doyle Jr. his town is Hitchite I.T.

                      Respectfully yours
                      Bedia Doyle

A full ~~brother~~ sister of leo Doyle is enrolled on Creek Card No. 4375

BIRTH AFFIDAVIT.

DEPARTMENT OF THE INTERIOR.
COMMISSION TO THE FIVE CIVILIZED TRIBES.

    IN RE APPLICATION FOR ENROLLMENT, as a citizen of the Creek Nation, of Leo Doyle, born on the 3 day of March, 1903

Name of Father: Sam Doyle   a citizen of the Creek Nation.
~~Eufaula~~ Hitchitee Town
Name of Mother: Bedia Doyle   a citizen of the United States Nation.

              Postoffice   Eufaula, Ind. Terr.

                      Child present
              AFFIDAVIT OF MOTHER.

UNITED STATES OF AMERICA, Indian Territory,
    Western   **DISTRICT.**

    I, Bedia Doyle, on oath state that I am 22 years of age and a citizen by *(blank)*, of the United States ~~Nation~~; that I am the lawful wife of Sam Doyle, who is a citizen, by blood of the Creek Nation; that a male child was born to me on 3 day of March, 1903, that said child has been named Leo Doyle, and was living March 4, 1905.

                      Bedia Doyle

Witnesses To Mark:

Applications for Enrollment of Creek Newborn
Act of 1905   Volume X

Subscribed and sworn to before me this 5 day of April, 1905.

Drennan C Skaggs
Notary Public.

AFFIDAVIT OF ATTENDING PHYSICIAN OR MID-WIFE.

UNITED STATES OF AMERICA, Indian Territory, }
Western   DISTRICT.

I, W. A. Tolleson, a physician, on oath state that I attended on Mrs. Bedia Doyle, wife of Sam Doyle on the 3 day of March, 1903; that there was born to her on said date a male child; that said child was living March 4, 1905, and is said to have been named Leo Doyle

W.A. Tolleson

Witnesses To Mark:
{

Subscribed and sworn to before me 6 day of April, 1905.

Drennan C Skaggs
Notary Public.

NC-766.

Muskogee, Indian Territory, October 18, 1905.

Nancy Tecumseh,
    c/o Nero Tecumseh,
        (No Address given.)

Dear Madam:

In the matter of the application for the enrollment of your minor children, Effie Tecumseh, born February 19, 1903, and Edward Tecumseh, born February 1, 1905, as citizens by blood of the Creek Nation this office is unable to identify you upon the final roll of citizens by blood of said nation.

It is necessary that you be so identified before the rights of said children can be finally determined. You are therefore requested to state the name under which you are finally enrolled, the names of your parents and other members of your family, the Creek

Applications for Enrollment of Creek Newborn
Act of 1905 Volume X

Indian town to which you belong and your final roll number as the same appears upon your allotment certificate and deeds.

Respectfully,

Commissioner.

HGH

REFER IN REPLY TO THE FOLLOWING:

N.C. 766

DEPARTMENT OF THE INTERIOR,
COMMISSIONER TO THE FIVE CIVILIZED TRIBES.

Muskogee, Indian Territory, December 15, 1905.

Nancy Tecumseh,
    Care Nero Tecumseh,
        Weleetka, Indian Territory.

Dear Madam:

    In the matter of the application for the enrollment of your minor children, Effie Tecumseh, born February 19, 1903, and Edward Tecumseh, born February 1, 1905, as citizens by blood of the Creek Nation, this office is unable to identify you upon the final roll of citizens by blood of the Creek Nation. It is necessary that you be so identified before the rights of said children can be finally determined; you are requested to state your maiden name, the names of your parents, the Creek Indian Town to which you belong and your roll number as the same appears upon your deeds to land in the Creek Nation.

    You are also requested to state whether you were ever the wife of Tecumseh Deere.

    This matter should receive your immediate attention.

Respectfully,
Tams Bixby   Commissioner.

BIRTH AFFIDAVIT.

DEPARTMENT OF THE INTERIOR.
COMMISSION TO THE FIVE CIVILIZED TRIBES.

    IN RE APPLICATION FOR ENROLLMENT, as a citizen of the Creek Nation, of Effie Tecumseh, born on the 19th day of February, 1903

Name of Father:	Nero Tecumseh	a citizen of the Creek	Nation.
Name of Mother:	Nancy Tecumseh	a citizen of the Creek	Nation.

Postoffice   Wealaka, I T

Applications for Enrollment of Creek Newborn
Act of 1905   Volume X

AFFIDAVIT OF MOTHER.

UNITED STATES OF AMERICA, Indian Territory,
Western DISTRICT.

I, Nancy Tecumseh , on oath state that I am 30 years of age and a citizen by blood , of the Creek   Nation; that I am the lawful wife of Nero Tecumseh , who is a citizen, by blood of the Creek   Nation; that a female   child was born to me on 19th day of February , 1903 , that said child has been named Effie Tecumseh , and is now living.

            Nancy Tecumseh

Witnesses To Mark:

Subscribed and sworn to before me this 17th day of April , 1905.

            Ralph Dresback
             Notary Public.

AFFIDAVIT OF ATTENDING PHYSICIAN OR MID-WIFE.

UNITED STATES OF AMERICA, Indian Territory,
Western DISTRICT.

I, Susanna Kelley , a   Midwife , on oath state that I attended on Mrs. Nancy Tecumseh , wife of Nero Tecumseh on the 19th day of February , 1903 ; that there was born to her on said date a Female   child; that said child is now living and is said to have been named Effie Tecumseh

            Susanna Kelly

Witnesses To Mark:

Subscribed and sworn to before me this 17th day of April , 1905.

            Ralph Dresback
             Notary Public.

Applications for Enrollment of Creek Newborn
Act of 1905 Volume X

BIRTH AFFIDAVIT.

DEPARTMENT OF THE INTERIOR.
COMMISSION TO THE FIVE CIVILIZED TRIBES.

IN RE APPLICATION FOR ENROLLMENT, as a citizen of the Creek Nation, of Edward Tecumseh, born on the 1st day of Feb, 1905

Name of Father:	Nero Tecumseh	a citizen of the	Creek	Nation.
Name of Mother:	Nancy Tecumseh	a citizen of the	Creek	Nation.

Postoffice   Wealaka, I T

AFFIDAVIT OF MOTHER.

UNITED STATES OF AMERICA, Indian Territory, }
    Western   DISTRICT.

I, Nancy Tecumseh, on oath state that I am 30 years of age and a citizen by Blood, of the Creek Nation; that I am the lawful wife of Nero Tecumseh, who is a citizen, by Blood of the Creek Nation; that a male child was born to me on 1st day of February, 1905, that said child has been named Edward Tecumseh, and is now living.

Nancy Tecumseh

Witnesses To Mark:
{

Subscribed and sworn to before me this 17th day of April, 1905.

Ralph Dresback
Notary Public.

AFFIDAVIT OF ATTENDING PHYSICIAN OR MID-WIFE.

UNITED STATES OF AMERICA, Indian Territory, }
    Western   DISTRICT.

I, Rosa Alexander, a Midwife, on oath state that I attended on Mrs. Nancy Tecumseh, wife of Nero Tecumseh on the 1st day of February, 1905; that there was born to her on said date a male child; that said child is now living and is said to have been named Edward Tecumseh

her
Rosa x Alexander
mark

Witnesses To Mark:
{ Daniel Beaver
  Nellie Dresback

Applications for Enrollment of Creek Newborn
Act of 1905 Volume X

Subscribed and sworn to before me this 17th day of April, 1905.

Ralph Dresback
Notary Public.

NC-767
DEPARTMENT OF THE INTERIOR,
COMMISSIONER TO THE FIVE CIVILIZED TRIBES.

Muskogee, Indian Territory, November 18, 1905.

In the matter of the application for the enrollment of Mary Tecumseh as a citizen by blood of the Creek Nation.

Austin Tecumseh, being duly sworn, testified as follows:

EXAMINATION BY THE COMMISSION:
Q What is your name? A Austin Tecumseh.
Q How old are you? A 28.
Q What is your postoffice address? A Wealaka.
Q You are a citizen of the Creek Nation? A Yes sir.

The witness is identified on Creek Indian card, Field No. 754, opposite Roll No. 2473.

Q You have a newborn child, for whom you made application this morning? A Yes sir.
Q What is the child's name? A Mary.
Q When was Mary born? A February 3.
Q What year? A 1904.
Q That child is living now? A Yes sir.
Q Who is the mother of Mary? A Rosa.
Q Have you received your deeds yet? A No.
Q Your wife, Rosa, made application on the 17th day of April, for the enrolment of this child, Mary, under the name Rosa Alexander, and gave your name, as the father, as Austin Alexander; is that correct? Is Austin Alexander your correct name? A It must be a mistake.
Q Your name is Austin Tecumseh? A Yes sir.
Q To what Town do you belong? A Concharte.
Q Who was the midwife in attendance when Mary was born? A Nancy.
Q Nancy Tecumseh? A Yes sir.

Applications for Enrollment of Creek Newborn
Act of 1905   Volume X

INDIAN TERRITORY, Western District.

    I, J. Y. Miller, a stenographer to the Commission to the Five Civilized Tribes, do hereby certify that the above and foregoing is a true and complete translation of my notes as same appear in my stenographic report of this case.

                                JY Miller

Sworn to and subscribed before me
  this the 18th day of November, 1905.

                                J McDermott

BIRTH AFFIDAVIT.

DEPARTMENT OF THE INTERIOR.
COMMISSION TO THE FIVE CIVILIZED TRIBES.

    IN RE APPLICATION FOR ENROLLMENT, as a citizen of the Creek Nation, of Mary Alexander, born on the 3rd day of Feby, 1904.

Name of Father: Austin Alexander   a citizen of the   Creek   Nation.
Name of Mother: Rosa Alexander   a citizen of the   Creek   Nation.

                      Postoffice   Wealaka, I T

AFFIDAVIT OF MOTHER.

UNITED STATES OF AMERICA, Indian Territory, ⎫
    Western   DISTRICT.   ⎬

    I, Rosa Alexander, on oath state that I am 20 years of age and a citizen by Blood, of the Creek Nation; that I am the lawful wife of Austin Alexander, who is a citizen, by Blood of the Creek Nation; that a female child was born to me on 3rd day of February, 1904, that said child has been named Mary Alexander, and is now living.

                                        her
                              Rosa x Alexander
Witnesses To Mark: mark
  ⎰ Nellie Dresback
  ⎱ Susanna Kelly

    Subscribed and sworn to before me this 17th day of April, 1905.

                            Ralph Dresback
                                  Notary Public.

Applications for Enrollment of Creek Newborn
Act of 1905 Volume X

AFFIDAVIT OF ATTENDING PHYSICIAN OR MID-WIFE.

UNITED STATES OF AMERICA, Indian Territory, ⎫
    Western   DISTRICT.   ⎬
                                  ⎭

I, Nancy Tecumseh , a   Midwife , on oath state that I attended on Mrs. Rosa Alexander , wife of   Austin Alexander on the 3rd day of February   , 1904 ; that there was born to her on said date a female child; that said child is now living and is said to have been named Mary Alexander

                                            Nancy Tecumseh

Witnesses To Mark:
{

Subscribed and sworn to before me this 17th day of April , 1905.

                                          Ralph Dresback
                                               Notary Public.

BIRTH AFFIDAVIT.

DEPARTMENT OF THE INTERIOR.
COMMISSION TO THE FIVE CIVILIZED TRIBES.

IN RE APPLICATION FOR ENROLLMENT, as a citizen of the Creek Nation, of Mary Tecumseh , born on the 3 day of Feb , 1904

Name of Father: Austin Tecumseh   a citizen of the   Creek   Nation.
Name of Mother: Rosa Tecumseh   a citizen of the   Creek   Nation.

                              Postoffice   Wealaka, I. T.

AFFIDAVIT OF ~~MOTHER~~. Father

UNITED STATES OF AMERICA, Indian Territory, ⎫
    Western   DISTRICT.   ⎬

I, Austin Tecumseh , on oath state that I am 28 years of age and a citizen by blood, of the   Creek Nation; that I am the lawful ~~wife~~ Husband   of Rosa Tecumseh , who is a citizen, by blood of the Creek   Nation; that a female   child was born to me on 3 day of   February   , 1904 , that said child has been named Mary Tecumseh , and is now living.

                                        Austin Tecumseh

Witnesses To Mark:
{

Applications for Enrollment of Creek Newborn
Act of 1905   Volume X

Subscribed and sworn to before me this 18 day of November, 1905.

         Edw C Griesel
         Notary Public.

BIRTH AFFIDAVIT.

DEPARTMENT OF THE INTERIOR.
COMMISSION TO THE FIVE CIVILIZED TRIBES.

IN RE APPLICATION FOR ENROLLMENT, as a citizen of the Creek Nation, of Mary Tecumseh, born on the 3 day of Feb, 1904

Name of Father: Austin Tecumseh	a citizen of the	Creek	Nation.
Name of Mother: Rosa Tecumseh	a citizen of the	Creek	Nation.

      Postoffice Wealaka, I T

AFFIDAVIT OF MOTHER.

UNITED STATES OF AMERICA, Indian Territory, ⎱
  Western   DISTRICT. ⎰   Child Present

  I, Rosa Tecumseh, on oath state that I am 22 years of age and a citizen by blood, of the Creek Nation; that I am the lawful wife of Austin Tecumseh, who is a citizen, by blood of the Creek Nation; that a female child was born to me on 3rd day of February, 1904, that said child has been named Mary Tecumseh, and is now living.

         Rosa Tecumseh

Witnesses To Mark:
{

Subscribed and sworn to before me this 18 day of November, 1905.

         Edw C Griesel
         Notary Public.

AFFIDAVIT OF ATTENDING PHYSICIAN OR MID-WIFE.

UNITED STATES OF AMERICA, Indian Territory, ⎱
  Western   DISTRICT. ⎰

  I, Nancy Tecumseh, a Midwife, on oath state that I attended on Mrs. Rosa Tecumseh, wife of Austin Tecumseh on the 3 day of February, 1904; that there was

Applications for Enrollment of Creek Newborn
Act of 1905   Volume X

born to her on said date a female child; that said child is now living and is said to have been named Mary Tecumseh

                                        Nancy Tecumseh

Witnesses To Mark:

{

    Subscribed and sworn to before me this 18 day of November, 1905.

                                        Edw C Griesel
                                        Notary Public.

NC-767.

                            Muskogee, Indian Territory, October 18, 1905.

Rosa Alexander,
    c/o Austin Alexander,
        Wealaka, Indian Territory.

Dear Madam:

    In the matter of the application for the enrollment of your minor child, Mary Alexander, born February 3, 1904, as a citizen by blood of the Creek Nation this office is unable to identify you upon the final roll of citizens by blood of the Creek Nation. It is necessary that you be so identified before the rights of said child can be finally determined.

    You are therefore requested to inform this office of the name under which you were finally enrolled, the names of your parents and other members of your family, the Creek Indian town to which you belong and your final roll number as the same appears upon your allotment certificate and deeds.

    You are also requested to inform this office of the name under which Austin Alexander, the father of your said child, was enrolled, the names of his parents and other members of his family, the Creek Indian town to which he belongs and his final roll number as the same appears upon his allotment certificate and deeds.

                                    Respectfully,
                                                               Commissioner.

Applications for Enrollment of Creek Newborn
Act of 1905   Volume X

DEPARTMENT OF THE INTERIOR,
COMMISSION TO THE FIVE CIVILIZED TRIBES.
Eufaula, I. T., April 6, 1905.

In the matter of the application for the enrollment of Laura White as a citizen by blood of the Creek Nation.

PHENIE WHITE, being duly sworn, testified as follows:

BY COMMISSION:
Q What is your name? A Phenie White.
Q How old are you? A Twenty-three.
Q What is your post office address? A Eufaula.
Q Are you a citizen of the Creek Nation? A Yes sir.
Q To what town do you belong? A Tuskegee.
Q Do you make application for the enrollment of your minor child, Laura White, as a citizen by blood of the Creek Nation? A Yes, sir.
Q Who is the father of the child? A Mack White.
Q Is he a citizen of the Creek Nation? A No, sir, state man.
Q Is he your lawful husband? A Yes, sir.
Q Do you know when Laura was born? A Yes, sir.
Q When? A The third day f March.
Q How do you fix the date? A I remembers[sic] well when she was born, the names of her parents and whether or not she was living on March 4, 1905. She was born the third day of March.
Q On what day of the week was she born? A On Saturday.
Q Are you positive that it was on Saturday? A Yes, sir, it was on Saturday.
Q Was the next day Sunday? A Yes, sir.
Q Was there any record made of the child's birth? A No, sir.
Q Who was present when the child was born? A My husband and Edgar Miller.
Q What is Edgar Miller's post office address? A Eufaula.
Q Who else was present? A Hannah Grayson.
Q Was the child born in the day time or at night? A In the day time.
Q What time of the day? A I don't know what time it was. It was early in the morning.
Q How old is the child now? A I don't know.
Q How many weeks old is it? a She will be five weeks old next Saturday.
Q Are you positive? A Yes, sir.

HANNAH GRAYSON?[sic] being duly sworn, testified as follows:

BY COMMISSION:
Q What is your name? A Hannah Grayson.
Q What is your age? A I don't know, about thirty.
Q What is your post office address? A Huttonville.
Q Are you a citizen of the Creek Nation? A Yes, sir.
Q To what town do you belong? A North Fork.
Q Do you know Mack and Phenie White? A Yes, sir.

Applications for Enrollment of Creek Newborn
Act of 1905   Volume X

Q Do you know a child of theirs named Laura White? A Yes, sir.
Q When was that child born? A Born in March.
Q What time in March? A Thirty--------I have forgotten----third of March.
Q How do you know it was the 3rd of March? A I know because I was there.
Q What day of the week was that? A On Friday.
Q Are you positive? A Yes, sir.
Q What time on Friday? A About ten o'clock.
Q In the morning? A Yes, sir.
Q How old is the child now? A A month old----a little over a month old, now, I guess.
Q How many weeks old is the child? A Four weeks old, going on five weeks old now.
Q You are positive are you? A Yes, sir.
Q You attended on Phenie White, did you, at the time the child was born? A Yes, sir.

MACK WHITE, being duly sworn, testified as follows:

BY COMMISSION:
Q What is your name? A Mack White.
Q How old are you? A Twenty-six.
Q What is your post office address? A Eufaula.
Q Are you a citizen of the Creek Nation? A No, sir.
Q Are you a United States citizen? A Yes, sir.
Q Have you a child named Laura White? A Yes, sir.
Q Who is the mother of that child? A Phenie.
Q Is she a citizen of the Creek Nation? A Yes, sir.
Q Do you know when Laura was born? A The 3rd day of March.
Q How do you fix the date? A I just remember it.
Q Did you make any record of the birth of the child? A No, sir.
Q What day of the week was it? A The 3rd day of March was on Friday if I am not mistaken.
Q Are you positive it was on Friday? A No, sir, I think it was on Friday.
Q How old is the child now? A About a month old.
Q How many weeks is it? A Weel[sic], she is five weeks old, I believe.
Q Is she over five weeks old? A She may be a day or two over five weeks old, I don,t[sic] know.
Q Will she be six weeks old next Friday? A Six weeks old next Friday.
Q Id[sic] could not have been born on the third day of March if it is six weeks old next Friday? A I ain't positive.
Q Are you positive that the child was born on the third day of March? A Yes, sir.

---oooOOOooo---

I, D. C. Skaggs, on oath state that the above and foregoing is a full and true transcript of my stenographic notes as taken in said cause on said date.

DC Skaggs

Applications for Enrollment of Creek Newborn
Act of 1905   Volume X

Subscribed and sworn to before me this 22 day of July, 1905.

J McDermott

NC-768

DEPARTMENT OF THE INTERIOR,
COMMISSIONER TO THE FIVE CIVILIZED TRIBES.

Muskogee, Indian Territory, December 5, 1905.

In the matter of the application for the enrollment of Laura White as a citizen by blood of the Creek Nation.

Phenia White, being duly sworn, testified as follows:

EXAMINATION BY THE COMMISSION:
Q What is your name? A Phenia White.
Q How old are you? A 23, I think.
Q What is your postoffice address? A Eufaula.
Q What is the name of your father? A Eli Jacob.
Q What is the name of your mother? A Millie.

The witness is identified as Phenia White, on Creek Indian card, Field No. 1135, opposite Roll No. 3674.

Q Have you a child named Laura White? A Yes sir.
Q Is that it, there? A Yes sir.
Q What is the name of the father of this child? A Mack White.
Q Is he a citizen of any tribe in Indian Territory? A No sir.
Q State man, is he? A Yes sir.
Q When was Laura White, the little girl here, born? A The 3rd day of March.
Q Sure of that? A Yes sir.
Q This year, 1905? A Yes sir.
Q How old is she now? A She was nine months the third day of this month.
[sic] On what day of the week was she born? A Friday.
Q What time of the day or night was she born? A In the morning.
Q What hour? A I don't know, sir; what hour.
Q Before breakfast or after breakfast? A About sun-up, about 6 o'clock.
Q What were you doing Thursday morning--anything that you remember? A No aie.
Q Did you eat your breakfast that morning? A I don't remember.
Q And then, Thursday dinner-time at noon; did you eat then? A I don't know, sir.
Q And then Thursday, after supper, six o'clock in the evening; did you eat then? A I don't know, sir.
Q Get your mind on that Thursday, the second of March, supper time--you don't know whether you ate any meal at all? A No sir.
Q After supper--did you begin to have this child then? A No, sir.

Applications for Enrollment of Creek Newborn
Act of 1905   Volume X

Q Did you have it before 12 o'clock of Thursday? A No sir.
Q Did you have it after 12 o'clock Thursday--going into Friday morning? A No sir.
Q Did breakfast time pass without having this child? A No sir, before breakfast.
Q Early Friday morning? A Yes sir.
Q Was anybody present when this child was born? A My husband and the midwoman.
Q What is the name? A Hannah Grayson.
Q She is not here today? A No sir, she is not here.
Q Was that all present, those two people? A Yes sir.
Q Was there anyone come in during the day? A No sir.
Q Anybody come in the next day? A I don't know, sir.
Q Were you in bed when you had this child? A Certainly.
Q How long had you been in bed? A One month.
Q Itsn'by[sic] usual for a woman to stay in bed so long. A no sir.
Q You must have been pretty sick? A Yes sir.
Q Didn't you have anybody else except Hannah Grayson? A Yes, sir.
Q Why didn't you have a doctor? A I wasn't really bad off. I was in bed four days after she was born.
Q That day did you get up? A I don't know, sir.
Q You only know that day; you don't know what day you got up: A I never kept account of the days.
Q Did you write it down? make a report? A Yes sir.
Q Got it with you? A No sir.
Q Who mad[sic] the record? who wrote it down? A I did.
Q How long after the birth of the child? A I don't know, about five or six day.s
Q With pen or pencil? A Pencil.
Q What kind of a book? A I forgot the name of the book
Q Is it the Bible? A Yes, it was the Bible.
Q Was anything else on the page you wrote? A Yes sir.
Q What is on it? A All my children are there.
Q That is the last entry in the book? A Yes sir.
Q What does the last entry say, what words are used? A "____was born March 3, 1905."
Q You say you write it four days after it was born? A I said it might have been four or five days.
Q You didn't name the child right away? A Yes sir.
Q You called it Laura right away, did you? A The woman named it.

Mack White, being duly sworn, testified as follows:

EXAMINATION BY THE COMMISSIONER:
Q What is your name? A Mack White.
Q How old are you? A 27 years old.
Q What is your postoffice address? A Eufaula.
Q State man, are you? A Yes sir.
Q Can you read and write? A Yes sir.
Q Mack, on what day of the week was the child born? A I don't remember the day.
Q Were you there? A Yes sir.

Applications for Enrollment of Creek Newborn
Act of 1905 Volume X

Q You don't remember the day of the week A No sir.
Q You remember the day of the month? A Yes sir.
Q How does it come you can remember the day of the month and can't remember the day of the week A It is easy.
Q Are you superstitious? you believe 13 is unlucky? A No sir.
Q You heard of it being unlucky for 13 to sit down at the table; havn't[sic] heard of that. A I never heard of it.
Q Haven't you ever heard that one should never begin anything on Friday? A Yes, I've heard of that.
Q Unlucky to be born on Friday? A No sir, I never heard of that.
Q If you had a child born on Friday, it seems to me it would be easier for you to remember that it was born on Friday than to remember March 3. A I can remember the day and month my parents said I was born, but I can't remember the day.
Q But you were born 37[sic] years ago; this child was born this year. A I didn't pay much attention to the date.
Q How did you pay attention to get March 3 fixed in your mind? A Because I know it was on March 3rd.
Q Because you thought it had to be born to be entitled? A No sir.
Q You were there, were you? A Yes sir.
Q Did you help the midwife deliver it? A No sir.
Q Stood around and look at it? A Yes sir.
Q Did you have a lamp lit? A I did during the night.
Q Was it when the baby was born? A No sir.
Q You put it out? A Yes sir.
Q How long had you put it out? A About an hour. An hour after sun-up; it was born sometime in the morning.
Q Of the fourth or fifth or morning of the third? A Morning of the third.
Q On the morning of the fourth of March the child was a day old? A Yes sir.

The first witness is advised that this Office would like to have her produce the record spoken of.

Phenia White, recalled:

BY THE COMMISSIONER:
Q You understand the nature of an oath? you understand that it is to hold up your hand to tell the truth? A Yes sir.
Q Now, look here: Down at Eufaula, Indian Territory on April 6, of this year, before a field party of the Commission, which was about a month after the child was born, when its birthday was fresh in your mind, you said it was born on Saturday; you swore it was born on Saturday; you sworn that the next day after it was born on Sunday; you swore also that you didn't know how old the child was. You sworn again, in answer to this question: "Who was present when the child was born?" "My husband and Edgar Miller." How do you account for all that contradiction? A There was a young man come but he didn't know nothing about him.
Q A minute ago, when I asked you who was present, you said your husband and the midwife. I said, "Is that all" and you said, "Yes." A There was present.

Applications for Enrollment of Creek Newborn
Act of 1905   Volume X

Q You said there was nobody present but your husband and the midwife; nine months ago you said your husband and Edgar Miller were there. Now you say the child was born on Friday and you are sure on what hour, this about nine months after the child's birth, and but one month after the child was born you were sure it was born on Saturday. What do you say to that? A If it was on Saturday I made a mistake. On Friday I know.

Q At one time, after the birth of the child, when it should have been fresh in your mind "Are you positive that it was on Saturday?" A "Yes, it was on Saturday." Q "Was the next day Sunday?" A "Yes, sir." You said under oath now--you swear positively tht[sic] it was on Friday. You were asked the question: "On what day of the week" A "On Saturday." Q Are you positive that it was on Saturday?" A "Yes, sir, it was on Saturday." A It was Friday, I know it, if I said, it was a mistake.

Q You were asked three plain questions, and then it was only after the child was born. It looks more likely for a mistake to be made now than it was then. (No answer)

Q I want you to think about the solemnity of an oath; what it means to swear to a lie, not to frighten you. I simply want you to tell the truth--now, here is another one: today you swore that you wrote down in a book four or five days after the child was born, you were asked this question: "Was there any record made of the child's birth?" A "No, sir." You see, you are getting yourself into it. You are just swearing up and down and crosswise. How do you account for that? One month after the child was born you swore that there was no record made of it; now, nine months after it was born you swear that you made a record. Did you write in the family Bible four days after the child was born? It couldn't be a mistake about that kind of business. You can't say you made and you didn't make it, both. Which one of these two statements is correct? A I did.

Q Why didn't you know about it four or five days after it was born? Why did you answer under oath? A Friday, man isn't like--everybody can't remember.

Q It is easier to remember four weeks than to remember months. If you couldn't remember at that early date, when it was so fresh in your mind, how can you remember now? At first you said there was no record. A-- (Answer not audible)

      Mack White, recalled.

BY THE COMMISSIONER:

Q You say you can't remember the day of the week this child was born? A No sir.

Q Did you ever remember it? A Yes, I guess I did.

Q You know it when it was born? A Yes sir.

Q About a month--on April 6, when she made these mistakes or contradictions, shw swore up and down and crosswise to what she knew; you knew then the day, you knew positively, but you now say it was Friday. Now in answer to the question: "Did you make any record of the birth of the child?" you answered: "No, sir." Did you know of any record at all at that time? A Yes sir.

Q Why didn't you say that you didn't, but your wife did, if that was the fact? A I don't know why I didn't.

INDIAN TERRITORY, Western District.
      I, J. Y. Miller, a stenographer to the Commissioner to the Five Civilized Tribes, do hereby certify that the above and foregoing is a true and complete translation of my notes as same appear in my stenographic report of this case.

Applications for Enrollment of Creek Newborn
Act of 1905   Volume X

JY Miller

Sworn to and subscribed before me
this the 8th day of December,
1905.   J McDermott

BIRTH AFFIDAVIT.

DEPARTMENT OF THE INTERIOR,
COMMISSIONER TO THE FIVE CIVILIZED TRIBES.

ENROLLMENT OF MINORS.   ACT OF CONGRESS, APPROVED APRIL 26, 1906.

IN RE APPLICATION FOR ENROLLMENT, as a citizen of the Creek Nation, of Laura White, born on the 3$\underline{rd}$ day of March, 1905

Name of Father: Mark H. White   a citizen of the United States Nation.
Name of Mother: Phenia White   a citizen of the   Creek   Nation.

Tribal enrollment of father   Tribal enrollment of mother   Creek

Postoffice   Eufaula I.T.

AFFIDAVIT OF MOTHER.

UNITED STATES OF AMERICA, Indian Territory,
   Western   District.

I, Phenia White, on oath state that I am 26 years of age and a citizen by blood, of the Creek Nation; that I am the lawful wife of M. H. White, who is a citizen, by marriage of the Creek Nation; that a female child was born to me on 3$\underline{rd}$ day of March, 1905, that said child has been named Laura White, and was living March 4, 1906.

Phenia White

WITNESSES TO MARK:

   Aug 1 1906

Subscribed and sworn to before me this 30th day of June, 1906.

Thos. F. *(Illegible)*
Notary Public.

Applications for Enrollment of Creek Newborn
Act of 1905 Volume X

AFFIDAVIT OF ATTENDING PHYSICIAN OR MID-WIFE.

UNITED STATES OF AMERICA, Indian Territory, }
Western Judicial   District.

I, Hannah Grayson , a mid-wife , on oath state that I attended on Phenia White , wife of Mark H. White on the 3rd day of March , 1906[sic] ; that there was born to her on said date a   Female   child; that said child was living March 4, 1906, and is said to have been named Laura White

　　　　　　　　　　　　　　　　　　　　　　her
　　　　　　　　　　　　　　　　　Hannah x Grayson
WITNESSES TO MARK:　　　　　　　　　　　mark
{ Governor Nero
{ Louis Dotson

Subscribed and sworn to before me this 12th day of July   , 1906.

　　　　　　　　　　　　　　　J. C. Smock
　　　　　　　　　　　　　　　　　　Notary Public.

BIRTH AFFIDAVIT.

DEPARTMENT OF THE INTERIOR.
COMMISSION TO THE FIVE CIVILIZED TRIBES.

IN RE APPLICATION FOR ENROLLMENT, as a citizen of the Creek Nation, of Laura White , born on the 3 day of March , 1905

Name of Father: Mac White　　　　　　a citizen of the United States Nation.
Name of Mother: Phenia White　　　　　a citizen of the   Creek   Nation.
Tuskegee Town
　　　　　　　　　　Postoffice   Eufaula, Ind. Ter.

AFFIDAVIT OF MOTHER.

UNITED STATES OF AMERICA, Indian Territory, }
　　Western　　　　DISTRICT.　　　　Child is present

I, Phenia White , on oath state that I am 23 years of age and a citizen by blood, of the Creek   Nation; that I am the lawful wife of Mac White , who is a citizen, by *(blank)* of the United States ~~Nation~~; that a female   child was born to me on 3 day of March , 1905 , that said child has been named Laura White , and was living March 4, 1905.

　　　　　　　　　　　　　　　Phenia White
Witnesses To Mark:
{

25

Applications for Enrollment of Creek Newborn
Act of 1905   Volume X

Subscribed and sworn to before me this 6 day of April, 1905.

         Drennan C Skaggs
         Notary Public.

AFFIDAVIT OF ATTENDING PHYSICIAN OR MID-WIFE.

UNITED STATES OF AMERICA, Indian Territory, ⎱
 Western   DISTRICT.   ⎰

  I, Hannah Grayson, a midwife, on oath state that I attended on Mrs. Phenia White, wife of Mac White on the 3 day of March, 1905; that there was born to her on said date a *(blank)* child; that said child was living March 4, 1905, and is said to have been named Laura White
                  her
               Hannah x Grayson
Witnesses To Mark: mark
 ⎰ Alex Posey
 ⎱ DC Skaggs

  Subscribed and sworn to before me 6 day of April, 1905.

         Drennan C Skaggs
         Notary Public.

NC-768.

        Muskogee, Indian Territory, October 18, 1905.

Phenie White,
  c/o Mack White,
    Eufaula, Indian Territory.

Dear Madam:

  Further evidence is desired in the matter of the application for the enrollment of your minor child Laura White as a citizen by blood of the Creek Nation. You are hereby notified to appear before the Commissioner to the Five Civilized Tribes at his office in Muskogee, Indian Territory, within fifteen days from date with at least two witnesses, who know the exact day and the exact time of day at which said Laura White was born, for the purpose of being examined under oath.

       Respectfully,

                Commissioner.

Applications for Enrollment of Creek Newborn
Act of 1905 Volume X

NC 768.

Muskogee, Indian Territory, June 21, 1906.

Phenia White,
    Eufaula, Indian Territory.

Dear Madam:

    In the matter of the application for the enrollment of your minor child, Laura White, as a citizen by blood of the Creek Nation, you are hereby advised that it is required that you furnish this office with the affidavits of yourself and the midwife who attended you at the birth of said child, said affidavits showing the name of the child, the names of its parents, the date of birth, and whether said child was living March 4, 1906, and for this purpose there is enclosed herewith a blank affidavit. This matter should receive your immediate attention.

                    Respectfully,

1 BA.   Commissioner.

BIRTH AFFIDAVIT.

DEPARTMENT OF THE INTERIOR.
COMMISSION TO THE FIVE CIVILIZED TRIBES.

    IN RE APPLICATION FOR ENROLLMENT, as a citizen of the Creek Nation, of Bertha Bruner, born on the 29 day of January, 1902

Name of Father: Daniel Bruner   a citizen of the   Creek   Nation.
Name of Mother: Betty Bruner   a citizen of the   Creek   Nation.

                    Postoffice   Okmulgee IT

AFFIDAVIT OF MOTHER.

UNITED STATES OF AMERICA, Indian Territory,
    Western   DISTRICT.

    I, Betty Bruner, on oath state that I am 35 years of age and a citizen by Blood, of the Creek Nation; that I am the lawful wife of Daniel Bruner, who is a citizen, by Blood of the Creek Nation; that a female child was born to me on 29 day of January, 1902, that said child has been named Bertha Bruner, and is now living.

Applications for Enrollment of Creek Newborn
Act of 1905 Volume X

                              her
                       Betty x Bruner
Witnesses To Mark: mark
{ Isom Peters
  Nellie Dresback

Subscribed and sworn to before me this 10 day of April, 1905.

                            Ralph Dresback
                            Notary Public.

AFFIDAVIT OF ATTENDING PHYSICIAN OR MID-WIFE.

UNITED STATES OF AMERICA, Indian Territory, }
    Western   DISTRICT.

I, Nancy Pigeon, a Midwife, on oath state that I attended on Mrs. Betty Bruner, wife of Daniel Bruner on the 29th day of January, 1902; that there was born to her on said date a female child; that said child is now living and is said to have been named Bertha Bruner

                            Nancy Pigeon
Witnesses To Mark:
{

Subscribed and sworn to before me this 10th day of April, 1905.

                            Ralph Dresback
                            Notary Public.

BIRTH AFFIDAVIT.

DEPARTMENT OF THE INTERIOR.
COMMISSION TO THE FIVE CIVILIZED TRIBES.

IN RE APPLICATION FOR ENROLLMENT, as a citizen of the Creek Nation, of Maggie Bruner, born on the 19 day of May, 1904

Name of Father: Daniel Bruner   a citizen of the Creek Nation.
Name of Mother: Betty Bruner   a citizen of the Creek Nation.

                  Postoffice   Okmulgee IT

Applications for Enrollment of Creek Newborn
Act of 1905   Volume X

AFFIDAVIT OF MOTHER.

UNITED STATES OF AMERICA, Indian Territory, ⎫
   Western   DISTRICT.   ⎬
                                                                ⎭

    I, Betty Bruner, on oath state that I am 35 years of age and a citizen by Blood, of the Creek Nation; that I am the lawful wife of Daniel Bruner, who is a citizen, by Blood of the Creek Nation; that a female child was born to me on 19 day of May, 1904, that said child has been named Maggie Bruner, and is now living.

                                                                     her
                                                       Betty x Bruner
Witnesses To Mark: mark
⎰ Isom Peters
⎱ Nancy Pigeon

    Subscribed and sworn to before me this 10 day of April, 1905.

                                           Ralph Dresback
                                                    Notary Public.

AFFIDAVIT OF ATTENDING PHYSICIAN OR MID-WIFE.

UNITED STATES OF AMERICA, Indian Territory, ⎫
   Western   DISTRICT.   ⎬

    I, Lucy Bruner, a Midwife, on oath state that I attended on Mrs. Betty Bruner, wife of Daniel Bruner on the 19th day of May, 1904; that there was born to her on said date a female child; that said child is now living and is said to have been named Maggie Bruner

                                                 her
                                       Lucy x Bruner
Witnesses To Mark: mark
⎰ John Bruner
⎱ Daniel *(Illegible)*

    Subscribed and sworn to before me this 17th day of April, 1905.

                                       Ralph Dresback
                                         Notary Public.

Applications for Enrollment of Creek Newborn
Act of 1905 Volume X

Muskogee, Indian Territory, August 12, 1905.

A. M. Milan,
    Morris, Indian Territory.

Dear Sir:

    Receipt is acknowledged of your letter of August 8, 1905, in which you ask that a power of attorney blank be sent you for a minor child, you also ask to be notified when the application for the enrollment of Cecil Doyle has been approved.

    You are advised that when the enrollment of said child has been approved by the Secretary of the Interior, the parties in interest will be duly notified.

    You are further advised that no reservation of land can be made at this time in the Creek Nation for new-born children and that this office has no blank powers of attorney of the nature requested.

                  Respectfully,

                                Acting Commissioner.

BIRTH AFFIDAVIT.

DEPARTMENT OF THE INTERIOR.
COMMISSION TO THE FIVE CIVILIZED TRIBES.

    IN RE APPLICATION FOR ENROLLMENT, as a citizen of the Creek Nation, of Cecil Lee Doyle, born on the 7 day of Sept, 1902

Name of Father: Sebron J Doyle   a citizen of the   Creek   Nation.
Name of Mother: Dell Doyle   a citizen of the   -----   Nation.

                  Postoffice   Hitchatee[sic], I.T.

AFFIDAVIT OF MOTHER.

UNITED STATES OF AMERICA, Indian Territory,
    Western   DISTRICT.

    I, Dell Doyle, on oath state that I am 22 years of age and now a citizen by *(blank)*, of the *(blank)* Nation; that I am the lawful wife of Sebron J Doyle, who is a citizen, by blood, of the Creek Nation; that a male child was born to me on 7 day of Sept, 1902, that said child has been named Cecil Lee Doyle, and was living March 4, 1905.

                              Dell Doyle

Witnesses To Mark:

Applications for Enrollment of Creek Newborn
Act of 1905   Volume X

Subscribed and sworn to before me this 5 day of April, 1905.

My Commission expires July 2/06   AM Milan
                                     Notary Public.

AFFIDAVIT OF ATTENDING PHYSICIAN OR MID-WIFE.

UNITED STATES OF AMERICA, Indian Territory,
Western   DISTRICT.

I, W.A. Tolleson, a physician, on oath state that I attended on Mrs. Dell Doyle, wife of Sebron J Doyle on the 7 day of Sept, 1902; that there was born to her on said date a male child; that said child was living March 4, 1905, and is said to have been named Cecil Lee Doyle

                                     W.A. Tolleson
Witnesses To Mark:

Subscribed and sworn to before me 8 day of April, 1905.

                                     MM Washington
                                     Notary Public.

N.C 771

DEPARTMENT OF THE INTERIOR,
COMMISSIONER TO THE FIVE CIVILIZED TRIBES.
Muskogee, I.T. September 5, 1905.

In the matter of the application for the enrollment of Henry Brown as a citizen by blood of the Creek Nation.

Thomas Brown being duly sworn testified as follows:

Q What is your name? A Thomas Brown
Q Are you a citizen of the Creek Nation? A Yes, I am a Euchee
Q What was the name of your father? A George Brown
Q What was the name of your mother? A Lizzie Brown
Q What is your post office address? A Wealaka
Q Have you a child named Henry Brown? A Yes, sir
Q What is the name of his mother? A Annie Brown now, used to be Annie Rowland. M. Rowland her husband was but he is dead

Applications for Enrollment of Creek Newborn
Act of 1905   Volume X

Q Before you married her? A Yes, sir
Q What was the name of her father? A John Buck
Q What was the name of her mother? A Rose Buk
Q Is that child Henry living? A Yes, this is the child right here
Q How old is he? A 12 months going on 13 now.
Q When was he born? A August 11, 1904.

I, Anna Garrigues, on oath state that the above and foregoing is a true and correct copy of my stenographic notes taken in said case on said date.

                                      Anna Garrigues

Subscribed and sworn to
before me this 5 September 1905.   Henry G Hains
                                        Notary Public.

Indian Territory }
   Western Dist

     I Annie Brown, a duly enrolled Creek Citizen make oath that a male child was born to me on August 11th 1904 and has been named Henry Brown, and is now living on this date: April 15th 1905
                                 signed   Annie Brown

Indian Territory } ss
   Western District

     Subscribed and sworn to before me this, 15th day of April 1905
                                 J.F. Panther
                                     Notary Public
                               My com exp. July 2-1906

Indian Territory } ss
   Western District

     We Rosa Buck and Solome Fleetwood, each for herself swear that we (acting as *(illegible)*) were present and bear witness to the fact of a male child being born to Annie Brown on Aug. 11th 1904 and said child is now living at this date (Apr. 15th 1905) and we are informed has been named Henry Brown.
                                      her
                              Rosa x Buck
Witness to mark   mark
   J.F. Panther   Solome Fleetwood

Applications for Enrollment of Creek Newborn
Act of 1905 Volume X

Indian Territory \ ss
Western District / Subscribed and sworn to before
me this 15th day of April 1905

                         J.F. Panther
                         Notary Public
                         My com exp. July 2-1906

NC 772.

DEPARTMENT OF THE INTERIOR,
COMMISSIONER TO THE FIVE CIVILIZED TRIBES.
MUSKOGEE, INDIAN TERRITORY,
September 20, 1906.

    In the matter of the application for the enrollment of Mattie and Samuel Davis, as citizens of the Creek Nation.

    Appearances: J.G. Lieber, representing M.L. Mott, Attorney for the Creek Nation.

    Benjamin Davis, being duly sworn, by H.G. Hains, a Notary Public, testified as follows:

Examination by Commissioner.
Q What is your name? A Benjamin Davis.
Q What is your age? A I don't exactly know.
Q What is your post office address? A Stidham.
Q What was it before that? A Checotah.
Q Q[sic] Tullahassee[sic] ever your post office address? A Yes sir.
Q Muskogee? A Yes sir.
Q What is the name of your father? A John Davis.
Q What is the name of your mother? A Sarah Bell.

    Witness presents deed to allotment and from the information given he is identified as Benjamin Davis, opposite Creek Indian roll number 361.

Q Are you married? A Yes sir.
Q What is the name of your wife? A Malinda.
Q What was her name before you married her? A Crabtree.
Q Where did she get that name? A From her husband, Braxton Crabtree.
Q Was Braxton Crabtree dead when you married her? A Yes sir.
Q Have you any children enrolled by Braxton Crabtree? Has she any? A Yes Willie, Bessie and Lynn.

Applications for Enrollment of Creek Newborn
Act of 1905   Volume X

Said Melinda[sic] is identified opposite Creek Indian roll number 4358.

Q Did you ever have any children by Melinda? A Yes sir.
Q What are their names? A Mattie and Samuel.
Q When was Mattie born? A   don't recollect.
Q How old is she? A She is nearly four years old. She was three years old in July.
Q Three years old on the 4th? A Yes sir.

     Melinda Davis, being duly sworn by H.G. Hains, a Notary Public, testified as follows, through Official Interpreter Lona Merrick.

Q What is your name? A Melinda Davis.
Q What was her[sic] name before it was Davis? A Melinda Crabtree?
Q What is your age? A About thirty.
Q What is your post office address? A Stidham.
Q What is the name of your father? A Tecumseh Phillips.
Q What is the name of your mother? A Wisey Phillips.

     Witness if identified as Malinda Crabtree, opposite Creek Indian Roll number 4258.

Q You were at one time the wife of Braxton Braxton[sic] Crabtree? A Yes.
Q Is he dead? A Yes sir.
Q Since his death have you married Benjamin Davis? A Yes sir.

     Said Benjamin Davis is identified opposite Creek Indian Roll number 61.

Q Have you had children by Benjamin Davis? A Yes sir.
Q Are these the children here? A Yes sir.
Q What are their names? A Mattie and Samuel.

     Witness is handed blanks for the affidavit of two disinterested witnesses relative to the birth of her child, Samuel to take the place of the midwife that was not present.
Q What town do you belong to? A Tulmochussee.

     Lona Merrick, being duly sworn, states that the above and foregoing is a true and correct transcript of her stenographic notes as taken in said cause on said date.

Lona Merrick

Subscribed and sworn to before me this 25th day of September, 1906.

Edward Merrick
Notary Public.

Applications for Enrollment of Creek Newborn
Act of 1905 Volume X

N.C. 772
SAM
AG

DEPARTMENT OF THE INTERIOR,
COMMISSIONER TO THE FIVE CIVILIZED TRIBES.

In the matter of the application for the enrollment of Samuel Davis as a citizen by blood of the Creek Nation.

DECISION.

The record in this case shows that on April 11, 1905, an application was made in affidavit form for the enrollment of Samuel Davis as a citizen by blood of the Creek Nation, under the provisions of the Act of Congress approved March 3, 1905 (33 Stats., 1048). Supplemental affidavits were filed September 19 1906 and February 19, 1907, and further proceedings were had September 20, 1906.

It appears from the evidence and the records in the possession of the office that Samuel Davis is the minor child of Benjamin Davis, whose name appears on a partial schedule of citizens by blood of the Creek Nation approved by the Secretary of the Interior March 13, 1902, opposite No. 61, and Malinda Davis, who is identified by the name of Malinda Crabtree, on a partial schedule of citizens by blood of the Creek Nation approved by the Secretary of the Interior March 13, 1902, opposite No. 4358.

The evidence shows that Samuel Davis was born February 24, 1905, and that said child was living March 4, 1905.

It is, therefore, ordered and adjudged that said Samuel Davis is entitled to be enrolled as a citizen by blood of the Creek Nation in accordance with the provisions of the Act of Congress approved March 3, 1905 (33 Stat. L., 1048), and the application for his enrollment as such is accordingly granted.

Tams Bixby COMMISSIONER.

Muskogee, Indian Territory.

BIRTH AFFIDAVIT.

DEPARTMENT OF THE INTERIOR.
COMMISSION TO THE FIVE CIVILIZED TRIBES.

IN RE APPLICATION FOR ENROLLMENT, as a citizen of the Creek Nation, of Samuel Davis, born on the 24 day of Feb., 1905

Name of Father: Benjamin Davis   a citizen of the   Creek   Nation.
Broken Arrow Town
Name of Mother: Melindy Davis (nee Crabtree) a citizen of the   Creek   Nation.
Tulmochussee Town

Postoffice   Stidham, Ind. Ter.

Applications for Enrollment of Creek Newborn
Act of 1905   Volume X

AFFIDAVIT OF MOTHER.

UNITED STATES OF AMERICA, Indian Territory, ⎫
Western   DISTRICT.   ⎬ Child is present

    I, Melindy Davis , on oath state that I am about 30 years of age and a citizen by blood , of the Creek Nation; that I am the lawful wife of Benjamin Davis , who is a citizen, by blood of the Creek Nation; that a male child was born to me on 24 day of February , 1905 , that said child has been named Samuel Davis , and was living March 4, 1905. That no one attended on me as midwife or physician at the birth of the child

                               her
                      Melindy x Davis
                            mark

Witnesses To Mark:
⎰ Alex Posey
⎱ DC Skaggs

    Subscribed and sworn to before me this 7 day of April , 1905.

                    Drennan C Skaggs
                    Notary Public.

BIRTH AFFIDAVIT.
DEPARTMENT OF THE INTERIOR,
COMMISSIONER TO THE FIVE CIVILIZED TRIBES.

ENROLLMENT OF MINORS.   ACT OF CONGRESS, APPROVED APRIL 26, 1906.

    IN RE APPLICATION FOR ENROLLMENT, as a citizen of the Creek Nation, of Samuel Davis , born on the 24 day of Feb. , 1905

Name of Father: Benjamin Davis   a citizen of the   Creek   Nation.
Name of Mother: Malinda   "   a citizen of the   "   Nation.

Tribal enrollment of father   Tribal enrollment of mother

                  Postoffice   Stidham I.T.

AFFIDAVIT OF MOTHER.

UNITED STATES OF AMERICA, Indian Territory, ⎫
Western   District.   ⎬ Child present

    I, Malinda Davis , on oath state that I am about 30 years of age and a citizen by blood , of the Creek Nation; that I am the lawful wife of Benjamin Davis , who is a citizen, by blood of the Creek Nation; that a male child was born to me on 24 day

Applications for Enrollment of Creek Newborn
Act of 1905 Volume X

of February, 1905, that said child has been named Samuel Davis, and was living March 4, 1906.

                                                her
WITNESSES TO MARK: Malinda x Davis
{ HG Hains   mark
  Lona Merrick

Subscribed and sworn to before me this   19" day of September, 1906.

                                       H.G. Hains
                                               Notary Public.

BIRTH AFFIDAVIT.

DEPARTMENT OF THE INTERIOR.
COMMISSION TO THE FIVE CIVILIZED TRIBES.

    IN RE APPLICATION FOR ENROLLMENT, as a citizen of the Creek Nation, of Samuel Davis, born on or about the 24 day of Februaru, 1907[sic]

Name of Father: Benjamin Davis   a citizen of the   Creek   Nation.
Name of Mother: Melindy   "   a citizen of the   "   Nation.

                        Postoffice   Muskogee

                                  Acquaintances
                 AFFIDAVIT OF ATTENDING PHYSICIAN OR MID-WIFE.

UNITED STATES OF AMERICA, Indian Territory, }
       Western   DISTRICT.

                                                                 we know
      We, William and Sarah McCombs, acquaintances, on oath state that I attended on Mrs. Melinda Davis, wife of Benjamin Davis on or about the 24 day of February, 1905; that there was born to her on said date a male child; that said child was living March 4, 1905, and is said to have been named Samuel Davis & that we both saw it about four weeks ago and it was about 2 years old; we came up on same train with parents of child from Eufaula

                                         Wm McCombs
Witnesses To Mark: Sarah McCombs

{

    Subscribed and sworn to before me   19" day of February, 1907.

                                           Henry G. Hains
                                               Notary Public.

Applications for Enrollment of Creek Newborn
Act of 1905 Volume X

BIRTH AFFIDAVIT.

DEPARTMENT OF THE INTERIOR,
COMMISSIONER TO THE FIVE CIVILIZED TRIBES.

ENROLLMENT OF MINORS. ACT OF CONGRESS, APPROVED APRIL 26, 1906.

IN RE APPLICATION FOR ENROLLMENT, as a citizen of the Creek Nation, of Mattie Davis, born on the 22 day of Nov., 1902

Name of Father: Benjamin Davis   a citizen of the   Creek   Nation.
Name of Mother: Malinda "   a citizen of the   "   Nation.

Tribal enrollment of father   Tribal enrollment of mother

Postoffice   Stidham I.T.

AFFIDAVIT OF MOTHER.

UNITED STATES OF AMERICA, Indian Territory,
Western District. } Child present

I, Malinda Davis, on oath state that I am about 30 years of age and a citizen by blood, of the Creek Nation; that I am the lawful wife of Benjamin Davis, who is a citizen, by blood of the Creek Nation; that a *(blank)* child was born to me on 22 day of November, 1902, that said child has been named Mattie Davis, and was living March 4, 1906.   her

                                     Malinda x Davis
WITNESSES TO MARK: mark
{ HG Hains
{ Lona Merrick

Subscribed and sworn to before me this 19 day of September, 1906.

                               HG Hains
                                   Notary Public.

Applications for Enrollment of Creek Newborn
Act of 1905   Volume X

BIRTH AFFIDAVIT.

Copy

DEPARTMENT OF THE INTERIOR.
COMMISSION TO THE FIVE CIVILIZED TRIBES.

IN RE APPLICATION FOR ENROLLMENT, as a citizen of the Creek Nation, of Samuel Davis, born on the 24 day of Feb., 1905

Name of Father: Benjamin Davis   a citizen of the   Creek   Nation. B.A. T.
Name of Mother: Melindy Davis (nee Crabtree) a citizen of the   Creek   Nation. Tulmochussee

Postoffice   Stidham, Ind. Ter.

AFFIDAVIT OF MOTHER.

UNITED STATES OF AMERICA, Indian Territory, }
   Western   DISTRICT.   }   Child is present

I, Melindy Davis , on oath state that I am about 30 years of age and a citizen by blood , of the Creek Nation; that I am the lawful wife of Benjamin Davis , who is a citizen, by blood of the Creek Nation; that a male child was born to me on 24 day of February , 1905 , that said child has been named Samuel Davis , and was living March 4, 1905. That no one attended on me as midwife or physician at the birth of the child
                                                                 her
                                                Melindy x Davis
                                                          mark

Witnesses To Mark:
 { Alex Posey
 { DC Skaggs

Subscribed and sworn to before me this 7 day of April , 1905.
Seal

                       Drennan C Skaggs
                       Notary Public.

Applications for Enrollment of Creek Newborn
Act of 1905   Volume X

BIRTH AFFIDAVIT.

DEPARTMENT OF THE INTERIOR.
COMMISSION TO THE FIVE CIVILIZED TRIBES.

IN RE APPLICATION FOR ENROLLMENT, as a citizen of the Creek Nation, of Mattie Davis, born on the 22 day of Nov., 1902

Name of Father: Benjamin Davis   a citizen of the Creek Nation.
Broken Arrow Town
Name of Mother: Melindy Davis (nee Crabtree) a citizen of the Creek Nation.
Tulmochussee Town
                    Postoffice   Stidham, Ind. Ter.

AFFIDAVIT OF MOTHER.

UNITED STATES OF AMERICA, Indian Territory,
    Western   DISTRICT.   Child is present

I, Melindy Davis, on oath state that I am about 30 years of age and a citizen by blood, of the Creek Nation; that I am the lawful wife of Benjamin Davis, who is a citizen, by blood of the Creek Nation; that a female child was born to me on 22 day of November, 1902, that said child has been named Mattie Davis, and was living March 4, 1905.
                                her
                      Melindy x Davis
Witnesses To Mark: mark
  { Alex Posey
  { DC Skaggs

Subscribed and sworn to before me this 7 day of April, 1905.

                      Drennan C Skaggs
                          Notary Public.

AFFIDAVIT OF ATTENDING PHYSICIAN OR MID-WIFE.

UNITED STATES OF AMERICA, Indian Territory,
    Western   DISTRICT.

I, Nancy Posey, a (blank), on oath state that I attended on Mrs. Melindy Davis, wife of Benjamin Davis on the 22 day of Nov, 1902; that there was born to her on said date a (blank) child; that said child was living March 4, 1905, and is said to have been named Mattie Davis
                                her
                      Nancy x Posey
                          mark

Applications for Enrollment of Creek Newborn
Act of 1905   Volume X

Witnesses To Mark:
{ Alex Posey
{ DC Skaggs

Subscribed and sworn to before me 7 day of April, 1905.

Drennan C Skaggs
Notary Public.

BIRTH AFFIDAVIT.

DEPARTMENT OF THE INTERIOR.
COMMISSION TO THE FIVE CIVILIZED TRIBES.

IN RE APPLICATION FOR ENROLLMENT, as a citizen of the Creek Nation, of Mattie Davis, born on or about the 22 day of November, 1902

Name of Father: Benjamin Davis   a citizen of the   Creek   Nation.
Name of Mother: Melindy   "   a citizen of the   "   Nation.

Postoffice   Muskogee

Acquaintance
AFFIDAVIT OF ~~ATTENDING PHYSICIAN OR MID-WIFE~~.

UNITED STATES OF AMERICA, Indian Territory, }
     Western   DISTRICT.   }

know
I, Sarah McCombs, an acquaintance, on oath state that I ~~attended on~~ Mrs. Malinda Davis, wife of Benjamin Davis and on or about the 22 day of November, 1902; that there was born to her on said date a female child; that said child was living March 4, 1905, and is said to have been named Mattie Davis & I saw said child alive about 4 weeks ago

Sarah McCombs

Witnesses To Mark:
{

Subscribed and sworn to before me 19 day of February, 1907.

Henry G. Hains
Notary Public.

Applications for Enrollment of Creek Newborn
Act of 1905   Volume X

(The letter below typed as given)

NC 772

      Muskogee I T Oct 18 1905

Malinda Davis

    Stidham I T

Dear Madam:

    in the matter of the application for the enrollment of your minor children Mattie Davis born November 22 1902, and Samuel Davis born February 24, 1905 as citizens by blood of the Creek Nation, this office is unable to identify Benjamin Davis the father of said children upon the final roll of citizens by blood of the Creek Nation It is necessary that the said Benjamin Davis be identified and you are requested to advise this office of the name under which he is finally enrolled the names of his parents and other members of his family the Creek Indian town to which he belongs and his final roll number as the same appears upon his allotment certificate and deeds.

    You are requested to furnish this office with the affidavits of two disinterested persons relative to the birth of the said Samuel Davis. Said affidavits to set forth said child's name the date of his birth the names of his parents and whether or not he was living on March 4, 1905.

                               Respt
                                   Comr

NC 772

                          Muskogee, Indian Territory, January 10, 1907.

Malinda Davis,
    Care of Benjamin Davis,
        Stidham, Indian Territory.

Dear Madam:

    In the matter of the application for the enrollment of your minor child Samuel Davis, born February 24, 1905, as a citizen by blood of the Creek Nation, you are advised that it will be necessary that you furnish this office with the affidavits of two disinterested persons relative to the birth of said Samuel Davis within ten days from this date; said affidavits to set forth said child's name, the date of his birth, the names of his parents and whether or not he was living on March 4, 1905. A blank form for such affidavits is herewith inclosed.

                          Respectfully,
                                     Commissioner.

1 D W

Applications for Enrollment of Creek Newborn
Act of 1905   Volume X

N.C. 722.

Eufaula, Indian Territory, February 13, 1907.

Commissioner to the Five Civilized Tribes,
    Muskogee, Indian Territory.

Sir:

I have the honor to report in the matter of the application for the enrollment of Samuel Davis, as a citizen by blood of the Creek Nation, that Benjamin and Melindy Davis, the parents of said child are now residents of Muskogee, Indian Territory; that the Creek Enrollment Field Party is unable to secure the evidence desired in said case. Copies of record are herewith enclosed.

                Respectfully,

                            Jesse McDermott
                            Clerk In Charge

NC 772.

Muskogee, Indian Territory, March 18, 1907.

Melindy Davis,
    c/o Benjamin Davis,
        Stidham, Indian Territory.

Dear Madam:

You are hereby advised that on March 4, 1907, the Secretary of the Interior approved the enrollment of your minor children, Mattie and Samuel Davis, as citizens by blood of the Creek Nation, and that the names of said children appear upon the roll of new born citizens by blood, enrolled under the act of Congress approved March 3, 1905, as numbers 1169 and 1286, respectively.

These children are now entitled to allotments, and applications therefor should be made without delay at the Creek Land Office, Muskogee, Indian Territory.

                Respectfully,
                            Commissioner.

Applications for Enrollment of Creek Newborn
Act of 1905   Volume X

DEPARTMENT OF THE INTERIOR,
COMMISSION TO THE FIVE CIVILIZED TRIBES.
Near Morse, I.T. April 28, 1905.

In the matter of the application for new born children concerning whose enrollment no affidavits could be obtained in time.

Chofulop, being duly sworn, testified as follows: Through Official Interpreter, Alex Posey.

Examination by the Commission:

Q What is your name? A Chofulop.
Q What is your age? (No answer)
Q What is your post office address? [sic] Morse, I.T

Statements: I am a member of the House of Kings of Nuyaka Town. Eundel and Millie Robert[sic], both of Neyaka[sic] Town, have a girl named Indy--it is over two years old, and the other child is unnamed and was born in February. It is a boy, both are living-- about the first of February the youngest was born. Post Office, Morse.

The father of the child is unknown, the mother Funcinda of Nuyaka Town,-- has a child over a year old--a girl unnamed, living Post Office, Morse.

Henry G. Hains, being duly sworn, on his oath, states that the above and foregoing is a true and correct transcript of his stenographic notes as taken in said cause on said date.

Henry G. Hains

Subscribed and sworn to before me this 10th day of May, 1905.

Drennan C Skaggs
Notary Public.

774
N.C. 1140 & 1141.

DEPARTMENT OF THE INTERIOR,
COMMISSIONER TO THE FIVE CIVILIZED TRIBES.
Okemah, I. T., October 20, 1905.

In the matter of the application for the enrollment of Indie Roberts as a citizen by blood of the Creek Nation.

KENDALL ROBERTS, being duly sworn, testified as follows

Through Alex Posey Official Interpreter::

Applications for Enrollment of Creek Newborn
Act of 1905   Volume X

BY THE COMMISSIONER:
Q What is your name? A Kendall Roberts.
Q How old are you? A About thirty-three.
Q What is your post office address? A Morse.
Q Are you a citizen of the Creek Nation? A Yes, sir.
Q To what town do you belong? A Nuyaka.
Q Have you a child named Indie Roberts? A Yes, sir. The child is a girl.
Q Have you made application for the child's enrollment as a Creek New-Born? A Yes, sir. I went before Tupper Dunn (notary) and executed affidavits about the child. I made application at the same time for another child named Cainey Roberts.
Q What was the name of the mother of Indie? A Mary Roberts was the mother of both children.
Q What was your wife's name before her marriage to you? A Mary West.
Q When was Indie born? A January 18, 1903.
Q Is the child also known as Indie Johnson? A No, sir. Indie Johnson is a child of my sister, Wiley Roberts. The child's father was Ahullie Johnson, who is now dead.
Q To what town does Wiley Roberts belong? A Nuyaka.
Q To what town did Ahullie Johnson belong? A Greenleaf.
Q Is Indie Johnson living? A No, sir, she is dead.
Q Did they have another child named Mandoche Johnson? A Yes, sir. That child is also dead. My child, Indie Roberts and Indie Johnson are two different children. Wiley's child was named after its father, Ahullie Johnson, and the mother is known as Wiley Roberts instead of Wiley Johnson.
Q Was your wife ever known as Willie? A No, sir.
Q Was Wiley ever known as Millie? A No, sir.
Q Have you any other children? A I have only one other child living.
Q What is its name? A Johnson Roberts.
Q Has your sister, Wiley Roberts, any other children? A No, sir. She only had two children, Indie and Mandoche.
Q Is your wife Mary Roberts enrolled as Mary Roberts? A Yes, sir.
Q Is your sister, Wiley Roberts, enrolled as Wiley Roberts or Wiley Johnson? A She is enrolled as Wiley Roberts. I notice you have my name spelled Cundal. That is not correct--it is Kendall.

I, D. C. Skaggs, on oath state that the above and foregoing is a full and true transcript of my stenographic notes as taken in said cause on said date.

DC Skaggs

Subscribed and sworn to before me this 30 day of Dec 1905.

Edw C Griesel
Notary Public.

Applications for Enrollment of Creek Newborn
Act of 1905   Volume X

NC-774
DEPARTMENT OF THE INTERIOR,
COMMISSIONER TO THE FIVE CIVILIZED TRIBES.

Muskogee, Indian Territory, December 4, 1905

In the matter of the application for the enrollment of Indie Roberts as a citizen by blood of the Creek Nation.

Kendall Roberts, being duly sworn, testified as follows (through Jesse McDermott, Official Interpreter):

EXAMINATION BY THE COMMISSIONER:
Q What is your name? A Kendall Roberts.
Q How old are you? A About 33.
Q What is your postoffice address? A Morse.
Q Have you a child named Indie Roberts? A Yes sir.
Q Is it a girl? A Yes sir.
Q When was she born? A I haven't the record with me, or I could tell you the exact date.
Who was the mother of this child? A Mary Roberts.
Q She signed an affidavit saying the child was born January 18, 1903; is that about correct? A Yes sir.
Q Is India living? A Yes sir.
Q Have you a child named Johnson Roberts that is already enrolled here? A Yes sir.
Q Is Johnson living? A Yes sir.
Q You have another named Cainey; is she living? A Yes sir.
Q That is all, is it? A Yes sir.
Q What is the name of Mary's father? A Tulmochus Harjo.

Said Kendal and Mary Roberts are identified on creek Indian care, Field No. 1344, opposite Roll Nos. 4295 and 4296, respectively

The witness is advised that there is on file in this Office the affidavit of the mother of Indie Roberts, in which she states that she attended on herself; that there was no midwife or physician in attendance at the birth of said child physician present at the birth of Indie. This Office requires the affidavit of two disinterested witnesses as to the birth of Indie Roberts. It should be furnished at once.

INDIAN TERRITORY, Western District.
I, J. Y. Miller, a stenographer to the Commissioner to the Five Civilized Tribes, do hereby certify that the above and foregoing is a true and complete translation of my notes as same appear in my stenographic report of this case.

JY Miller

Applications for Enrollment of Creek Newborn
Act of 1905   Volume X

Sworn to and subscribed before me
this the 6th day of December,
1905.   J McDermott
                                              Notary Public.

AFFIDAVIT OF DISINTERESTED WITNESSES.

United States of America,
  Indian Territory,
  Western District.

We, the undersigned, on oath state that we are personally acquainted with Mary Roberts   , wife of   Kendall Roberts   ; and that there was born to her on or about the   18   day of   January , 1903, a   girl   child; that said child was living March 4, 1905. and is said to have been named   Indy Roberts   . We further state that we have no interest in this case.

                                  Ella West
                                  (Name Illegible)

(2) Witnesses to mark

_____

_____

Subscribed and sworn to before me this 20 of December , 1905.

My Commission expires *(Illegible)* 15, 1904   *(Name Illegible)*
                                              Notary Public.

BIRTH AFFIDAVIT.
DEPARTMENT OF THE INTERIOR,
COMMISSION TO THE FIVE CIVILIZED TRIBES.
                    Copy

In Re Application for Enrollment, as a citizen of the Creek Nation, of Indie Roberts , born on the 18 day of January , 1903

Name of Father: Kendall Roberts   a citizen of the   Creek   Nation.
Name of Father: Mary Roberts   a citizen of the   Creek   Nation.

                        Post-office   Morse, I.T.

_____

Applications for Enrollment of Creek Newborn
Act of 1905 Volume X

AFFIDAVIT OF MOTHER.

~~Copy~~

UNITED STATES OF AMERICA, }
   INDIAN TERRITORY,
   Western   District.

   I, Mary Roberts , on oath state that I am 29 years of age and a citizen by blood , of the Creek Nation; that I am the lawful wife of Kendall Roberts , who is a citizen, by blood of the Creek Nation; that a female child was born to me on 18 day of January , 1903 , that said child has been named Indie Roberts , and ~~is now~~ was living. March I attending myself her

                                  Mary x Roberts
WITNESSES TO MARK: mark
  { Kendall Roberts
    Wiley Roberts
(Seal)

   Subscribed and sworn to before me this 17 day of April , 1905.

My Com Exp Aug. 19-1908   Tupper Dunn
                                        NOTARY PUBLIC.

BIRTH AFFIDAVIT.

DEPARTMENT OF THE INTERIOR.
COMMISSION TO THE FIVE CIVILIZED TRIBES.

   IN RE APPLICATION FOR ENROLLMENT, as a citizen of the Creek Nation, of Cainey Roberts , born on the 10 day of February , 1905

Name of Father: Kendall Roberts   a citizen of the   Creek   Nation.
Name of Mother: Mary Roberts   a citizen of the   Creek   Nation.

                          Postoffice   Morse I. T.

AFFIDAVIT OF MOTHER.

UNITED STATES OF AMERICA, Indian Territory, }
   Western   DISTRICT.

   I, Mary Roberts , on oath state that I am 29 years of age and a citizen by blood, of the Creek Nation; that I am the lawful wife of Kendall Roberts , who is a citizen, by blood of the Creek Nation; that a male child was born to me on 10 day of February , 1905 , that said child has been named Cainey Roberts , and was living March 4, 1905.

Applications for Enrollment of Creek Newborn
Act of 1905   Volume X

Witnesses To Mark:
{ Kendall Roberts
  Wiley Roberts

        her
      Mary x Roberts
        mark

Subscribed and sworn to before me this 17 day of April, 1905.

My Com Exp Aug. 19-1908   Tupper Dunn
             Notary Public.

AFFIDAVIT OF ATTENDING PHYSICIAN OR MID-WIFE.

UNITED STATES OF AMERICA, Indian Territory,
  Western **DISTRICT.**

  I, Wiley Roberts, a Midwife, on oath state that I attended on Mrs. Mary Roberts, wife of Kendall Roberts on the 10 day of February, 1905 ; that there was born to her on said date a male child; that said child was living March 4, 1905, and is said to have been named Cainey Roberts

            Wiley Roberts
Witnesses To Mark:
{

Subscribed and sworn to before me 17 day of April, 1905.

My Com Exp Aug. 19-1908   Tupper Dunn
             Notary Public.

BIRTH AFFIDAVIT.

DEPARTMENT OF THE INTERIOR.
COMMISSION TO THE FIVE CIVILIZED TRIBES.

  IN RE APPLICATION FOR ENROLLMENT, as a citizen of the Creek Nation, of Indie Roberts, born on the 18 day of January, 1903

Name of Father: Kendall Roberts   a citizen of the Creek Nation.
Name of Mother: Mary Roberts   a citizen of the Creek Nation.

        Postoffice Morse I. T.

Applications for Enrollment of Creek Newborn
Act of 1905   Volume X

AFFIDAVIT OF MOTHER.

UNITED STATES OF AMERICA, Indian Territory,
Western   DISTRICT.

    I, Mary Roberts, on oath state that I am 29 years of age and a citizen by blood, of the Creek Nation; that I am the lawful wife of Kendall Roberts, who is a citizen, by blood of the Creek Nation; that a female child was born to me on 18 day of January, 1903, that said child has been named Indie Roberts, and was living March 4, 1905.

                                      her
                            Mary x Roberts
Witnesses To Mark: mark
  { Kendall Roberts
    Wiley Roberts

    Subscribed and sworn to before me this 17 day of April, 1905.

My Com Exp Aug. 19-1908   Tupper Dunn
                                    Notary Public.

NC-775

                        Muskogee, Indian Territory, October 18, 1905.

Susanna Kelly,
    c/o Wesley Kelly,
        Wealaka, Indian Territory.

Dear Madam:

    In the matter of the application for the enrollment of your minor daughter, Rosella Kelly, born May 14, 1904, as a citizen by blood of the Creek Nation this office is unable to identify you upon the final roll of citizens by blood of the Creek Nation.

    It is necessary that you be identified before the rights of said child can be finally determined. You are therefore requested to inform this office of the name under which you are finally enrolled, the names of your parents and other members of your family, the Creek Indian town to which you belong and your final roll number as the same appears upon your allotment certificate and deeds.

                            Respectfully,

                                          Commissioner.

Applications for Enrollment of Creek Newborn
Act of 1905 Volume X

BIRTH AFFIDAVIT.

DEPARTMENT OF THE INTERIOR.
COMMISSION TO THE FIVE CIVILIZED TRIBES.

IN RE APPLICATION FOR ENROLLMENT, as a citizen of the Creek Nation, of Rosella Kelly, born on the 14 day of May, 1904

Name of Father: Wesley Kelley	a citizen of the Creek	Nation.
Name of Mother: Susanna Kelly	a citizen of the Creek	Nation.

Postoffice   Wealaka IT

AFFIDAVIT OF MOTHER.

UNITED STATES OF AMERICA, Indian Territory,
WESTERN   DISTRICT.

I, Susanna Kelly, on oath state that I am 31 years of age and a citizen by Blood, of the Creek Nation; that I am the lawful wife of Wesley Kelly, who is a citizen, by Blood of the Creek Nation; that a female child was born to me on 14 day of May, 1904, that said child has been named Rosella Kelly, and is now living.

Susanna Kelley

Witnesses To Mark:

Subscribed and sworn to before me this 17th day of April, 1905.

Ralph Dresback
Notary Public.

AFFIDAVIT OF ATTENDING PHYSICIAN OR MID-WIFE.

UNITED STATES OF AMERICA, Indian Territory,
WESTERN   DISTRICT.

I, Rosa Alexander, a midwife, on oath state that I attended on Mrs. Susanna Kelly, wife of Wesley Kelly on the 14 day of May, 1904 ; that there was born to her on said date a female child; that said child is now living and is said to have been named Rosella Kelly

her
Rosa x Alexander
mark

Witnesses To Mark:
  C.J. Neuhard
  Nero Tecumseh

Applications for Enrollment of Creek Newborn
Act of 1905   Volume X

Subscribed and sworn to before me this 17th day of April, 1905.

                                          Ralph Dresback
                                          Notary Public.

NC 776

DEPARTMENT OF THE INTERIOR,
COMMISSIONER TO THE FIVE CIVILIZED TRIBES.

In the matter of the application for the enrollment of OPHILA HARJO as a citizen of the Creek Nation.

SAMPSON HARJO, being first duly sworn by Edward Merrick, a Notary Public, testifies as follows:

<u>BY THE COMMISSIONER</u>:

Q What is your name? A Sampson Harjo.
Q What is your postoffice address? A Grayson.
Q How old are you? A I was born June 24, 1863.
Q We have here the affidavits of Mahalay Harjo-- A Yes sir.
Q And Mary Sayles, executed on April 14, 1905 in the matter of the date of birth of Ophelia Harjo, and the affidavit of Simon Harjo and L. Alexander filed with this office on April 22, 1905 in the matter of the date of birth of Ophila Harjo; state whether or not you have a child by the name of Ophelia or Ophila Harjo? A Yes sir, Ophelia.
Q The correct name of the child is Ophelia, O-p-h-e-l-i-a? A Yes sir, Ophelia.
Q How do you spell it? A O-p-h-l-a.
Q Now is it O-p-h-i-l-a- or O-p-h-e-l-i-a, Ophila or Ophelia? A It is Ophelia.
Q When was Ophelia born? A On the 11th day of March, 1905.
Q 1905? A Yes sir, I think that is the date; she will be three years old this March, she was born the 11th of March, 1904.
Q Is she living now? A Yes sir, talks well too.
Q Is she your child? A Yes sir.
Q What is her mother's name? A Mahalay Harjo.
Q Are you a citizen of the Creek Nation? A Yes sir, full blood.
Q Full blood? A Yes sir.
Q Have you received your allotment? A Not yet, it is pending.
Q Are you on the roll? A I am on the roll.
Q You have an application for enrollment pending? A Yes sir. I am a member of Arbaka, Deep Fork Town.
Q You have an application pending, that is all you have? A Yes sir.

Applications for Enrollment of Creek Newborn
Act of 1905   Volume X

Q You havent[sic] received your allotment yet? A No sir.

WITNESS EXCUSED.

—

Cora Moore, being first duly sworn, states that as stenographer to the Commissioner to the Five Civilized Tribes she reported the proceedings had in the above entitled cause on February 14, 1907, and that the above and foregoing is a true and correct transcript of her stenographic notes taken in said cause on said date.

Cora Moore

Subscribed and sworn to before me February 15, 1907.

Edward Merrick
Notary Public.

NC 776

WSC
CM

DEPARTMENT OF THE INTERIOR,
COMMISSIONER TO THE FIVE CIVILIZED TRIBES.

In the matter of the application for the enrollment of Ophila Harjo as a citizen by blood of the Creek Nation.

DECISION.

The record in this case shows that on April 21, 1905, application was made, in affidavit form, for the enrollment of Ophelia Harjo as a citizen by blood of the Creek Nation, under the provisions of the act of Congress approved March 3, 1905 (33 Stat. 1048). The parents of the applicant not being duly enrolled citizens of the Creek Nation there was no authority of law to consider this application under the provisions of the Act of Congress approved March 3, 1905 (33 Stat. 1048), but it is considered as a continuing application for the enrollment of said Ophelia Harjo as a citizen by blood of the Creek Nation under the provisions of the Act of Congress approved March 3, 1905 (33 Stat. 1048). The affidavits of Simon Harjo and L. Alexander in the matter of the birth of the applicant herein, filed with this office on April 22, 1905, are attached to and made a part of the record herein. Further proceedings were had February 15, 1907. It appears from the evidence that the proper name of the applicant is Ophila Harjo and further reference will be made to her under that name.

It also appears from the evidence in this case that the applicant herein was born on the 11th day of March, 1904, and was living on the date of the last proceedings had herein.

It further appears from the evidence and the records in the possession of this office that the applicant herein is the minor child of Simon Harjo, an alleged citizen of the Creek Nation, and Mahaley Harjo, a non-citizen, and possesses no right to enrollment

Applications for Enrollment of Creek Newborn
Act of 1905   Volume X

as a citizen of the Creek Nation not possessed by her parents. It further appears that application was made on June 1, 1904 for the enrollment of the aforesaid Simon Harjo as a citizen by blood of the Creek Nation; that said application was on November 11, 1905 denied by the Commissioner to the Five Civilized Tribes and on November 13, 1905 the decision therein was forwarded to the Department of the Interior for approval. February 1, 1907 (I.T.D. 1828-1907) the Department remanded the record and decision of this office in this matter and ordered a readjudication of the same. In accordance therewith further proceedings were had on February 14 and 15, 1907, and on February 25, 1907 the Commissioner to the Five Civilized Tribes rendered his decision again denying said application for enrolment and forwarded the decision, together with the entire record in the case, to the Department on the same day.

It is, therefore, ordered and adjudged that the applicant, Ophila Harjo, is not entitled to be enrolled as a citizen by blood of the Creek Nation under the provisions of the Act of Congress approved April 26, 1905 (34 Stat. 137), and the application for her enrollment as such is accordingly denied.

Tams Bixby   COMMISSIONER.

Muskogee, Indian Territory.
FEB 27 1907

NC 766

Muskogee, Indian Territory, February 27, 1907.

M. L. Mott,
    Attorney for Creek Nation,
        Muskogee, Indian Territory.

Dear Sir:

There is herewith enclosed one copy of the decision of the Commissioner to the Five Civilized Tribes, in the matter of the application for the enrollment of Ophila Harjo, as a citizen by blood of the Creek Nation, denying said application.

The decision, with a copy of the proceedings had in the case, is this day transmitted to the Secretary of the Interior for his review and decision. The final decision of the Secretary will be made known to you as soon as the Commissioner is informed of the same.

Respectfully,

Commissioner.

LM 210

Applications for Enrollment of Creek Newborn
Act of 1905 Volume X

Nc 766

Muskogee, Indian Territory, February 27, 1907.

Mahaley Harjo,
    Care of Simon Harjo,
        Grayson, Indian Territory.

Dear Madam:

    There is herewith enclosed one copy of the decision of the Commissioner to the Five Civilized Tribes, in the matter of the application for the enrollment of your minor child Ophila Harjo, as a citizen by blood of the Creek Nation, denying said application.

    The decision, with a copy of the proceedings had in the case, is this day transmitted to the Secretary of the Interior for his review and decision. The final decision of the Secretary will be made known to you as soon as the Commissioner is informed of the same.

                Respectfully,

                              Commissioner.

LM 206.
Register.

Muskogee, Indian Territory, February 27, 1907.

The Honorable,
    The Secretary of the Interior.
Sir:

    There is herewith transmitted record of proceedings in the matter of the application for the enrollment of Ophila Harjo, as a citizen by blood of the Creek Nation, including the decision of the Commissioner to the Five Civilized Tribes denying said application.

                Respectfully,

                              Commissioner.

LM 212
Through the Commissioner
    of Indian Affairs.

Applications for Enrollment of Creek Newborn
Act of 1905 Volume X

DEPARTMENT OF THE INTERIOR
WASHINGTON

JP
FHE

I.T.D. 7764-1907.

LES

March 4, 1907.

Direct.

Commissioner to the Five Civilized Tribes,
    Muskogee, Indian Territory.
Sir:

    The Department has considered the following citizenship cases received with your letters of February 25, 26 and 27 1907, and Indian Office letter of March 2, 1907 (Land 21229 et al), copy inclosed, and in accordance with the recommendation made by you and the Indian Office the application in each case is rejected:

Title of case.

George and Julia McIntosh, deceased (freedmen)
Belle and Delpha May Brown (Freedmen)
Peggy McCoy (Freedman)
Lena McGirt (Creek)
Julia Grayson deceased (Creek)
Cesarpe, Ithas Harjo and Mewike (Creeks)
<u>Ophila Harjo (Creek)</u>
Louana Johnson (Creek)
Sampson Harjo (Creek)
Ivy Richardson (Cherokee freedman)
Hester and Myrtle Powell (Cherokee freedman)
George Sutherland (Cherokee)
Lawrence Smith (Creek freedman)
John W. Vaughn et al., (Cherokees)
Louis A. Lafallier, (Cherokee)

A copy hereof has been sent to the Indian Office.

Respectfully,
E. A. Hitchcock,
Secretary.

i inclosure. WCF 4/4/06.

Applications for Enrollment of Creek Newborn
Act of 1905   Volume X

LAND

DEPARTMENT OF THE INTERIOR
OFFICE OF INDIAN AFFAIRS
WASHINGTON.

References
at bottom
of letter.

The Honorable,
    The Secretary of The Interior.
Sir:

    There are forwarded herewith several reports of Commissioner Bixby and records in the following named citizenship cases, together with the Commissioner's decision denying the applications for enrollment of the persons involved in each case:

Cherokee citizens by blood	John W. Vaughn, et al.,
Cherokee citizens by intermarriage	George Sutherland
	Louis A Lafallier
Cherokee freedmen	Hester ad[sic] Myrtle Powell
	Ivy Richardson
Creek citizens by blood	Sampson Harjo
	Louanna Johnson
	Ophila Harjo
	Cosarpe, Ithas Harjo, and Mewile
	Julia Grayson
	Lena McGirt
	Belle Brown and Delpha May Brown
	Lawrence Smith
	George and Julia McIntosh
	Peggy McCoy

    The Office has examined the record in each of the above cases and recommends for approval the decisions of the Commissioner denying the applications.

    There are also forwarded herewith briefs and affidavits to be considered in connection with the following cases, which have heretofore been forwarded to the Department:

Chickasaw citizens by blood	M.D. Carson et al.
Chickasaw intermarried citizen	Martin M. Yoakum

Applications for Enrollment of Creek Newborn
Act of 1905   Volume X

Choctaw citizen by blood   Hazy Ann Vandergriff

Choctaw intermarried citizen   Mattie Doak

Choctaw intermarried citizen   Emma Crawford

Choctaw intermarried citizen   Mary Jane Williams

Very respectfully,
C. F. Larrabee,

AJW-EH   Acting Commissioner.

21229-1907	21271-1907	21265-1907
21226	21270	21221
21230	21269	21222
21236	21227	21224
21237	21268	21248
21273	21267	21223
21272	21266	21225

NC 776.

Muskogee, Indian Territory, March 16, 1907.

Mahaley Harjo,
   c/o Simon Harjo,
      Grayson, Indian Territory.

Dear Madam:

    You are hereby advised that the Secretary of the Interior under date of March 4, 1907, affirmed the decision of the Commissioner to the Five Civilized Tribes, denying the application for the enrollment of your minor child, Ophila Harjo, as a citizen by blood of the Creek Nation.

Respectfully,

LM   Commissioner.

Applications for Enrollment of Creek Newborn
Act of 1905 Volume X

THE WESTERN UNION TELEGRAPH COMPANY.
----------INCORPORATED----------
24,000 OFFICES IN AMERICA.   CABLE SERVICE TO ALL THE WORLD.
ROBERT C. CLOWRY, President and General Manager.

Receiver's No.	Time Filed	Check
		Government Paid

SEND the following message subject to the terms on back hereof, which are hereby agreed to.

February 5,   190 7

To   Jesse McDermott,
_____Creek Enrollment Party,_____
_____Checotah, Indian Territory._____
_____Ascertain whether Ophila Harjo, minor child of Samuel or Simon_____
_____Harjo, postoffice, Grayson, was living March 4, 1906._____
_____Secure proof of marriage of Simon to Mahaley Harjo._____
_____BIXBY._____
O.B.G.R.   Commissioner.

READ THE NOTICE AND AGREEMENT ON BACK

BIRTH AFFIDAVIT.

DEPARTMENT OF THE INTERIOR.
COMMISSION TO THE FIVE CIVILIZED TRIBES.

IN RE APPLICATION FOR ENROLLMENT, as a citizen of the Creek Nation, of Martha Tiger, born on the 11 day of March, 1904

Name of Father: Daniel Tiger   a citizen of the   Creek   Nation.
(Tuskegee)
Name of Mother: Sarah " (Hawkins)   a citizen of the   "   Nation.
(Tuskegee)

Postoffice   Bristow

Applications for Enrollment of Creek Newborn
Act of 1905 Volume X

AFFIDAVIT OF MOTHER.

Child Present

UNITED STATES OF AMERICA, Indian Territory, ⎱
    Western   DISTRICT. ⎰

    I, Sarah Tiger nee Hawkins , on oath state that I am 38 years of age and a citizen by blood , of the Creek Nation; that I am the lawful wife of Daniel Tiger , who is a citizen, by blood of the Creek Nation; that a female child was born to me on 11 day of Mar. , 1904 , that said child has been named Martha Tiger , and is now living.

                                  Her
                             Sarah x Tiger
Witnesses To Mark: mark
  ⎰ Jesse McDermott
  ⎱ Edw C Griesel

    Subscribed and sworn to before me this 17 day of April , 1905.

    (Seal)   Edw C Griesel
                                        Notary Public.

AFFIDAVIT OF ATTENDING PHYSICIAN OR MID-WIFE.

UNITED STATES OF AMERICA, Indian Territory, ⎱
    Western   DISTRICT. ⎰

    I, Nellie Tiger , a Mid wife , on oath state that I attended on Mrs. Sarah Tiger , wife of Daniel Tiger on the 11 day of March , 1904 ; that there was born to her on said date a female child; that said child is now living and is said to have been named Martha Tiger

                                  Her
                             Nellie x Tiger
Witnesses To Mark: mark
  ⎰ Jesse McDermott
  ⎱ Edw C Griesel

    Subscribed and sworn to before me this 17 day of April , 1905.

    (Seal)   Edw C Griesel
                                        Notary Public.

Applications for Enrollment of Creek Newborn
Act of 1905 Volume X

J.D.

REFER IN REPLY TO THE FOLLOWING:

NC-778.

DEPARTMENT OF THE INTERIOR,
COMMISSIONER TO THE FIVE CIVILIZED TRIBES.

Muskogee, Indian Territory, October 18, 1905.

Fannie Hawkins,
    Bristow, Indian Territory.

Dear Madam:

    In the matter of the application for the enrollment of your minor son Louis Hamilton, born March 8, 1904, as a citizen by blood of the Creek Nation this office is unable to identify the father of said child upon the final roll of citizens by blood of the Creek Nation.

    It is necessary that he be identified and you are requested to advise this office of the name under which he is finally enrolled, the names of his parents and other members of his family, the Creek Indian town to which he belongs and his final roll number as the same appears upon his allotment certificate and deeds.

                  Respectfully,
                    Tams Bixby
                                  Commissioner.

NC-778

Muskogee, Indian Territory, December 15, 1905

Fannie Hawkins,
    Bristow, Indian Territory.

Dear Madam:

    In the matter of the application for the enrollment of your minor child, Louis Hamilton, born March 8, 1904, as a citizen by blood of the Creek Nation, this Office is unable to identify Ed Hamilton, the father of said child, on its final rolls of citizens by blood of the Creek Nation.

    If Ed Hamilton is a citizen of the Creek Nation as stated in your affidavit, you are requested to inform this office as to the names of his parents, the Creek Indian Town to which he belongs, and, if possible, his name and roll number as same appear on his allotment certificate and deeds to land in the Creek Nation. If he is not a citizen of the Creek Nation, you should advise this Office of that fact without delay.

                  Respectfully,
                                  Commissioner.

Applications for Enrollment of Creek Newborn
Act of 1905 Volume X

N C 778 (COPY)

Bristow, Indian Territory, September 10, 1906

Commissioner to the Five Civilized Tribes,
    Muskogee, Indian Territory

Dear Sir:

    There are herewith enclosed affidavits of the mother and midwife in the matter of the application for the enrollment of Louis Hawkins, as a citizen by blood of the Creek nation[sic]. In the original application, the record shows the child's name as Louis Hamilton, but the mother states that Tom Flynn called the name Hamilton and that is why the Notary Public made out the affidavit under that name.

                      Respectfully,
                      (Signed) Jesse McDermott
                      Clerk in Charge.

NC 778.

Muskogee, Indian Territory, September 13, 1906.

Jesse McDermott,
    Creek Enrollment Field Party,
        Bristow, Indian Territory.

Dear Sir:

    Replying to your letter of September 5, 1906, you are advised that on April 22, 1905, application was made for the enrollment, as a citizen of the Creek Nation of Louis Hamilton, born March 8, 1904, to Ed Hamilton, unidentified as a citizen of the Creek Nation, and Fannie Hawkins, who is identified opposite Creek Indian Roll number 6063.

    You are advised that further proof is required in said case, and the parents have been notified to appear at this office to be examined under oath.

                      Respectfully,
                                Commissioner.

Applications for Enrollment of Creek Newborn
Act of 1905 Volume X

NBC 778.

Muskogee, Indian Territory, September 14, 1906.

Fannie Hamilton,
    c/o Ed Hamilton,
        Bristow, Indian Territory.

Dear Madam:

In the matter of the application for the enrollment of your minor child, Louis Hamilton, as a citizen of the Creek Nation, you are advised that you will be allowed fifteen days from date hereof within which to appear at this office for the purpose of being examined under oath.

                Respectfully,

                              Commissioner.

BIRTH AFFIDAVIT.

DEPARTMENT OF THE INTERIOR.
COMMISSION TO THE FIVE CIVILIZED TRIBES.

IN RE APPLICATION FOR ENROLLMENT, as a citizen of the Creek Nation, of Louis Hawkins, born on the 8 day of March, 1904

Name of Father: Eddie Jack	a citizen of the Creek	Nation.
Roll #2733		
Name of Mother: Fannie Hawkins	a citizen of the Creek	Nation.
Roll #2063		

                Postoffice   Bristow I.T.

AFFIDAVIT OF MOTHER.

                Illegitimate Child

UNITED STATES OF AMERICA, Indian Territory, }
    Western   DISTRICT.

I, Fannie Hawkins, on oath state that I am 20 years of age and a citizen by blood, of the Creek Nation; that I am not the lawful wife of Eddie Jack, who is a citizen, by blood of the Creek Nation; that a male child was born to me on 8 day of March, 1904, that said child has been named Louis Hawkins, and was living March 4, 1905.

                                          her
                              Fannie x Hawkins

Witnesses To Mark: mark
    { Jesse McDermott
      E.H. Putt

Applications for Enrollment of Creek Newborn
Act of 1905 Volume X

Subscribed and sworn to before me this 10" day of Sept , 1906.

My Commission
Expires July 25" 1907

J McDermott
Notary Public.

AFFIDAVIT OF ATTENDING PHYSICIAN OR MID-WIFE.

UNITED STATES OF AMERICA, Indian Territory,
Western DISTRICT.

I, Nellie Tiger , a midwife , on oath state that I attended on Mrs. Fannie Hawkins , not the wife of Eddie Jack on the 8 day of March , 1904 ; that there was born to her on said date a male child; that said child was living March 4, 1905, and is said to have been named Louis Hawkins

         her
Nellie x Tiger
       mark

Witnesses To Mark:
  Jesse McDermott
  E.H. Putt

Subscribed and sworn to before me this 10" day of Sept , 1906.

J McDermott
Notary Public.

BIRTH AFFIDAVIT.

DEPARTMENT OF THE INTERIOR.
COMMISSION TO THE FIVE CIVILIZED TRIBES.

IN RE APPLICATION FOR ENROLLMENT, as a citizen of the Creek Nation, of Louis Hamilton , born on the 8 day of March , 1904

Name of Father: Ed Hamilton   a citizen of the   Creek   Nation.
Tuskegee
Name of Mother: Fannie Hawkins   a citizen of the   Creek   Nation.
Tuskegee

        Postoffice   Bristow

AFFIDAVIT OF MOTHER.
Child Present

UNITED STATES OF AMERICA, Indian Territory,
Western DISTRICT.

I, Fannie Hawkins , on oath state that I am 19 years of age and a citizen by blood , of the Creek Nation; that I am ~~the~~ not the lawful wife of Ed Hamilton , who

Applications for Enrollment of Creek Newborn
Act of 1905   Volume X

is a citizen, by blood of the Creek Nation; that a male child was born to me on 8 day of March , 1904 , that said child has been named Louis Hamilton , and is now living.

                                        Her
Witnesses To Mark: Fannie x Hawkins
{ Jesse McDermott   mark
{ EC Griesel

Subscribed and sworn to before me this 17 day of April , 1905.

                                                   Edw C Griesel
                                                   Notary Public.

AFFIDAVIT OF ATTENDING ~~PHYSICIAN~~ OR MID-WIFE.

UNITED STATES OF AMERICA, Indian Territory,
     Western   DISTRICT.

I, Nellie Tiger , a Midwife , on oath state that I attended on ~~Mrs~~. Fannie Hawkins , not the wife of Ed Hamilton on the 8 day of March , 1904 ; that there was born to her on said date a male child; that said child is now living and is said to have been named Louis Hamilton

                                        Her
Witnesses To Mark: Nellie x Tiger
{ Jesse McDermott   mark
{ EC Griesel

Subscribed and sworn to before me this 17 day of April , 1905.

                                                   Edw C Griesel
                                                   Notary Public.

(The above Birth Affidavit given again.)

Applications for Enrollment of Creek Newborn
Act of 1905   Volume X

BIRTH AFFIDAVIT.

DEPARTMENT OF THE INTERIOR.
COMMISSION TO THE FIVE CIVILIZED TRIBES.

IN RE APPLICATION FOR ENROLLMENT, as a citizen of the Creek Nation, of Charles Call, born on the 25th day of Sept, 1901

Name of Father: John M. Call   ~~a citizen of the~~ ———— Nation.
Name of Mother: Pearl Call   a citizen of the   Creek   Nation.

                        Postoffice   Bixby, Ind. Ter.
4/22/05 Child present J.D.

AFFIDAVIT OF MOTHER.

UNITED STATES OF AMERICA, Indian Territory, }
    Western   DISTRICT.

I, Pearl Call, on oath state that I am 28 years of age and a citizen by blood, of the Creek Nation; that I am the lawful wife of John M. Call, who is a non citizen, ~~by (blank) of the (blank) Nation~~; that a male child was born to me on 25th day of September, 1901, that said child has been named Charles Call, and is now living.

                                  Pearl Call
Witnesses To Mark:
{

Subscribed and sworn to before me this 21st day of April, 1905.

                                    J.F. Panther
                                    Notary Public.

AFFIDAVIT OF ATTENDING PHYSICIAN OR MID-WIFE.

UNITED STATES OF AMERICA, Indian Territory, }
    Western   DISTRICT.

I, Dollie Bowman, a *(blank)*, on oath state that I attended on Mrs. Pearl Call, wife of John M. Call on the 25th day of Sept, 1901; that there was born to her on said date a male child; that said child is now living and is said to have been named Charles Call

                                  Dollie Bowman
Witnesses To Mark:
{

Applications for Enrollment of Creek Newborn
Act of 1905 Volume X

Subscribed and sworn to before me this 21st day of April, 1905.

                                                  J.F. Panther
                                                  Notary Public.

DEPARTMENT OF THE INTERIOR.
COMMISSION TO THE FIVE CIVILIZED TRIBES.

In the matter of the death of Lizzie White a citizen of the Creek Nation, who formerly resided at or near Mellette, Ind. Ter., and died on the 22" day of Feby, 1906

AFFIDAVIT OF RELATIVE.

UNITED STATES OF AMERICA, Indian Territory,
    Western   DISTRICT.

I, Choctaw Givens, on oath state that I am 59 years of age and a citizen by blood, of the Creek Nation; that my postoffice address is Mellette, Ind. Ter.; that I am Grandfather of Lizzie White who was a citizen, by blood, of the Creek Nation and that said Lizzie White died on the 22" day of Feby, 1906

                                        Choctaw Givens   his x

Witnesses To Mark:
    John W Robertson
    L.K. Massey

Subscribed and sworn to before me this 31 day of Jan, 1907.

                                        L.G. McIntosh
                                              Notary Public.

My Com expires Apr. 10.1907

AFFIDAVIT OF ACQUAINTANCE.

UNITED STATES OF AMERICA, Indian Territory,
    Western   DISTRICT.

I, Robert Benton, on oath state that I am 40 years of age, and a citizen by blood of the Creek Nation; that my postoffice address is Mellette, Ind. Ter.;

Applications for Enrollment of Creek Newborn
Act of 1905   Volume X

that I was personally acquainted with   Lizzie White   who was a citizen, by blood, of the Creek Nation; and that said   Lizzie White   died on the   22"   day of Feby, 1906

                                        Robert Benton his x

Witnesses To Mark:
{ John W Robertson
  L.K. Massey

Subscribed and sworn to before me this 31 day of Jan, 1907.

                              L.G. McIntosh
My Com expires   Notary Public.
Apr. 10.1907

BIRTH AFFIDAVIT.
                       DEPARTMENT OF THE INTERIOR.
              COMMISSION TO THE FIVE CIVILIZED TRIBES.

      IN RE APPLICATION FOR ENROLLMENT, as a citizen of the Creek Nation, of Lizzie White, born on the 17 day of December, 1904

Name of Father: George White   a citizen of the   Creek   Nation.
Name of Mother: Sarah White   a citizen of the   Creek   Nation.

                        Postoffice   Mellette I.T.

                        AFFIDAVIT OF MOTHER.

UNITED STATES OF AMERICA, Indian Territory,
        Western   **DISTRICT.**

      I, (<u>Decease</u>)   , on oath state that I am ....years of age and a citizen by ...., of the .... Nation; that I am the lawful wife of ...., who is a citizen, by .... of the .... Nation; that a .... child was born to me on .... day of ...., 1........; that said child has been named ...., and was living March 4, 1905.

Witnesses To Mark:
{ ....
  ....

      Subscribed and sworn to before me this .... day of ...., 1905.

                                       Notary Public.

Applications for Enrollment of Creek Newborn
Act of 1905 Volume X

AFFIDAVIT OF ATTENDING PHYSICIAN OR MID-WIFE.

UNITED STATES OF AMERICA, Indian Territory,
Western DISTRICT.

my wife
I, George White , a ~~(blank)~~ , on oath state that I attended on ^ Mrs. Sarah White , ~~wife of~~ (blank) on the 17 day of December , 1904 ; that there was born to her on said date a Female child; that said child was living March 4, 1905, and is said to have been named Lizzie White

George White his x

Witnesses To Mark:
{ L K Massey
  Hozen Green

Subscribed and sworn to before me this 31 day of Jan, 1907.

My Com expires
Apr. 10.1907

L.G. McIntosh
Notary Public.

DEPARTMENT OF THE INTERIOR.
COMMISSION TO THE FIVE CIVILIZED TRIBES.

In the matter of the death of Sarah White a citizen of the Creek Nation, who formerly resided at or near Mellette , Ind. Ter., and died on the 22" day of October , 1906

AFFIDAVIT OF RELATIVE.

UNITED STATES OF AMERICA, Indian Territory,
Western DISTRICT.

I, Choctaw Givens , on oath state that I am 59 years of age and a citizen by blood , of the Creek Nation; that my postoffice address is Mellette , Ind. Ter.; that I am the father of Sarah White who was a citizen, by blood , of the Creek Nation and that said Sarah White died on the 22" day of October , 1906

Choctaw Givens his x

Witnesses To Mark:
{ L K Massey
  Hozen Green

Applications for Enrollment of Creek Newborn
Act of 1905   Volume X

Subscribed and sworn to before me this 31 day of Jan, 1907.

                        L.G. McIntosh
                        Notary Public.

AFFIDAVIT OF ACQUAINTANCE.

UNITED STATES OF AMERICA, Indian Territory,
    Western   DISTRICT.

    I, Robert Benton, on oath state that I am 40 years of age, and a citizen by blood of the Creek Nation; that my postoffice address is Mellette, Ind. Ter.; that I was personally acquainted with Sarah White who was a citizen, by blood, of the Creek Nation; and that said Sarah White died on the 22" day of October, 1906

                        Robert Benton his x

Witnesses To Mark:
  L K Massey
  Hozen Green

Subscribed and sworn to before me this 31 day of Jan, 1907.

                        L.G. McIntosh
Apr. 10 1907 My Com   Notary Public.
expires

BIRTH AFFIDAVIT.
DEPARTMENT OF THE INTERIOR.
COMMISSION TO THE FIVE CIVILIZED TRIBES.

    IN RE APPLICATION FOR ENROLLMENT, as a citizen of the Creek Nation, of Lizzie White, born on the 17 day of Dec., 1904

Name of Father: George White (or Field)   a citizen of the Creek Nation.
Hillabee Town
Name of Mother: Sarah White (or Yahola)   a citizen of the Creek Nation.
Tuckabatche Town
                    Postoffice   Mellette, Ind. Ter.

Applications for Enrollment of Creek Newborn
Act of 1905   Volume X

AFFIDAVIT OF MOTHER.

UNITED STATES OF AMERICA, Indian Territory, ⎫
Western   DISTRICT.   ⎬

I, Choctaw Givens , on oath state that I am about 57 years of age and a citizen by blood , of the Creek Nation; that I am the ~~lawful wife~~ father of Sarah White , who is a citizen, by blood of the Creek Nation; that a female child was born to ~~me~~ her on 17 day of December , 1904 , that said child has been named Lizzie White , and was living March 4, 1905. That the mother refuses to make application for the enrollment of the child.

                                                his
                                    Choctaw x Givens

Witnesses To Mark: mark
⎰ Alex Posey
⎱ DC Skaggs

Subscribed and sworn to before me this 7 day of April , 1905.

                                      Drennan C Skaggs
                                      Notary Public.

BIRTH AFFIDAVIT.

DEPARTMENT OF THE INTERIOR.
COMMISSION TO THE FIVE CIVILIZED TRIBES.

IN RE APPLICATION FOR ENROLLMENT, as a citizen of the Creek Nation, of Lizzie White, born on the 17 day of Dec , 1904

Name of Father: George White   a citizen of the   Creek   Nation.
Name of Mother: Sarah White   a citizen of the   Creek   Nation.

                          Postoffice   Mellette I T

AFFIDAVIT OF MOTHER.

UNITED STATES OF AMERICA, Indian Territory, ⎫
Western   DISTRICT.   ⎬

I, Sarah White , on oath state that I am about 28 years of age and a citizen by blood , of the Creek Nation; that I am the lawful wife of George White , who is a citizen, by blood of the Creek Nation; that a female child was born to me on 17 day of Dec , 1904 , that said child has been named Lizzie White , and was living March 4, 1905.

                                      Sarah Yarhalar[sic]

Applications for Enrollment of Creek Newborn
Act of 1905   Volume X

Witnesses To Mark:
{

Subscribed and sworn to before me this 5 day of Nov , 1905.

LG McIntosh
Notary Public.

AFFIDAVIT OF ATTENDING PHYSICIAN OR MID-WIFE.

UNITED STATES OF AMERICA, Indian Territory, }
     Western   DISTRICT.

I, Selie Hill , a midwife , on oath state that I attended on Mrs. Sarah White , wife of George White on the 17 day of Dec , 1904 ; that there was born to her on said date a Female child; that said child was living March 4, 1905, and is said to have been named Lizzie White

Selie Hill   her x

Witnesses To Mark:
{ WM *(Illegble)*
   L.G. McIntosh

Subscribed and sworn to before me this 5 day of Nov , 1905.

LG McIntosh
Notary Public.

BIRTH AFFIDAVIT.

Department of the Interior,
COMMISSION TO THE FIVE CIVILIZED TRIBES.

IN RE APPLICATION FOR ENROLLMENT, as a citizen of the Creek Nation, of Lizzie White , born on the 17 day of Nov , 1905

Name of Father: George White   a citizen of the   Creek   Nation.
Name of Mother: Sarah White   a citizen of the   Creek   Nation.

Post-Office: Mellette I.T.

Applications for Enrollment of Creek Newborn
Act of 1905   Volume X

AFFIDAVIT OF MOTHER.

UNITED STATES OF AMERICA, ⎫
    INDIAN TERRITORY,
  Western   District. ⎭

    I, Sarah White , on oath state that I am about 30 years of age and a citizen by blood , of the Creek Nation; that I am the lawful wife of George White , who is a citizen, by blood of the Creek Nation; that a Female child was born to me on 17 day of Nov , 1905 , that said child has been named Lizzie White , and ~~is now living~~. was living on 4th Mch 1905

Sarah White

WITNESSES TO MARK:
{

    Subscribed and sworn to before me this 26 day of Feb., 1906.

L.G. McIntosh
Notary Public.

AFFIDAVIT OF ATTENDING PHYSICIAN OR MID-WIFE.

UNITED STATES OF AMERICA, ⎫
    INDIAN TERRITORY,
  Western   District. ⎭

    I, Kizzie Givens , a midwife , on oath state that I attended on Mrs. Sarah White , wife of George White on the   17 day of Nov , 1905 ; that there was born to her on said date a Female child; that said child ~~is now living~~ was living on 4th March 1905 and is said to have been named Lizzie White

Kizzie Givens   her x

WITNESSES TO MARK:
{ John Gambler
  L.G. McIntosh

    Subscribed and sworn to before me this 26 day of Feb, 1906.

L.G. McIntosh
Notary Public

My com. expires
Apr 10 1907

Applications for Enrollment of Creek Newborn
Act of 1905 Volume X

NC 780

DEPARTMENT OF THE INTERIOR, COMMISSIONER TO THE FIVE CIVILIZED TRIBES.

In the matter of the application for the enrollment of Lizzie White, as a citizen by blood of the Creek Nation.

DECISION.

The record shows that an application was made, in affidavit form, on April 11, 1905 for the enrollment of Lizzie White as a citizen by blood of the Creek Nation. Supplemental affidavits filed November 9, 1905 and March 1, 1906 are attached to and made a part of the record herein.

It appears from the evidence in this case and the records of this office that the said Lizzie White, is the child of George and Sarah White, whose names appear as George White and Sarah Yarhola on a partial schedule of citizens by blood of the Creek Nation, approved by the Secretary of the Interior, March 28, 1902, opposite roll numbers 8359 and 7312. It appears that the supplemental affidavit filed March 1, 1906, gives the date of the birth of the said Lizzie White, as December 17, 1905, but a preponderance of the evidence establishes the date of the birth of the said applicant as December 17, 1904.

It if further established by the evidence that the said Lizzie White was living March 5, 1905.

The Act of Congress approved March 3, 1905, (33 Stats. 1048) provides in part as follows:

"That the Commission to the Five Civilized Tribes is authorized for sixty days after the date of the approval of this Act to receive and consider applications for enrollments of children born subsequent to May twenty five, nineteen hundred and one, and prior to March fourth, nineteen hundred and five, and living on said latter date, to citizens of the Creek tribe of Indians whose enrollment has been approved by the Secretary of the Interior prior to the approval of this act; and to enroll and make, allotments to such children."

It is therefore, ordered and adjudged that the said Lizzie White is entitled to be enrolled as a citizen by blood of the Creek Nation, in accordance with the provisions of law above quoted, and the application for his enrollment as such is accordingly granted.

Muskogee, Indian Territory,
JAN 17 1907   Tams Bixby   COMMISSIONER.

Applications for Enrollment of Creek Newborn
Act of 1905   Volume X

NC-780.

Muskogee, Indian Territory, October 18, 1905

Choctaw Givens,
    Mellette, Indian Territory.

Dear Sir:

    In the matter of the application for the enrollment of your minor grandchild, Lizzie White, born December 17, 1904 this office requires the affidavit of the mother of said child and the attending physician or midwife who attended at her birth.

    For that purpose there is inclosed herewith a blank form for proof of birth which you are requested to have properly executed and when so executed return it to this office in the inclosed envelope. Be careful to see that all blank spaces are properly filled, all names written in full and that the notary public, before whom the affidavits are sworn to, attaches his name and seal to each affidavit. In case any signature is by mark the same must be attested by two disinterested witnesses.

                        Respectfully,

                                          Commissioner.

B C
Env.

NC-780

Muskogee, Indian Territory, December 16, 1905.

Sarah White,
    Care of Choctaw Givens,
        Mellette, Indian Territory.

Dear Madam:

    In your affidavit on file at this Office in the matter of the application for the enrollment of your minor child, Lizzie White, born December 17, 1904, as a citizen by blood of the Creek Nation, you state that you are the lawful wife of George White, and you signed your name to said affidavit "Sarah Yarhalar."

    If you are in fact the lawful wife of said George White, it necessarily follows that your name is Sarah White, and not Sarah Yarhalar. There is herewith enclosed blank form of birth affidavit which you are requested to execute, being careful to sign you name thereto as Sarah White. You will then return said affidavit to this Office in the enclosed envelope.

    This matter should receive your immediate attention.

Applications for Enrollment of Creek Newborn
Act of 1905   Volume X

Respectfully,

Commissioner.

1 B A

N C 780

Muskogee, Indian Territory, March 7, 1907.

Sarah White,
    Care of George White,
        Mellette, Indian Territory.

Dear Madam:

    You are hereby advised that on March 2, 1907 the Secretary of the Interior approved the enrollment of your minor child, Lizzie White as a citizen by blood of the Creek Nation, and that the name of said child appears upon the roll of citizens by blood of the Creek Nation enrolled under the Act of Congress approved March 3, 1905, as number 1236.

    This child is now entitled to allotment and application therefor should be made without delay at the Creek Land Office, Muskogee, Indian Territory.

Respectfully,

Commissioner.

NC. 781.

Muskogee, Indian Territory, July 15, 1905.

Chief Clerk,
    Cherokee Enrollment Division,
        Muskogee, Indian Territory.

Dear Sir:

    April 22, 1905, application was made to the Commission to the Five Civilized Tribes for the enrollment of Ione Berryhill, born June 5, 1904, as a citizen by blood of the Creek Nation. It is stated in said application that the father of said child is James Berryhill, a citizen of the Creek Nation, and that the mother is Elnora Berryhill, a citizen of the Cherokee Nation.

Applications for Enrollment of Creek Newborn
Act of 1905   Volume X

You are requested to inform the Creek Enrollment Division as to whether application has been made for the enrollment of said Ione Berryhill as a citizen of the Cherokee Nation, and if so, what disposition has been made of the same.

Respectfully,

Commissioner.

REFER IN REPLY TO THE FOLLOWING:

DEPARTMENT OF THE INTERIOR,   JR
COMMISSIONER TO THE FIVE CIVILIZED TRIBES.

Muskogee, Indian Territory, July 18, 1905.

Chief Clerk,
    Creek Enrollment Division,
        Muskogee, Indian Territory.

Dear Sir:

Replying to your letter of July 15, 1905, (NC. 781) asking to be advised whether or not any application has ever been made for the enrollment, as a citizen of the Cherokee Nation, of Ione Berryhill, a child of James Berryhill, a citizen of the Creek Nation, and Elnora Berryhill, a citizen of the Cherokee Nation, you are advised that from an examination of the records of the Cherokee Enrollment Division it does not appear that any application has ever been made for the enrollment of said child as a citizen of that nation.

Respectfully,
Tams Bixby

GHL   Commissioner.

NC-781.

Muskogee, Indian Territory, October 18, 1905.

Elnore[sic] Berryhill,
    c/o James Berryhill,
        Summett[sic], Indian Territory.

Dear Madam:

In the matter of the application for the enrollment of your minor child Ione Berryhill, born June 5, 1904, as a citizen by blood of the Creek Nation this office requires evidence of your marriage to James Berryhill, the father of said child.

Applications for Enrollment of Creek Newborn
Act of 1905   Volume X

Such evidence may consist of either the original or a certified copy of the marriage license and certificate.

Respectfully,

Commissioner.

CERTIFICATE OF RECORD.

United States of America, ⎱
   INDIAN TERRITORY,   ⎬ ss.
   Northern District.   ⎰

I, *CHARLES A. DAVIDSON*, Clerk of the United States Court in the Northern District, Indian Territory, do hereby certify that the instrument hereto attached was filed for record in my office the   30   day of   Mch   1900 at .... M., and duly recorded in Book   2 , Marriage Record, Page   316

WITNESS my hand and seal of said Court at Muscogee, in said Territory, this   30   day of   Mch   A. D. 190 0

                Chas A. Davidson   Clerk.
                By...Deputy.

MARRIAGE LICENSE

⚜⚜⚜

United States of America, ⎱
   INDIAN TERRITORY,   ⎬ ss.
   Northern District.   ⎰

To Any Person Authorized by Law to Solemnize Marriage---Greeting:

You are Hereby Commanded to Solemnize the Rite and publish the Banns of Matrimony between Mr.   James Berryhill   of   Muskogee , in the Indian Territory, aged   19   years and Miss Elnora Alberty   of   Muskogee   in the Indian Territory aged   18   years according to law, and do you officially sign and return this License to the parties therein named.

WITNESS my hand and official seal at Muscogee Indian Territory this   23   day of   March   A.D. 190 0

                Chas. A. Davidson
                Clerk of the U.S. Court

By   P M Ford   Deputy

Applications for Enrollment of Creek Newborn
Act of 1905 Volume X

CERTIFICATE OF MARRIAGE.

United States of America, ⎫
INDIAN TERRITORY, ⎬ ss.
Northern District. ⎭

I, Elder D D Hall , *a Minister of the Gospel, DO HEREBY CERTIFY that on the* 25 *day of* March *A. D.* 1900, *I did duly and according to law as commanded in the foregoing License, solemnize the Rite and publish the Banns of Matrimony between the parties therein named.*

WITNESS my hand this 25 *day of* March A. D. 1900

My credentials are recorded in the office of the Clerk of the United States Court, Indian Territory, Northern District, Book C *, Page* 285 .

Elder D D Hall
A Minister of the Gospel

Note—This License and Certificate of Marriage must be returned to the Office of the Clerk of the United States Court in the Northern District, Indian Territory, from whence it was issued, within sixty days from the date thereof, or the party to whom the license was issued will be liable in the amount of the One Hundred Dollars ($100.00)

BIRTH AFFIDAVIT.

DEPARTMENT OF THE INTERIOR.
COMMISSION TO THE FIVE CIVILIZED TRIBES.

IN RE APPLICATION FOR ENROLLMENT, as a citizen of the Creek Nation, of Ione Berryhill, born on the 5 day of June , 1904

Name of Father: James Berryhill   a citizen of the Creek Nation.
Name of Mother: Elnora Berryhill   a citizen of the Cherokee Nation.

Postoffice Summit, I.T.

AFFIDAVIT OF MOTHER.

UNITED STATES OF AMERICA, Indian Territory, ⎫
     Western   DISTRICT. ⎭

I, Elnora Berryhill , on oath state that I am 23 years of age and a citizen by blood , of the Cherokee Nation; that I am the lawful wife of James Berryhill , who is

Applications for Enrollment of Creek Newborn
Act of 1905   Volume X

a citizen, by blood of the Creek Nation; that a Female child was born to me on 5th day of June , 1904 , that said child has been named Ione Berryhill , and is now living.

Elnora Berryhill

Witnesses To Mark:
{

    Subscribed and sworn to before me this 17th day of April , 1905.

W. A. Cain
Notary Public.

AFFIDAVIT OF ATTENDING PHYSICIAN OR MID-WIFE.

UNITED STATES OF AMERICA, Indian Territory,
    Western   DISTRICT. }

    I, Mrs. N. J. Miller , a Midwife , on oath state that I attended on Mrs. Elnora Berryhill , wife of James Berryhill on the 5th day of June , 1904 ; that there was born to her on said date a Female child; that said child is now living and is said to have been named Ione Berryhill

Nancy J Miller

Witnesses To Mark:
{

    Subscribed and sworn to before me this 17 day of April, 1905.

W. A. Cain
Notary Public.

NC-784 2

Muskogee, Indian Territory, October 18, 1905.

Choctaw Givens,
    Mellette, Indian Territory.

Dear Sir:

    In the matter of the application for the enrollment of your minor grandson Jefferson Yahola, born April 11, 1902, as a citizen by blood of the Creek Nation this

Applications for Enrollment of Creek Newborn
Act of 1905   Volume X

office requires the affidavits of the mother of said child and the attending physician or midwife who attended at his birth.

For that purpose there is inclosed herewith a blank form for proof of birth which you are requested to have properly executed and when so executed return it to this office in the inclosed envelope. Be careful to see that all blank spaces are properly filled, all names written in full and that the notary public, before whom the affidavits are sworn to, attaches his name and seal to each affidavit. In case any signature is by mark the same must be attested by two disinterested witnesses.

                    Respectfully,

                                        Commissioner.
B C
Env.

NC-782

Muskogee, Indian Territory, December 15, 1905.

Sarah White,
    Care of Choctaw Givens,
        Mellette, Indian Territory.

Dear Madam:

In the matter of the application for the enrollment of your minor child, Jefferson Yarhola, born April 11, 1902, as a citizen by blood of the Creek Nation blood of the Creek Nation, what purports to be the affidavit of two disinterested witnesses is defective, inasmuch as it appears from the body of said affidavit that the affiant is Tayo Washington, while the names signed thereto are Sallie Tiger and Solie Hill. The erasures and interlincations[sic] on the form of which said affidavit is prepared, render same absolutely unintelligible.

There is herewith enclosed a blank form of affidavit for disinterested witnesses which you are requested to have executed and returned to this Office in the enclosed envelope.

                    Respectfully,

                                        Commissioner.

Applications for Enrollment of Creek Newborn
Act of 1905   Volume X

N C 782

JWH

Muskogee, Indian Territory, March 1, 1907.

Sarah White,
    Mellette, Indian Territory.

Dear Madam :--

    You are hereby advised that on February 15, 1907, the Secretary of the Interior approved the enrollment of your minor child, Jefferson Harhola[sic], as a citizen by blood of the Creek Nation, and that the name of said child appears upon the roll of New Born citizens by blood of the Creek Nation, enrolled under the Act of Congress approved March 3, 1905, as number 1170.

    This child is now entitled to allotment and application therefor should be made without delay at the Creek Land Office, Muskogee, Indian Territory.

                   Respectfully,

                            Commissioner.

AFFIDAVIT OF DISINTERESTED WITNESS.

UNITED STATES OF AMERICA,
Western DISTRICT,   SS
INDIAN TERRITORY.

    We, the undersigned, on oath state that we are personally acquainted with ---
--------Sarah White, formerly ---------- the wife of Sampson Yahola, deceased --- ; that there was born to her a Male child on or about the 11th day of April, 1902 ---; that the said child has been named Jefferson Yahola . and was living March 4, 1906.

Witnesses: John Bright
          (Illegible) Bright

                        Sarah White

Subscribed and sworn to before me this 6 day of Sept. 1906.

                        L. G. McIntosh
                           Notary Public.

My commission
expires Apr. 10. 1907

Applications for Enrollment of Creek Newborn
Act of 1905 Volume X

BIRTH AFFIDAVIT.

DEPARTMENT OF THE INTERIOR.
COMMISSION TO THE FIVE CIVILIZED TRIBES.

IN RE APPLICATION FOR ENROLLMENT, as a citizen of the Creek Nation, of Jefferson Yahola, born on the 11 day of Apr, 1902

Name of Father: Sampson Yahola   a citizen of the   Creek   Nation.
Name of Mother: Sarah Yahola   a citizen of the   Creek   Nation.

Postoffice   Mellette I.T.

AFFIDAVIT OF MOTHER.

UNITED STATES OF AMERICA, Indian Territory,
    Western   DISTRICT.

     I, Sarah Yahola, on oath state that I am about 28 years of age and a citizen by blood, of the Creek Nation; that I am the lawful wife of Sampson Yahola (Dead), who is a citizen, by blood of the Creek Nation; that a male child was born to me on 11 day of Apr, 1902, that said child has been named Jefferson Yahola, and was living March 4, 1905.

                                         Sarah Yarhalar
Witnesses To Mark: now Sarah White

     Subscribed and sworn to before me this 5 day of Nov., 1905.

                                         L.G. McIntosh
                                         Notary Public.

AFFIDAVIT OF ATTENDING PHYSICIAN OR MID-WIFE.

UNITED STATES OF AMERICA, Indian Territory,
    Western   DISTRICT.

     I, Taye Washington, a to old to *(illegible)*, ~~on oath state that I attended~~ she on Mrs. Sarah Yahola now White, wife of Sampson Yahola now George White on the 11 day of Apr, 1902; that there was born to her on said date a male child; that said child was living March 4, 1905, and is said to have been named Jefferson Yahola

                                   Sallie *(Illegible)* her x
Witnesses To Mark: Solie Hill her x
   WM *(Illegible)*
   L G McIntosh

Applications for Enrollment of Creek Newborn
Act of 1905   Volume X

Subscribed and sworn to before me 11 day of Nov., 1905.

          L.G. McIntosh
          Notary Public.

BIRTH AFFIDAVIT.

DEPARTMENT OF THE INTERIOR.
COMMISSION TO THE FIVE CIVILIZED TRIBES.

IN RE APPLICATION FOR ENROLLMENT, as a citizen of the Creek Nation, of Jefferson Yahola, born on the 11 day of April, 1902

Name of Father: Sampson Yahola (deceased) a citizen of the Creek Nation. Hutchechuppa Town
Name of Mother: Sarah White (nee Yahola) a citizen of the Creek Nation. Tuckabatche Town
       Postoffice Mellette, Ind. Ter

AFFIDAVIT OF MOTHER.

UNITED STATES OF AMERICA, Indian Territory, }
 Western DISTRICT.   Child is not present

  I, Choctaw Givens, on oath state that I am about 57 years of age and a citizen by blood, of the Creek Nation; that I am the lawful ~~wife~~ father of Sarah White, who is a citizen, by blood of the Creek Nation; that a male child was born to ~~me~~ her on 11 day of April, 1902, that said child has been named Jefferson Yahola, and was living March 4, 1905. That the mother refuses to make application for the enrollment of the child.
          his
        Choctaw x Givens
Witnesses To Mark: mark
 { Alex Posey
   DC Skaggs

Subscribed and sworn to before me this 7 day of April, 1905.

         Drennan C Skaggs
         Notary Public.

Applications for Enrollment of Creek Newborn
Act of 1905   Volume X

BIRTH AFFIDAVIT.

DEPARTMENT OF THE INTERIOR.
COMMISSION TO THE FIVE CIVILIZED TRIBES.

IN RE APPLICATION FOR ENROLLMENT, as a citizen of the Creek Nation, of Floyd Ila Johnson, born on the *(blank)* day of *(blank)*, 1*(blank)*

Name of Father: Elijah T. Johnson   a citizen of the United States ~~Nation~~.
Name of Mother: Lorena Johnson   a citizen of the   Creek   Nation.

Postoffice   Checotah, I.T.

AFFIDAVIT OF MOTHER.

UNITED STATES OF AMERICA, Indian Territory, ⎱
    Western   DISTRICT.   ⎰

I, Lorena Johnson, on oath state that I am 23 years of age and a citizen by Blood, of the Creek Nation; that I am the lawful wife of Elijah Johnson, who is a citizen, ~~by~~ of the United States ~~Nation~~; that a Male child was born to me on 7$^{\underline{th}}$ day of April, 1903, that said child has been named Floyd Ila Johnson, and was living March 4, 1905.

                                    Lorena Johnson
Witnesses To Mark:
{

Subscribed and sworn to before me this 22 day of April, 1905.

                                    J.B. Lucas
                                         Notary Public.

AFFIDAVIT OF ATTENDING PHYSICIAN OR MID-WIFE.

UNITED STATES OF AMERICA, Indian Territory, ⎱
    Western   DISTRICT.   ⎰

I, Rachael Thornsbury, a Midwife, on oath state that I attended on Mrs. Lorena Johnson, wife of Elijah T. Johnson on the 7th day of April, 1903 ; that there was born to her on said date a male child; that said child was living March 4, 1905, and is said to have been named Floyd Ila Johnson   her
                                    Rachael Thornsbury x
Witnesses To Mark: mark
  { Chas. R. Furman
  { J B Lucas

85

Applications for Enrollment of Creek Newborn
Act of 1905   Volume X

Subscribed and sworn to before me this 22 day of April, 1905.

> J.B. Lucas
> Notary Public.

NC 784.

Muskogee, Indian Territory, July 15, 1905.

Chief Clerk,
    Seminole Enrollment Division,
        Muskogee, Indian Territory.

Dear Sir:

    April 24, 1905, application was made to the Commission to the Five Civilized Tribes for the enrollment of Willey Deere, born October 30, 1903, as a citizen by blood of the Creek Nation. It is stated in said application that the father of said child is John Deere, a citizen of the Seminole Nation, and that the mother is Lizzie Deere, identified as Lizzie Berryhill, a citizen of the Creek Nation.

    You are requested to inform the Creek Enrollment Division as to whether application has been made for the enrollment of said Willey Deere as a citizen of the Seminole Nation, and if so, what disposition has been made of the same.

> Respectfully,
> Commissioner.

W.F.

DEPARTMENT OF THE INTERIOR.
COMMISSION TO THE FIVE CIVILIZED TRIBES.

Muskogee, Indian Territory, July 19, 1905.

Chief Clerk,
    Creek Enrollment Division.

Dear Sir:

    Receipt is acknowledged of your letter of July 15, 1905 (NC-784) stating that application was made to the Commission to the Five Civilized Tribes for the enrollment of Willey Deere, born October 30, 1903, child of John Deere, a citizen of the Seminole

Applications for Enrollment of Creek Newborn
Act of 1905   Volume X

Nation, and Lizzie Deere, identified as Lizzie Berryhill, a citizen of the Creek Nation, as a citizen by blood of the Creek Nation and requesting to be informed as to whether application has been made for the enrollment of said Willey Deere as a citizen of the Seminole Nation, and if so, what disposition has been made of the same.

In reply to your letter you are advised that it does not appear from an examination of the records of this office that application was made for the enrollment of said Willey Deere as a citizen of the Seminole Nation.

Respectfully,
Tams Bixby   Commissioner.

J.D.

REFER IN REPLY TO THE FOLLOWING:
NC-784.

DEPARTMENT OF THE INTERIOR,
COMMISSIONER TO THE FIVE CIVILIZED TRIBES.

Muskogee, Indian Territory, October 18, 1905.

Lizzie Deere,
    c/o John Deere,
        Burney, Indian Territory.

Dear Madam:

In the matter of the application for the enrollment of your minor child Willey Deere, born October 30, 1903, as a citizen by blood of the Creek Nation, this office requires the affidavits of two disinterested witnesses relative to the birth of said child.

Said affidavits must set forth said child's name, the date of his birth, the names of his parents and whether or not he was living on March 4, 1905.

Respectfully,
Tams Bixby   Commissioner.

Applications for Enrollment of Creek Newborn
Act of 1905   Volume X

NC 784.

Muskogee, Indian Territory, August 21, 1906.

Chief Clerk,
    Seminole Enrollment Division,
        Muskogee, Indian Territory.

Dear Sir:

    Application has been made for the enrollment as a citizen of the Creek Nation of Willy Deere, born October 30, 1903, to John Deere, a citizen of the Seminole Nation, and Lizzie Deere, a citizen of the Creek Nation.

    You are requested to advise this office if application has been made for the enrollment of said child as a citizen of the Seminole Nation, and if so, please furnish the present status of said application.

                Respectfully,
                             Commissioner.

A.B.

REFER IN REPLY TO THE FOLLOWING:

DEPARTMENT OF THE INTERIOR,
COMMISSIONER TO THE FIVE CIVILIZED TRIBES.

Muskogee, Indian Territory, August 24, 1906.

Chief Clerk,
    Creek Enrollment Division,
        Muskogee, Indian Territory.

Dear Sir:

    Receipt is hereby acknowledged of your letter of August 21, 1906, asking if application has been made for enrollment as a citizen of the Seminole Nation of Willy Deere, child of John Deere, a citizen of the Seminole Nation, and Lizzie Deere, a citizen of the Creek Nation.

    You are advised that it does not appear from the records of this office that application has been made on behalf of Willy Deere for enrollment as a new born citizen of the Seminole Nation under the Act of Congress approved March 3, 1905.

                Respectfully,
                      Wm. O. Beall
                      Acting Commissioner.

Applications for Enrollment of Creek Newborn
Act of 1905   Volume X

NC 784.

Muskogee, Indian Territory, October 31, 1906.

Chief Clerk,
    Seminole Enrollment Division,
        Muskogee, Indian Territory.

Dear Sir:

    There is on file in this office an application for the enrollment of Willey Deere, born October 30, 1903, to John Deere, a citizen of the Seminole Nation, and Lizzie Deere, identified as Lizzie Berryhill on the rolls of citizens by blood of the Creek Nation, opposite roll number 8239.

    You are advised that the name of said child is contained in a partial list of new born citizens by blood of the Creek Nation, approved by the Secretary of the Interior October 15, 1906, opposite roll number 1066.

        Respectfully,

                Commissioner.

Western District
Indian Territory   SS

    We, the undersigned, on oath state that we are personally acquainted with   Lizzie Deere   wife of   John Deere   and that on or about the   30   day of Oct , 19 03, a male child was born to them and has been named   Willey Deere   that said child was living March 4, 1905.

    We further state that we have no interest in the above case.

                            his
                      Joseph x Tiger
                          mark
Witness to mark: Lillie Tiger

_____

J McDermott
(Name Illegible)

_____   H G Hains

Subscribed and sworn to before
me this 9" day of   Jan 19 06

My Commission
Expires July 25' 1907

Applications for Enrollment of Creek Newborn
Act of 1905   Volume X

B.A. 2153 B.

DEPARTMENT OF THE INTERIOR,
COMMISSION[sic] TO THE FIVE CIVILIZED TRIBES.
April 24, 1905.

In the matter of the application for the enrollment of Wiley Deere as a citizen by blood of the Creek Nation.

Lizzie Deere being duly sworn, testified as follows:

Q What is your name? A Lizzie Deere.
Q What is your age? A 26.
Q What is your post office address? A Burney.
Q What is the name of Willey Deere's father? A John Deere.
Q You have a child by that name? A Yes sir.
Q When was Willey born? A I don't know.
Q Did you have the date of his birth written in a record or book of any kind? A Yes sir?[sic] I have it in a book.
Q Is this paper copied from the book you speak of? A Yes sir.

The following record appears on the paper referred to:
"Willey Deere was born the 30th day of October, 1903."

Q What is the name of Willey's father? A John Deere.
Q Is he a citizen of the Creek Nation? A He is a citizen of the Seminole Nation.
Q Are you a citizen of the Creek Nation? A Yes sir.
Q What is the name of your father? A Tobe Berryhill.

Witness is identified as Lizzie Berryhill on Creek Indian card, Field No. 3013, and her name is contained in the partial list of Creek Indians by blood, approved by the Secretary of the Interior, March 28, 1902, Roll No. 8239.

Q In case it should be found that your child Willey Deere is entitled to enrollment in either of the Creek or Seminole Nation, in which Nation do you elect to have him enrolled and receive his allotment of land. [sic] In the Creek Nation.

Lona Merrick being duly sworn, states that the above and foregoing is a true and correct transcript of her stenographic notes taken of said proceedings on said dates.

Lona Merrick

Subscribed and sworn to before me this 24, day of April, 1905.

My commission expires
April 11, 1909.

Zera E. Parrish
Notary Public.

Applications for Enrollment of Creek Newborn
Act of 1905   Volume X

BIRTH AFFIDAVIT.

DEPARTMENT OF THE INTERIOR.
COMMISSION TO THE FIVE CIVILIZED TRIBES.

IN RE APPLICATION FOR ENROLLMENT, as a citizen of the Creek Nation, of Willey Deere, born on the 30 day of October , 1903

Name of Father: John Deere   a citizen of the   Seminole   Nation.
Name of Mother: Lizzie Deere   a citizen of the   Creek   Nation.

Postoffice   Burney

Child present and appears to be about 1 1/2 years

AFFIDAVIT OF MOTHER.

UNITED STATES OF AMERICA, Indian Territory, }
     Western   DISTRICT.

I, Lizzie Deere , on oath state that I am 26 years of age and a citizen by blood , of the Creek Nation; that I am the lawful wife of John Deere , who is a citizen, by blood of the Seminole Nation; that a male child was born to me on 30 day of October , 1903 , that said child has been named Willey Deere , and was living March 4, 1905. No one attended me when child was born

              her
            Lizzie x Deere
Witnesses To Mark: mark
 { Lona Merrick
  Edward Merrick

Subscribed and sworn to before me this 24th day of April , 1905.

           Edward Merrick
            Notary Public.

Applications for Enrollment of Creek Newborn
Act of 1905   Volume X

N C 786

JWH

Muskogee, Indian Territory, March 9, 1907.

Cora Ellis Starr,
    %Charley Starr,
        Shawnee, Oklahoma.

Dear Madam :--

    You are hereby advised that on March 2, 1907, the Secretary of the Interior approved the enrollment of your minor child, Jesse Starr, Jr., as a citizen by blood of the Creek Nation, and that the name of said child appears upon the roll of new born citizens by blood of the Creek Nation, enrolled under the Act of Congress approved March 3, 1905, as number 1271,

    This child is now entitled to allotment and application therefor should be made without delay at the Creek Land Office, Muskogee, Indian Territory.

                Respectfully,
                          Commissioner.

DEPARTMENT OF THE INTERIOR,
COMMISSION TO THE FIVE CIVILIZED TRIBES,
April 18, 1904, Bristow, I.T.

    In the matter of the application for the enrollment of Henry, Annie and Gertrude Starr, as citizens by blood of the Creek Nation.

    Cora Ella Starr, being duly sworn by E.C. Griesel, a Notary Public, testified as follows:

By Commission:
Q What is your name? A Cora Ella Starr.
Q What is your age? A About 37.
Q What is your post office? A Shawnee, Okla.
Q You are a citizen of the Creek Nation, are you? A Yes sir.
Q What town do you belong to? A Little River Tulsa.
Q What is the name of your father? A Gobbler.
Q What is the name of your mother? A Har-ko-the-way.
Q Are the parents Creek citizens? A My mother is a Creek and my father a Shawnee.
Q You are the mother of Gertrude, Henry and Annie Starr, are you? A Yes sir.
Q When were these children born? A (Witness here presents record: above referred to).
Q If it should be found that your children, Henry, Annie and Gertrude Starr are entitled to enrollment in both the Creek and Shawnee Nations, in which Nation do you elect to have them enrolled and receive their allotments of land? A In the Creek Nation.

Applications for Enrollment of Creek Newborn
Act of 1905   Volume X

Q Who drew the money for these children? A Dick Ellis my uncle drew the first payment and brought it to us. I and Dick Ellis went together and drew the last payment. John Goat was the one who paid us the last time.

    E.C. Griesel being duly sworn, on his oath, states that the above and foregoing is a true and correct transcript of his stenographic notes as taken in said cause on said date.

Edw C Griesel

Subscribed and sworn to before me this 5 day of May, 1905.

Zera E Parrish
Notary Public.

DEPARTMENT OF THE INTERIOR
COMMISSION TO THE FIVE CIVILIZED TRIBES
Okmulgee, Indian Territory, May 22, 1901.

    In the matter of the application of Cora Ellis for the enrollment of herself and children Clara Starr, Henry Starr, Annie Starr and Gertrude Starr as citizens of the Creek Nation.

    Cora Ellis being duly sworn by the Commission testified as follows: Examination by the Commission conducted through Mr. Starr, sworn Creek interpreter.

Examination by the Commission.

Q What is your name? A Cora Ellis.
Q What is your age? A Don't know.
Q About how old are you? A About 35 or 36.
Q Are you a citizen of the Creek Nation? A Yes sir.
Q What town do you belong to? A Little River Tulsa.
Q Are you married? A Yes sir.
Q What is the name of your husband? A Charlie Starr.
Q How long have you been married to Charlie Starr? A About 18 years ago.
Q Have you any children? A Yes sir.
Q What is the name, age and sex of the oldest child? A Clara Starr.
Q Aged 14? A yes sir.
Q Female. What is the name, age and sex of the next oldest? A Henry Starr.
Q Aged 11. Is that right? A 11.
Q 11, male. What is the name, age and sex of the next oldest? A Annie Starr.
Q Aged 6? A Yes sir, six.
Q Female. What is the name of the next oldest? A Gertrude.
Q Gertrued[sic] Starr. Aged 3. Is that right? A Yes sir.
Q Female? A Yes sir.
Q Are these all the children you have? A Yes sir.

Applications for Enrollment of Creek Newborn
Act of 1905   Volume X

Q Who was your father? A Gobler.
Q Is he living or dead? A He's dead.
Q Was he an Indian or a white man? A Injun.
Q To what tribe did he belong? A Shawnee tribe.
Q Was your father a full blood Shawnee Indian? A Yes sir.
Q Who was your mother? A Ellie.
Q Is she living or dead? A She's dead.
Q Was she an Indian or a white woman? A Indian.
Q To what tribe did she belong? A Creek.
Q To what town in the Creek tribe did she belong? A Little River Tulsa.
Q Was your mother a full blood Creek Indian? A Yes sir.
Q Where do you reside? A In Oklahoma, Pottowattomie[sic] County.
Q How long have you resided in Oklahoma? A Three years ago since moved back to Oklahoma.
Q Been living there for the past three years. Where did you reside before you moved to Oklahoma? A In the Creek Nation.
Q How long did you live in the Creek Nation before you moved to Oklahoma? A About 5 or 6 years.
Q Where did you reside prior to the time that you married this man Starr? A Lived in Oklahoma.
Q Were you born and raised in Oklahoma? A Yes sir.
Q Did you marry this man Shaw in Oklahoma? [sic] Yes sir.
Q When did you first move to the Creek Nation? A About 8 years ago.
Q Did you remain in the Creek Nation continuously from the time you moved here until you returned to Oklahoma? A Yes sir.
Q Did you have a home in the Creek Nation? A Yes sir.
Q Have you at this time any home or farm or improvement of any kind in the Creek Nation? A No sir.
Q Did you ever own a home or a farm or anaimprovement[sic] of any kind in the Creek Nation? A Owned a home a farm in the Creek Nation but a white fellow took it away from us.
Q How long has it been since this white man took yes place away from you? A Four years ago.
Q You state that you returned to Oklahoma about three years ago. Can you give the exact date that you left the Creek Nation and took up your residence in Oklahoma? A In March but don't know what day of the month.
Q What year? A Don't know it.
Q How many years has it been since you moved to Oklahoma this last time? A Two years.
Q What is the name of your husband? A Charlie Starr.
Q What is his occupation? A Farming.
Q How many crops have you or your husband or both of you raised in Oklahoma since you returned there from the Creek Nation? A Two crops.
Q Then do you mean to say that you removed from the Creek Nation in March, 1899? A Yes sir.
Q Where were you residing on the 28th day of June, 1898? A In Oklahoma.

Applications for Enrollment of Creek Newborn
Act of 1905 Volume X

Q Where was your child, Gertrude, born in Oklahoma or the Creek Nation? A In Oklahoma.
Q Have you ever resided in the Creek Nation since your child Gertrude was born? A No sir.
Q Can you give the exact date of the birth of your child Gertrude? A I can't tell.
Q Gave you no record of the date of the birth of your child? A No sir.
Q How do you know the child is three years old then? A I just keep it in my head.
Q Is your husband a citizen of the Shawnee Tribe of Indians? A Yes sir.
Q Do you reside in Oklahoma with your husband? A Yes sir.
Q Have you lived with him continuously since you were married? A Yes sir.
Q Did he take his allotment as a Shawnee Indian in Oklahoma? A Yes sir.
Q When did he take his allotment? A About 11 or 12 years ago.
Q Did you ever take an allotment as a Shawnee Indian either for yourself or your children for whom you now make application for enrollment? A Only one allotment.
Q For which child did you take an allotment as a Shawnee Indian? A Clara.
Q That is your oldest child for whom you now make application for enrollment as a citizen of the Creek Nation is it not? A Yes sir.
Q Did you not take an allotment as a Shawnee Indian for yourself? A No sir.
Q Was your child Henry Starr born before or after the allotments were made to the Shawnee Indians in Oklahoma? A He was born after the Shawnee allotment.
Q Why was it you did not take an allotment for yourself as a Shawnee Indian in Oklahoma? A I don't know.
Q Did you make any effort to obtain an allotment in Oklahoma as a Shawnee Indian? A Never tried.
Q Did you draw the $29, payment made by the Creeks in 1890 as a citizen of the Creek Nation? A Yes sir.
Q Did you draw the money yourself or did some one draw it for you? A No didn't draw it myself.
Q Who drew the money for you? A Dick Ellis.
Q Did Dick Ellis ever pay you any money which he claimed to have drawn for you and your children as citizens of the Creek Nation? A Yes sir.
Q How many children did you have living at the time the $29, payment was made by the Creeks in 1890? A Three.
Q How much money did Dick Ellis give you which he claimed to have drawn for you and your children as citizens of the Creek Nation at the time the $29.00 payment was made in 1890? A We got $110.00 from him.

The 1890 authenticated roll of the Creek Nation is examined and the name of the applicant and her children is not found thereon.

Q Did you draw the $14.40 payment for yourself and children as citizens of the Creek nation which payment was made by the Creeks in 1895? A Yes sir.
Q How many children did you have living at the time the $14.40 payment was made by the Creeks? A Four.
Q Give their names? A Clara, Henry, Annie and Frank.

Applications for Enrollment of Creek Newborn
Act of 1905 Volume X

The 1895 authenticated roll of Little River Tulsa Town, Creek Nation, examined and the names of Cora Ellis, No. 369, Clara Starr No. 370, Henry Starr No. 371, Frank Starr No. 372, and Annie Starr No. 373 are found thereon.

Q Were you living in the Creek Nation at the time this $14.40 payment was made?
A Yes sir.
Q Does your daughter Clara now hold an allotment as a member of the Shawnee Tribe of Indians? A Yes sir.
Q Is there anything else which you desire to say with reference to your application for the enrollment of yourself and children as citizens of the Creek Nation? A No sir.
Q Have you any further testimony which you desire to introduce in behalf of your application for enrollment of yourself and children as citizens of the Creek Nation?
A Wants witnesses but don't know nobody here.
Q What witnesses do you desire to introduce? A Haven't got anybody that I know of.

Myra Young have been first duly sworn upon her oath states that as stenographer to the Commission to the Five Civilized Tribes she reported in full all proceedings had in the above entitled cause on the 22nd day of May, 1901, and that the above and foregoing is a full, true and correct transcript of her stenographic notes of said proceedings on said date.

Myra Young

Subscribed and sworn to before me this 23rd day of May, 1901, at Okmulgee, Indian Territory.

(Name Illegible)
Acting Chairman.

En. 123
AN.C. 786.

DEPARTMENT OF THE INTERIOR,
COMMISSIONER TO THE FIVE CIVILIZED TRIBES.
Muskogee, Indian Territory, March 28, 1906.

In the matter of the application for the enrollment of Cora Ellis Starr and her children, Clara Starr, Henry Starr, Annie Starr, Gertrude Starr and Jesse J. Starr as citizens by blood of the Creek Nation.

CHARLES STARR, being duly sworn, testified as follows:

Q What is your name? A Charles Starr.
Q What is your age? A Forty six next September.
Q What is your post office address? A Shawnee, Oklahoma.
Q What is your purpose in appearing here this morning, did you get a letter from some one? A Yes, I got that letter.

Applications for Enrollment of Creek Newborn
Act of 1905   Volume X

Q What letter? A From the Commissioner of Indian Affairs at Washington care of the Indian Agent at Shawnee and he read it to me and he said that I had to move over here in the Creek Nation and take my children and he wrote to the Dawes Commission and got an answer and told me to bring my children right away to the land office.
Q You present here a letter from the Acting Commissioner of Indian Affairs addressed to you through the superintendent of Shawnee Indian schools and that is the letter you refer to is it? A Yes
Q Did you see a letter that was addressed to Cora Starr from this office dated November 11, 1903 in which she was told that this office required certain evidence in order to show whether she intended to move to the Creek Nation or not? A I believe I seen one.
Q Is your purpose in coming here now to testify and show that your wife, Cora Starr and her children have removed to the Creek Nation. Have you come to the Creek Nation to make it your home? A Yes, sir The United States Indian Agent over there told me to come here.
Q he advised you to come over here and establish a home? a Yes, sir.
Q When did you come to establish this as your home? A I have been over here a week now.
Q What place in the Creek Nation have you decided upon to make you place of residence? A I haven't found any yet; I am just looking around because I don't know where the vacant land is, I can't find it. I haven't a map.
Q Then you have not as yet established a home in the Creek Nation? A No, sir.
Q You have come over here to find a home but haven't yet done so? [sic] I haven't found one yet.
Q Where have you been the past week? A Near Paden.
q Are you visiting there? A No, not visiting; I am over to see if I can find some vacant land.
Q Are you a citizen of the Shawnee tribe? A Yes, sir
Q Have you received an allotment of land in the Shawnee Nation? A Yes
Q Where is that allotment, near what place? A It is five miles south east from Shawnee.
Q What has been your post office over there? A Shawnee.
Q What is the name of your wife? A Cora Starr, used to be Cora Ellis.
Q You and our wife are living together at the present time? A Yes
Q You have never separated? A No, sir
Q How many children have you? A Five.
Q From this woman? A Yes, sir
Q Are these five children all living? A Yes, sir. I used to have six
Q What are the names of the five living children? [sic] Clara the oldest, Henry, Annie, Gertrude and Jesse. Cora is the one died and she got an allotment in Shawnee.
Q Which of these children received allotment in the Shawnee? [sic] Clara and Cora.
Q Where are these allotments for Cora and Clara situated? A On same place where I have my allotment.
Q When did you receive your own allotment over there, do you remember the date? A No, I can't.
Q Did you get an allotment for Cora and Clara at the same time you did for yourself? A Yes, sir.
Q Why didn't you apply for an allotment for your other children and your wife? A Time Henry was born they told me it was too late.

Applications for Enrollment of Creek Newborn
Act of 1905   Volume X

Q Is your wife a citizen of the Shawnee Nation? A Creek and part Shawnee.

It appears from the 1895 authenticated roll of the Creek Nation, Little River Tulsa town, that the name of Cora Ellis Starr, Clara Starr, Henry Starr, Frank Starr and Annie Starr are listed thereon.

Q Who is Frank Starr? A I forgot about that boy; that is my boy.
Q Is he living? A No, he is dead when I lived in the Creek Nation. I used to live in the Creek Nation.
Q What year did he die? A I can't tell what year. He died right after the last payment in the Creek Nation.
Q Did he die before the Creek land office opened? A Before then.
Q Did he receive an allotment in the Shawnee Nation? A No, sir
Q Died too soon? A Yes, sir.
Q All these four and that Frank didn't get any allotment in the Shawnee Nation? A Only Cora and Clara.
Q You were advised in letter to you wife dated November 11, 1904 that under the provision of section 21 of the act of Congress approved June 28, 1898 no person shall be enrolled who has not removed to and in good faith settled in the nation in which he claims citizenship. You state that you have come over here to make a home in the Creek Nation as soon as you have made a home here, in about thirty days from the present time you are notified that you must appear here again and give in you testimony to show that you have actually established your residence in the Creek Nation. That is in order that your wife and children may obtain the rights which they claim here.

CORA ELLIS STARR, being duly sworn, testified as follows through her husband Charles Starr who was duly worn to correctly interpret for her.

Q What is your name? A Cora Ellis Starr.
Q How old are you? A Thirty nine.
Q What is your post office address, how can we reach you in the next thirty days?
A Shawnee.

Charles Starr states: We have got to go home. I just left my home as soon as I got this letter and come right here and I have to go home first and try to get some one to rent my place then I can come back to the Creek Nation.

Charles Starr recalled.

Q Then you haven't come over here to establish your home at the present time, you intend to go back to Shawnee and wait until you rent your land before you establish a home here? A Yes, may be I will go by myself and leave my folks here.
Q You will have to decide what you will do? A That is what I do, I go home by myself and it didnt[sic]'t take me long, three of four days and then I come back to Paden where I leave my folks.

Applications for Enrollment of Creek Newborn
Act of 1905   Volume X

Q You state now that you have brought your family over here to establish a home and that you will go back to your former home near Shawnee in order to rent your land there and that you will be gone only a few days? A Yes, sir at Paden.

CORA ELLIS STARR, Recalled.

Q Then your post office address from now on will be Paden? A Yes
Q Do you now live at Paden and is it your intention to make that point your home? A Yes
Q Are you going to keep these children, Henry, Gertrude, Annie and Jessie here in the Creek Nation? A Yes, sir.
Q How old is your youngest child, Jesse J. Starr? A He will be five years old the 22nd of July.
Q As your husband was advised a moment ago you are also advised that in order that you and your four children, Henry, Gertrude, Annie and Jesse J. Starr may receive rights in the Creek Nation, it will be necessary for you to establish a home here and if after such a home has been established for a period of thirty days, you are required to appear here at the office of the Commissioner and testify to the fact that you have made a home and intend to live here in the Creek Nation.

JENNIE HARPER, being duly sworn, testified as follows:

Q What is your name? A Jennie Harper, used to be Jennie Chisholm.
Q What is your age? A About 44 or 45
Q What is your post office address? A Paden.
Q Are you a citizen of the Creek Nation? A Yes, sir.
Q You appear here as a witness for Charles Starr and his family do you? A Yes, sir.
Q Are they now residents of the Creek Nation? A Yes, sir.
Q Where are they living? A Right close to Paden since a *(illegible)*. They used to live in the Creek Nation and then they moved to Shawnee.
Q Are they living with you or have they a home of their own? A Camping out close by me.
Q Have they stated in your presence that they have come here to the Creek Nation to establish a home? A Yes, sir
Q You have been acquainted with them for some time have you? A Yes sir, she is a little relation to me; she is a cousin of mine.

As was stated to Charles Starr and his wife they will be required to come here 30 days from date and give in the testimony to show they have actually established a residence in the Creek Nation and intend to live here.

I, Anna Garrigues, on oath state that the above and foregoing is a true and correct transcript of my stenographic notes as taken in said cause on said date.

                                        Anna Garrigues

Applications for Enrollment of Creek Newborn
Act of 1905   Volume X

Subscribed and sworn to before
me this 28 day of March 1906.   J McDermott
                                                                          Notary Public.

En. 123
N.C. 786

DEPARTMENT OF THE INTERIOR,
COMMISSIONER TO THE FIVE CIVILIZED TRIBES.
Muskogee, Indian Territory, April 28, 1906.

In the matter of the application for the enrollment of Cora Ellis Starr and her children, Henry Starr, Annie Starr, Gertrude Starr and Jesse J. Starr as citizens by blood of the Creek Nation.

CORA ELLIS STARR, being duly sworn, testified as follows through William Hodjoe sworn Creek interpreter.

Q What is your name? A Cora Ellis Starr.
Q What is your post office address? A Paden.
Q What is your age? A I don't really know but about forty
Q Are you the identical Cora Ellis Starr who appeared before this office on March 28, 1906 and testified in the matter of the application for yourself and children as citizens of the Creek Nation? A Yes.
Q What is your purpose in appearing here today? A I came over here to see if I am going to be enrolled as a Creek.
Q Have you established your residence at Paden and is it your intention to make that your permanent place of residence? A Yes.
Q What is the name of your husband? A Charlie Starr.
Q Has he also moved his residence to Paden? A Yes, he has changed to Paden.
Q Are these child[sic], Henry, Annie, Gertrude and Jesse J. Starr living? A Yes, sir.

I, Anna Garrigues, on oath state that the above and foregoing is a true and correct transcript of my stenographic notes as taken in said case on said date.

                                                                          Anna Garrigues
Subscribed and sworn to before
me this 28 day of April 1906.   Henry G. Hains
                                                                          Notary Public.

Applications for Enrollment of Creek Newborn
Act of 1905   Volume X

En. 123.

DEPARTMENT OF THE INTERIOR,
COMMISSIONER TO THE FIVE CIVILIZED TRIBES.
Paden, I. T., May 31, 1906.

SUPPLEMENTAL TESTIMONY in the matter of the application for the enrollment of Cora Ellis, Clara Starr, Henry Starr, Annie Starr and Gertrude Starr as citizens by blood of the Creek Nation.

CORA ELLIS, being duly sworn, testified as follows:

Through Charlie Starr, who is duly sworn as Shawnee interpreter:

BY THE COMMISSIONER:
Q What is your name? A Cora Ellis.
Q How old are you? A Somewhere about forty.
Q What is your post office address? A Paden.
Q Are you a citizen of the Creek Nation? A Yes, sir.
Q To what town do you belong? A Tulsa Little River.
Q You appeared before the Commission at Okmulgee, on the 22nd of May, 1901, and made application for the enrollment of yourself and your children, Clara, Henry, Annie and Gertrude Starr, did you not? A Yes, sir.
Q Where was your residence at that time? A I had moved back to Shawnee about that time.
Q Where are you now living? A I am still staying right here now.
Q In the Creek Nation? A Yes, sir.
Q Have you in good faith returned to the Creek Nation to make it your home? A Yes, sir, that is what I am here for now--to live here.
Q Do you hold any allotment for yourself or children as a Shawnee? A No, sir. Clara has an allotment as a Shawnee and a little girl named Cora Starr is allotted over there.
Q Have you established a home in the Creek Nation? A No, sir, I have just been living in a tent. I haven't made any improvements yet because I don't know where I am going to get my allotment.
Q Do you own a home or any improvements in the Shawnee Reservation? A No, sir.
Q How long has it been since you removed from the Shawnee Reservation to the Creek Nation? A I couldn't say how long but it was right after the last Creek Payment.
Q Was that the $1400 Payment? A I think it was. It was the last Creek Payment.
Q One of your children that you mad application for in 1901 has been allotted as a Shawnee has it? A Yes, sir, one, Clara.
Q Henry, Annie and Gertrude Starr are not allotted as Shawnees? A No, sir, they haven't any allotment.
Q Have you any children born to you since that time for whom you now desire to make application? A Only Jesse. I made application for him last year at Bristow.
Q Have you appeared before the Commission recently to see about your rights in the Creek Nation? A Yes, sir, I appeared before the Commission at Muskogee on the 28th day of last March, and the Commission told me to stay here in the Creek Nation and I have been here ever since, and on the 28th day of April I reported to the Commission and

Applications for Enrollment of Creek Newborn
Act of 1905   Volume X

the Commission said the first statements you made the 28th of March we sent to Washington and now we have to send the statements you make now to Washington and then we will notify you and you can come and file, and I have already picked out my land and am only waiting to hear from the Commission.

I, D. C. Skaggs, on oath state that the above and foregoing is a full and true transcript of my stenographic notes as taken on said date.

DC Skaggs

Subscribed and sworn to before me this 12th day of June, 1906.

Alex Posey
Notary Public.

Cr. En. 123.

DEPARTMENT OF THE INTERIOR,
COMMISSIONER TO THE FIVE CIVILIZED TRIBES.

In the matter of the application of Cora Ellis Starr for the enrollment of herself and her children, Clara Starr, Henry Starr, Annie Starr, Gertrude Starr and Jesse J. Starr, as citizens by blood of the Creek Nation.

DECISION.

The record in this case shows that on May 22, 1901, Cora Ellis Starr appeared before the Commission to the Five Civilized Tribes, at Okmulgee, Indian Territory, and made application for the enrollment of herself and her children, Clara, Henry, Annie and Gertrude Starr, as citizens by blood of the Creek Nation and that on April 22, 1905, there was filed with this office a birth affidavit in re application for enrollment of Jesse J. Starr, minor child of Cora Ellis Starr, as a citizen by blood of the Creek Nation. Further proceedings were had in this matter, April 18, 1905 and March 28, April 28 and May 31, 1906. Affidavits in the matter of the birth of said Henry, Annie and Gertrude Starr, filed with this office May 20, 1905, are attached to and made part of the record herein.

The evidence in this case shows that the principal applicant, Cora Ellis Starr, is identified on the 1895 authenticated roll of citizens by blood of the Creek Nation, Little River Tulsa Town, as Cora Ellis; that the names of her minor children, Clara, Henry and Annie Starr, also appear on said roll, that the minor applicants, Gertrude and Jesse J. Starr, were born on the following dates respectively, September 16, 1897 and July 22, 1901; that Charlie Starr, the father of the minor applicants herein, is a member of the Shawnee tribe of Indians and that all of said applicants were living on April 28, 1906.

The evidence further shows that the principal applicant, herein was born and raised in Oklahoma Territory; that she removed to the Creek Nation in the year 1893, lived in said nation five or six years and then removed to Oklahoma; that on or about March 21, 1906, she, and the minor applicants herein, returned to the Creek Nation and established their residence in said nation where they have since resided.

Applications for Enrollment of Creek Newborn
Act of 1905   Volume X

The evidence also shows that said Clara Starr has received an allotment as a member of the Shawnee Tribe of Indians, but that none of the other applicants herein has received an allotment as a member of said tribe.

Paragraph 8 of section 21 of the act of Congress approved June 28, 1898 (30 Stats., 495), provides:

> "The several tribes may, by agreement, determine the right of persons who for any reason may claim citizenship in two or more tribes, and to allotment of lands and distribution of moneys belonging to each tribe; but if no such agreement be made, then such claimant shall be entitled to such rights in one tribe only, and may elect in which tribe he will take such right; but if he fail or refuse to make such selection in due time, he shall be enrolled in the tribe with whom he as resided, and there be given such allotment and distributions, and not elsewhere."

The Department under date of September 17, 1902 (I.T.D. 4991-1902), in the case involving the application of Nancy Sky for the enrollment of herself and child, Motley Sky, (both being of Shawnee blood), as citizens of the Cherokee Nation, held that,

> "Said section of the act of June 28, 1898, is applicable only when an applicant claims citizenship in two nations of the Five Civilized Tribes over which you have jurisdiction. Sky, however, having become an adopted citizen of the Peoria tribe and having received an allotment of land in that nation, lost her citizenship in the Cherokee Nation, and, of course, for that reason her child has no rights there. The application is rejected accordingly."

It is, therefore, ordered and adjudged that there is no authority of law for the enrollment of said Clara Starr as a citizen by blood of the Creek Nation and the application for her enrollment as such is accordingly denied.

It is further ordered and adjudged that said Cora Ellis Starr, Henry Starr, Annie Starr, Gertrude Starr and Jesse J. Starr are entitled to be as citizens by blood of the Creek Nation in accordance with the provisions of the acts of Congress approved June 28, 1898 (30 Stats., 495), March 1, 1901 (31 Stats., 861) and March 3, 1905 (33 Stats., 1060) and the application for their enrollment as such is accordingly granted.

Tams Bixby   Commissioner.

Muskogee, Indian Territory,
JUL 14 1906

Applications for Enrollment of Creek Newborn
Act of 1905 Volume X

DEPARTMENT OF THE INTERIOR
OFFICE OF INDIAN AFFAIRS

> DEPARTMENT
> RECEIVED
> **JUN 22 1922**
> ENCL. TO
> NO. **3837**
> Supt. Five Civilized Tribes

WASHINGTON, D. C.   JUNE 16 , *19* 22

I,   E. B. Meritt,   Assistant   , **Commissioner of Indian Affairs,** do hereby certify that the paper....... hereto attached is a   -   true copy....... of the original....... as the same appears on file   -   in this Office.

IN TESTIMONY WHEREOF, I have hereunto subscribed my name, and caused the seal of this office to be affixed on the day and year first above written.

E. B. Meritt

Assistant *Commissioner.*

BIRTH AFFIDAVIT.

DEPARTMENT OF THE INTERIOR.
COMMISSION TO THE FIVE CIVILIZED TRIBES.

IN RE APPLICATION FOR ENROLLMENT, as a citizen of the CREEK Nation, of Bessie Adella Mackay , born on the 22^d day of August, 1902

Name of Father: George Mackay "decd"   a citizen of the   Creek   Nation.
                            (nee McNulty)
Name of Mother: Cherokee Mackay   a citizen of the United States Nation.

Postoffice   Checotah Ind. Ter.

Applications for Enrollment of Creek Newborn
Act of 1905   Volume X

AFFIDAVIT OF MOTHER.

UNITED STATES OF AMERICA, Indian Territory, ⎫
   WESTERN   DISTRICT. ⎭

     I, Cherokee Mackay (nee McNulty) , on oath state that I am 39 years of age and a citizen by Blood , of the Creek Nation; that I ~~am~~ was the lawful wife of George Mackay (deceased) , who ~~is~~ was a citizen, by *(blank)* of the United States Nation; that a Female child was born to me on 22^d day of August , 1902 , that said child has been named Bessie Adella Mackay , and is now living.

                                      Cherokee Mackey (nee McNulty)
Witnesses To Mark:
{

     Subscribed and sworn to before me this 6th day of April , 1905.

     My Commission Expires July 1, 1908.   J.B. Morrow
                                                Notary Public.

AFFIDAVIT OF ATTENDING PHYSICIAN OR MID-WIFE.

UNITED STATES OF AMERICA, Indian Territory, ⎫
   WESTERN   DISTRICT. ⎭

     I, Mary Watts , a Midwife , on oath state that I attended on Mrs. Cherokee Mackay (nee McNulty) , wife of George Mackay "decd" on the 22^d day of August , 1902 ; that there was born to her on said date a Female child; that said child is now living and is said to have been named Bessie Adella Mackay

                                        her
                                Mary x Watts
Witnesses To Mark: mark
 { JB Morrow
   AA Smith

     Subscribed and sworn to before me this 6th day of April , 1905.

     My Commission Expires July 1, 1908.   J.B. Morrow
                                                Notary Public.

Applications for Enrollment of Creek Newborn
Act of 1905   Volume X

N.C. 788.

DEPARTMENT OF THE INTERIOR,
COMMISSIONER TO THE FIVE CIVILIZED TRIBES.
Senora, I. T., March 20, 1906.

In the matter of the application for the enrollment of Beaden Hope as a citizen by blood of the Creek Nation.

WILLIE HOPE, being duly sworn, testified as follows:

BY THE COMMISSIONER:
Q What is your name? A Willie Hope.
Q How old are you? A About twenty-five.
Q What is your post office address? A Dustin.
Q Are you a citizen of the Creek Nation? A Yes, sir.
Q Do you know Robert and Emma Hope? A Yes, sir.
Q Are they related to you? A Yes, sir, Robert is my brother.
Q Have they a child names Beaden Hope? A Yes, sir.
Q What was Emma Hope's maiden name? A Emma Davis.
Q Is she enrolled under that name? A Yes, sir.
Q Do you know her parents? A I know her father.
Q What is his name? A Jeff Davis.
Q Do you know to what Creek Town she belonged? A No, sir. She may belong to Quasarte or Hitchitee.
Q What is her post office address? A I don't know.
Q Is the child living? A Yes, sir.

~~This testimony is made part of the record in N. C. 919.~~

---oooOOOooo---

I, D. C. Skaggs, on oath state that the above and foregoing is a full and true transcript of my stenographic notes as taken in said cause on said date.

DC Skaggs

Subscribed and sworn to before me this 21 day of March, 1906.

Alex Posey
Notary Public.

Applications for Enrollment of Creek Newborn
Act of 1905 Volume X

Indian Territory)
) SS
Western District)

    We, the undersigned, on oath state that we are personally acquainted with Emma Hope   wife of   Robert Hope   and that on or about the   19   day of March , 1902, a   male   child was born to them and has been named   Beaden Hope   ; and that said child was living March 4, 1905.

    We further state that we have no interest in the above case.

                                       her
                              Martha x Haynes
                                    mark
                                    his
                              Paris x Rodgers
                                    mark

Witnesses to mark:
    Alex Posey
    D C Skaggs

    Subscribed and sworn to before me this 20 day of March 1906.

                                    Alex Posey
                                        Notary Public.

BIRTH AFFIDAVIT.

DEPARTMENT OF THE INTERIOR.
COMMISSION TO THE FIVE CIVILIZED TRIBES.

    IN RE APPLICATION FOR ENROLLMENT, as a citizen of the Creek Nation, of Beaden Hope, born on the 19th day of March , 1902

Name of Father: Robert Hope   a citizen of the   Creek   Nation.
Name of Mother: Emma Hope   a citizen of the   Creek   Nation.

                             Postoffice   Senora I. T.

Applications for Enrollment of Creek Newborn
Act of 1905   Volume X

AFFIDAVIT OF MOTHER.

UNITED STATES OF AMERICA, Indian Territory,　}
　　Western　　　　　　DISTRICT.

    I, Emma Hope , on oath state that I am Nineteen years of age and a citizen by Blood , of the Creek Nation; that I am the lawful wife of Robert Hope , who is a citizen, by Blood of the Creek Nation; that a Male child was born to me on 19th day of March , 1902 , that said child has been named Beaden Hope , and was living March 4, 1905.

                                        Her
                              Emma x Hope
Witnesses To Mark: mark
  { Louise McIntosh
    Leulah C Fowler

    Subscribed and sworn to before me this 19th day of April , 1905.
MY COMMISSION EXPIRES JULY 13th, 1908.
                          J W Fowler
                              Notary Public.

AFFIDAVIT OF ATTENDING PHYSICIAN OR MID-WIFE.

UNITED STATES OF AMERICA, Indian Territory,　}
　　Western　　　　　　DISTRICT.

    No dr or midwife, alone a , on oath state that I attended on Mrs. , wife of on the day of , 190 ; that there was born to her on said date a male child; that said child was living March 4, 1905, and is said to have been named

Witnesses To Mark:
  {

    Subscribed and sworn to before me 5 day of April, 1905.

                            Drennan C Skaggs
                              Notary Public.

NC-788.

                    Muskogee, Indian Territory, October 18, 1905.

Emma Hope,
      Senora, Indian Territory.

Dear Madam:

Applications for Enrollment of Creek Newborn
Act of 1905   Volume X

In the matter of the application for the enrollment of your minor child Beaden Hope, born March 19, 1902, as a citizen by blood of the Creek Nation, this office is unable to identify you upon the final roll of citizens by blood of the Creek Nation.

It is necessary that you be so identified before the rights of said child can be finally determined. You are therefore requested to advise this office of the name under which you are finally enrolled, the names of your parents and other members of your family, the Creek Indian town to which you belong and your final roll number as the same appears upon your allotment certificate and deeds.

You are requested to furnish this office with the affidavits of two disinterested persons relative to the birth of said Beaden Hope. Said affidavits must set forth said child's name, the date of his birth, the names of his parents and whether or not he was living on March 4, 1905.

                  Respectfully,

                              Commissioner.

J.D.

REFER IN REPLY TO THE FOLLOWING:
NC-788

DEPARTMENT OF THE INTERIOR,
COMMISSIONER TO THE FIVE CIVILIZED TRIBES.

Muskogee, Indian Territory, December 14, 1905.

Emma Hope,
    Care of Robert Hope,
        Senora, Indian Territory.

Dear Madam:

In the matter of the application for the enrollment of your minor child, Beaden Hope, born March 19, 1902, as a citizen by blood of the Creek Nation, this Office is unable to identify you upon the final roll of citizens by blood of the Creek Nation. It is necessary that you be so identified before the rights of your said child can be finally determined. You are therefore requested to write this Office at an early date, giving your maiden name, the names of your parents and other members of your family, the Creek Indian Town to which you belong, and, if possible, your name and roll number as same appear on your allotment certificate or deeds to land in the Creek Nation.

You are further requested to furnish this Office with the affidavits of two disinterested persons relative to said child's birth. A blank for that purpose is herewith enclosed.

This matter should receive your immediate attention.

Applications for Enrollment of Creek Newborn
Act of 1905   Volume X

Respectfully,

Dis   Tams Bixby   Commissioner.

BIRTH AFFIDAVIT.

DEPARTMENT OF THE INTERIOR.
COMMISSION TO THE FIVE CIVILIZED TRIBES.

IN RE APPLICATION FOR ENROLLMENT, as a citizen of the Creek Nation, of Sarah Ingram, born on the 20 day of March, 1902 and died Sept. 6, 1902

Name of Father: Thomas Ingram   a citizen of the   Creek   Nation.
Coweta Town
Name of Mother: Jeanetta Ingram   a citizen of the   Creek   Nation.
Quasarte No. 1
                   Postoffice   Stidham, Ind. Ter.

AFFIDAVIT OF MOTHER.

UNITED STATES OF AMERICA, Indian Territory,
    Western   DISTRICT.

I, Jeanetta Ingram, on oath state that I am 28 years of age and a citizen by blood, of the Creek Nation; that I am the lawful wife of Thomas Ingram, who is a citizen, by blood of the Creek Nation; that a female child was born to me on 20 day of March, 1902, that said child has been named Sarah Ingram, and was living March 4, 1905. died September 6, 1902.

                              her
                         Jeanetta x Ingram
Witnesses To Mark: mark
  Alex Posey
  D.C. Skaggs

Subscribed and sworn to before me this 7 day of April, 1905.

                         Drennan C Skaggs
                              Notary Public.

Applications for Enrollment of Creek Newborn
Act of 1905   Volume X

AFFIDAVIT OF ATTENDING PHYSICIAN OR MID-WIFE.

UNITED STATES OF AMERICA, Indian Territory, }
Western   DISTRICT.

I, Thomas Ingram , a~~ ~~ *(blank)* , on oath state that I attended on ^ my wife Mrs. Jeanetta Ingram , ~~wife of~~ *(blank)* on the 20 day of March , 1902 ; that there was born to her on said date a female child; that said child ~~was living March 4, 1905~~ died Sept. 6, 1901 and ~~is said to have been~~ was named Sarah Ingram

Thomas Ingram

Witnesses To Mark:
{

Subscribed and sworn to before me 7 day of April, 1905.

Drennan C Skaggs
Notary Public.

NC 789   JLD

DEPARTMENT OF THE INTERIOR,
COMMISSIONER TO THE FIVE CIVILIZED TRIBES.

In the matter of the application for the enrollment of Sarah Ingram, deceased, as a citizen by blood of the Creek Nation.

. . . .

STATEMENT AND ORDER.

The record in this case shows that on April 11, 1905, application was made, in affidavit form, for the enrollment of Sarah Ingram, deceased, as a citizen by blood of the Creek Nation, under the provisions of the Act of Congress approved March 3, 1905.

It appears from the affidavit filed in this matter that said Sarah Ingram, deceased, was born March 20, 1902, and died September 6, 1902.

The Act of Congress approved March 3, 1905, (33 Stats., 1048), provides:

"That the Commission to the Five Civilized Tribes is authorized for sixty days after the date of the approval of this act to receive and consider applications for enrollment, of children, <u>born subsequent to May twenty-fifth, nineteen hundred and one, and prior to March fourth, nineteen hundred and five, and living on said latter date,</u> to citizens of the Creek tribe of Indians whose enrollment has been approved by the Secretary of the Interior prior to the approval of this act; and to enroll and make allotments to such children."

It is, therefore, ordered that the application for the enrollment of Sarah Ingram, deceased, as a citizen by blood of the Creek Nation be, and the same is, hereby dismissed.

Tams Bixby Commissioner.

Applications for Enrollment of Creek Newborn
Act of 1905 Volume X

Muskogee, Indian Territory.
JAN 4 – 1907

BIRTH AFFIDAVIT.

DEPARTMENT OF THE INTERIOR.
COMMISSION TO THE FIVE CIVILIZED TRIBES.

   IN RE APPLICATION FOR ENROLLMENT, as a citizen of the Creek Nation, of Sudie Ingram, born on the 11 day of Feb., 1904

Name of Father: Thomas Ingram   a citizen of the   Creek   Nation.
Coweta Town
Name of Mother: Jeanetta Ingram   a citizen of the   Creek   Nation.
Quasarte No. 1
                    Postoffice   Stidham, Ind. Ter.

AFFIDAVIT OF MOTHER.

UNITED STATES OF AMERICA, Indian Territory,
      Western   DISTRICT.   Child is present

   I, Jeanetta Ingram, on oath state that I am 28 years of age and a citizen by blood, of the Creek Nation; that I am the lawful wife of Thomas Ingram, who is a citizen, by blood of the Creek Nation; that a female child was born to me on 11 day of February, 1904, that said child has been named Sudie Ingram, and was living March 4, 1905.
                                                 her
                                    Jeanetta x Ingram
Witnesses To Mark: mark
   D.C. Skaggs
   Alex Posey

   Subscribed and sworn to before me this 7 day of April, 1905.

                         Drennan C Skaggs
                         Notary Public.

AFFIDAVIT OF ATTENDING PHYSICIAN OR MID-WIFE.

UNITED STATES OF AMERICA, Indian Territory,
      Western   DISTRICT.

                                        my wife
   I, Thomas Ingram, a (blank), on oath state that I attended on ^ Mrs. Jeanetta Ingram, wife of (blank) on the 11 day of Feb., 1904; that there was born to her on

Applications for Enrollment of Creek Newborn
Act of 1905 Volume X

said date a female child; that said child was living March 4, 1905, and is said to have has been named Sarah Ingram

                                        Thomas Ingram

Witnesses To Mark:

{

    Subscribed and sworn to before me 7 day of April, 1905.

                                        Drennan C Skaggs
                                            Notary Public.

NC-789.

                              Muskogee, Indian Territory, October 18, 1905.

Janetta[sic] Ingram,
      c/o Thomas Ingram,
          Stidham, Indian Territory.

Dear Madam:

    In the matter of the application for the enrollment of your minor child Sudie Ingram, born February 11, 1904, this office desires the affidavit of the mid-wife or physician who attended at the birth of said child and a blank for that purpose is inclosed herewith.

    In the event that there was no physician or midwife in attendance at the birth of said child it will be necessary for you to furnish this office with the affidavits of two disinterested persons relative to the birth of said child. Said affidavits must set forth said child's name, the date of her birth, the names of her parents, and whether or not she was living on March 4, 1905.

                                Respectfully,

                                                      Commissioner.

B C
Env.

BIRTH AFFIDAVIT.
      NC-789   **DEPARTMENT OF THE INTERIOR.**
                     COMMISSION TO THE FIVE CIVILIZED TRIBES.

    IN RE APPLICATION FOR ENROLLMENT, as a citizen of the Ceek[sic] Nation, of Sudie Ingram , born on the 11 day of February, 1904

Name of Father: Thomas J. Ingram   a citizen of the   Creek   Nation.
Name of Mother: Janetta Ingram   a citizen of the   Creek   Nation.

                                  Postoffice   Stidham I.T.

Applications for Enrollment of Creek Newborn
Act of 1905   Volume X

AFFIDAVIT OF MOTHER.

UNITED STATES OF AMERICA, Indian Territory, ⎫
   Western   DISTRICT. ⎬   Child present

    I, Janetta Ingram , on oath state that I am 28 years of age and a citizen by Blood , of the Creek Nation; that I am the lawful wife of Thomas J. Ingram , who is a citizen, by Blood of the Creek Nation; that a Female child was born to me on 11 day of February , 1904 , that said child has been named Sudie Ingram , and was living March 4, 1905.

                                              Jennatte[sic] Ingram

Witnesses To Mark:
{

    Subscribed and sworn to before me this 11 day of November , 1905.
My commission
expires May 19 1908   Preston Janway
                                                      Notary Public.

AFFIDAVIT OF ATTENDING PHYSICIAN OR MID-WIFE.

UNITED STATES OF AMERICA, Indian Territory, ⎫
   Western Dist   DISTRICT. ⎬

    We, John McIntosh and Mary McIntosh , a citizens , on oath state that we attended on Mrs. *(blank)* , wife of Thomas J. Ingram know Janetta Ingram and who *(illegible)* there was on the 11 day of February , 1904 ; that there was born to her on said date a female child; that said child was living March 4, 1905, and is said to have been named Sudie Ingram

                                              John McIntosh
Witnesses To Mark: Mary McIntosh
{

    Subscribed and sworn to before me 11 day of November, 1905.

                                              Preston Janway
                                                  Notary Public.

Applications for Enrollment of Creek Newborn
Act of 1905 Volume X

BIRTH AFFIDAVIT.

DEPARTMENT OF THE INTERIOR.
COMMISSION TO THE FIVE CIVILIZED TRIBES.

IN RE APPLICATION FOR ENROLLMENT, as a citizen of the Creek Nation, of John B. King, born on the 19 day of August, 1903

Name of Father: W. L. King a ^ non citizen of the x x Nation.
Name of Mother: Elizabeth King a citizen of the Creek Nation.

Postoffice Henryetta I.T.

AFFIDAVIT OF MOTHER.

UNITED STATES OF AMERICA, Indian Territory,
Western DISTRICT.

I, Elizabeth King, on oath state that I am Twenty years of age and a citizen by Blood, of the Creek Nation; that I am the lawful wife of W. L. King, who is a non citizen, by x x of the x x Nation; that a male child was born to me on 19th day of August, 1903, that said child has been named John B. King, and was living March 4, 1905.

Elizabeth King

Witnesses To Mark:
{

Subscribed and sworn to before me this 19th day of April, 1905.

MY COMMISSION EXPIRES JULY 13th, 1908. J W Fowler
Notary Public.

AFFIDAVIT OF ATTENDING PHYSICIAN OR MID-WIFE.

UNITED STATES OF AMERICA, Indian Territory,
Western DISTRICT.

I, Nancy E. King, a midwife, on oath state that I attended on Mrs. Elizabeth King, wife of W. L. King on the 19th day of August, 1903; that there was born to her on said date a male child; that said child was living March 4, 1905, and is said to have been named John B. King

Nancy E King

Witnesses To Mark:
{

Applications for Enrollment of Creek Newborn
Act of 1905   Volume X

Subscribed and sworn to before me this 19<u>th</u> day of April, 1905.

MY COMMISSION EXPIRES JULY 13th, 1908.   J W Fowler
                                                                             Notary Public.

BIRTH AFFIDAVIT.

DEPARTMENT OF THE INTERIOR.
COMMISSION TO THE FIVE CIVILIZED TRIBES.

IN RE APPLICATION FOR ENROLLMENT, as a citizen of the Creek Nation, of Henry Lee King, born on the 28 day of December, 1901

Name of Father: W. L. King	a ^non citizen of the ——————Nation.
Name of Mother: Elizabeth King	a citizen of the Creek Nation.

Postoffice   Henryetta I.T.

AFFIDAVIT OF MOTHER.

UNITED STATES OF AMERICA, Indian Territory, }
          Western   DISTRICT.

I, Elizabeth King, on oath state that I am Twenty years of age and a citizen by Blood, of the Creek Nation; that I am the lawful wife of W. L. King, who is a non citizen, by ——of the x x Nation; that a male child was born to me on 28<u>th</u> day of December, 1901, that said child has been named Henry Lee King, and was living March 4, 1905.

                                                                         Elizabeth King

Witnesses To Mark:
{

Subscribed and sworn to before me this 19<u>th</u> day of April, 1905.

MY COMMISSION EXPIRES JULY 13th, 1908.   J W Fowler
                                                                             Notary Public.

AFFIDAVIT OF ATTENDING PHYSICIAN OR MID-WIFE.

UNITED STATES OF AMERICA, Indian Territory, }
          Western   DISTRICT.

I, Nancy E. King, a midwife, on oath state that I attended on Mrs. Elizabeth King, wife of W. L. King on the 28<u>th</u> day of December, 1901; that there was born to her on said date a male child; that said child was living March 4, 1905, and is said to have been named Henry Lee King

Applications for Enrollment of Creek Newborn
Act of 1905   Volume X

Witnesses To Mark:
{

Nancy E King

Subscribed and sworn to before me this 19th day of April, 1905.

MY COMMISSION EXPIRES JULY 13th, 1908.

J W Fowler
Notary Public.

DEPARTMENT OF THE INTERIOR,
COMMISSION TO THE FIVE CIVILIZED TRIBES.
Eufaula, I. T., April 7, 1905.

In the matter of the application for the enrollment of William Chotky as a citizen by blood of the Creek Nation.

G. W. GRAYSON, being duly sworn, testified as follows:

BY COMMISSION:
Q What is your name? A G. W. Grayson.
Q How old are you? A Sixty-one.
Q What is your post office address? A Eufaula.
Q Are you a citizen of the creek[sic] Nation? A Yes, sir.
Q To what town do you belong? A Coweta.
Q Do you make application for the enrollment of William Chotky as a citizen by blood of the Creek Nation? A I do.
Q What relation is the child to you? A None whatever.
Q Who are the parents of the child? A Chotky, alias Cotsilee, is the father. The mother's name I do not know, but she is a member of Okfuske Canadian Town and is a daughter of Mrs. John Kelley. The father of the child is not dead. Some days before his death I mentioned the matter of the Commission coming down here to enroll new-born children and that he would have to enroll his child. I told him one of the main questions asked would be the date of its birth. He told me that the child would be two years old on the 7th of April this year. The father died two or three days afterwards.
Q Was he a citizen of the Creek Nation? A He was a Seminole citizen. He has worked as my hired man for quite a good while. I understand that the mother of the child and her relatives are all opposed to and will not have anything to do with the enrollment of new-born children, and I make this statement in order that the child may, at som e time, get its rights as a Creek citizen.
Q Is the child now living? [sic] It is living with its mother.

Applications for Enrollment of Creek Newborn
Act of 1905   Volume X

Q What is her post office address? A Eufaula.

---oooOOOooo---

I, D. C. Skaggs, on oath state that the above and foregoing is a full and true transcript of my stenographic notes as taken in said cause on said date.

DC Skaggs

Subscribed and sworn to before me this 22 day of July, 1905.

J McDermott
Notary Public.

DEPARTMENT OF THE INTERIOR,
COMMISSION TO THE FIVE CIVILIZED TRIBES.
Eufaula, I. T., May 18, 1905.

In the matter of the application for the enrollment of William Tiger as a citizen by blood of the Creek Nation.

JEANETTA BROOK, being duly sworn, testified as follows:

BY COMMISSION:
Q What is your name? A Jeanetta Brook.
Q How old are you? A Thirty-two.
Q What is your post office address? A Eufaula.
Q Are you a citizen of the Creek Nation? A Yes, sir.
Q To what town do you belong? A Hickory Ground.
Q Are you acquainted with Chotka and Lucy Tiger? A Yes, sir.
Q Have they a child named William? A Yes, sir.
Q How old is the child? A He is a little over two years old.
Q Both of its parents living? A The father is dead. The mother is living.
Q Was the father a citizen of the Creek Nation? A No, sir, he was a Seminole.
Q To what town does Lucy belong? A Okfuske Canadian.
Q Who are Lucy's parents? A John Kelly is her step-father. Saleeche is her mother's name.

Application was made by G. W. Grayson of Eufaula, I. T., for the enrollment of William Tiger as a citizen by blood of the Creek Nation.

---oooOOOooo---

Applications for Enrollment of Creek Newborn
Act of 1905   Volume X

I, D. C. Skaggs, on oath state that the above and foregoing is a full and true transcript of my stenographic notes as taken in said cause on said date.

DC Skaggs

Subscribed and sworn to before me this 2 day of April 1906.

Alex Posey
Notary Public.

N.C. 791.

DEPARTMENT OF THE INTERIOR,
COMMISSIONER TO THE FIVE CIVILIZED TRIBES.
Creek Enrollment Field Party.
Eufaula, I. T., September 2, 1905.

In the matter of the application for the enrollment of William Chotky as a citizen by blood of the Creek Nation.

G. W. GRAYSON, INDIAN TERRITORY

BY COMMISSION:
Q What is your name? A G. W. Grayson.
Q What is your age? A Sixty-one.
Q What is your post office address? A Eufaula.
Q Are you a citizen of the Creek Nation? A Yes, sir.
Q To what town do you belong? A Coweta.
Q Do you know William Chotky? A Yes, sir.
Q Did you make application for the enrollment of William Chotky as a citizen by blood of the Creek Nation at the time the Commission was receiving applications for enrollment of new born children of Creek Citizens? A I did.
Q Have you found out anything further about the parents of this child? A I have learned that the name of the mother is Lucy.
Q Do you know what her full name is? A I think she is related to a family of Indians in that immediate neighborhood who known usually as Deere, and her name may be Lucy Deere.
Q Do you know to what Creek Town she belongs? A Okfuske Canadian, I believe they call it.
Q What is the name of her mother? A I do not know her name but do know that she is the present wife of John Kelley
Q Do you know the name of her father? A Yes, sir. He was a soldier in the confederate service, in my company, and was named Fus-hut-che Marthlochee.
Q What the father of William Chotky known by any other name than Chotky or Chosilee? A Since I first appeared before you in behalf of the applicant I have been told that he is enrolled in the Seminole enumeration as Chotky Tiger.
Q Do you know whether or not he was ever enrolled in the Creek Nation? A No, sir.

Applications for Enrollment of Creek Newborn
Act of 1905 Volume X

Q How long had he lived in the Creek Nation at the time of his death? A Some where near four or five years.
Q Have you seen the mother of the child since making application for its enrollment? A Yes, sir, quite often.
Q Do you know whether or not she would be disposed to give the Commission any information about the child? A She is now living with her step-father, John Kelley, who is opposed to enrolling the new-born children and advises the Okfuskes not to enroll and if he were present when she was asked for information it is very likely she would decline to give such information.
Q In the event it is found that the child is entitled to enrollment in either the Creek or Seminole Nations in which nation do you think the mother would elect to have the child enrolled? A I am quite sure that she would elect to have it enrolled in the Creek Nation. She, nor any of her people, never having lived in the Seminole Country.
Q Do you know who attended on lucy at the time the child was born? A My present recollection is that Lucy's mother, Mrs. Kelley, in answer to my question on the subject, informed me that she had waited on Lucy as mid-wife at the birth of the child.
Q You do not think it would be posible[sic] to secure any information from neighbors or the relatives of Lucy as to this child? A No, sir, I do not think they would be disposed to give you any information.
q[sic] The child is now living is it? A It was a few days since. Yes, sir, it is now living.

---oooOOOooo---

I, D. C. Skaggs, on oath state that the above and foregoing is a full and true transcript of my stenographic notes as taken in said cause on said date.

DC Skaggs

Subscribed and sworn to before me this 16 day of Oct, 1905.

Edw C Griesel
Notary Public.

N.C. 791.   I.S.N.
DEPARTMENT OF THE INTERIOR,
COMMISSIONER TO THE FIVE CIVILIZED TRIBES.

In the matter of the application for the enrollment of William Chotky, as a citizen by blood of the Creek Nation.

Applications for Enrollment of Creek Newborn
Act of 1905 Volume X

DECISION.

The record in this case shows that on April 7, 1905, one G. W. Grayson appeared before the Commission to the Five Civilized Tribes ar Eufaula, Indian Territory, and made application for the enrollment of William Chotky, as a citizen by blood of the Creek Nation. Further proceedings were had May 18 and September 2, 1905. There are also attached to and made part of the record in this case, two affidavits in the matter of the birth of William Chotky, one filed with this office April 11, 1905, and the other filed October 17, 1905.

It appears from the evidence herein and from the records in the possession of this office that said William Chotky is the minor child of Chotky Tiger, deceased, a duly enrolled citizen by blood of the Seminole Nation, and Lucy Deere, whose name appears on a partial schedule of citizens by blood of the Creek Nation, approved by the Secretary of the Interior November 14, 1902, opposite number 9155.

The evidence further shows that William Chotky was born in the Creek Nation on or about April 7, 1903, and was living, in said nation, on the date of the last proceedings herein.

Section 21 of the act of Congress, approved June 28, 1898 (30 Stats., 495) provided, in part, as follows:

"The several tribes, may by agreement, determine the right of persons who for any reason may claim citizenship in two or more tribes, and to allotment of lands and distribution of moneys belonging to each tribe; but if no such agreement be made, then such claimant shall be entitled to such rights in one tribe only, and may elect in which tribe he will take such right; but if he fail or refuse to make such selection in due time, he shall be enrolled in the tribe with whom he has resided, and there be given such allotment and distributions, and not elsewhere."

It is therefore ordered and adjudged that said William Chotky is entitled to be enrolled as a citizen by blood of the Creek Nation, in accordance with the provisions of the acts of Congress approved June 28, 1898 (30 Stats., 495) and March 3, 1905 (33 Stats., 1071), and the application for his enrollment as such is accordingly granted.

                                          Tams Bixby
                                          Commissioner.

Muskogee, Indian Territory.
JUN 28 1906

Applications for Enrollment of Creek Newborn
Act of 1905   Volume X

BIRTH AFFIDAVIT.

DEPARTMENT OF THE INTERIOR.
COMMISSION TO THE FIVE CIVILIZED TRIBES.

IN RE APPLICATION FOR ENROLLMENT, as a citizen of the Creek Nation, of William Chotky, born on the 7 day of April, 1903

Name of Father: Chotky (or Cots-il-ee) deceased a citizen of the Seminole   Nation.
Name of Mother: Unknown   a citizen of the   Creek   Nation.
Okfusky[sic] Canadian Town

Postoffice   Eufaula, Ind. Ter.

AFFIDAVIT OF MOTHER.

UNITED STATES OF AMERICA, Indian Territory,
Western   DISTRICT.   Child is not present

I, G. W. Grayson, on oath state that I am 61 years of age and a citizen by blood, of the Creek Nation; that I am ~~the lawful wife~~ no relation of Chotky (or Cots-il-ee), who is a citizen, by blood of the Seminole Nation; that a male child was born to ~~me~~ his wife on 7 day of April, 1903, that said child has been named William Chotky, and was living March 4, 1905. That the mother of the child refuses to make application for its enrollment, and the father of the child is now dead.

G.W. Grayson

Witnesses To Mark:
{

Subscribed and sworn to before me this 7 day of April, 1905.

Drennan C Skaggs
Notary Public.

BIRTH AFFIDAVIT.

DEPARTMENT OF THE INTERIOR.
COMMISSION TO THE FIVE CIVILIZED TRIBES.

IN RE APPLICATION FOR ENROLLMENT, as a citizen of the Creek Nation, of William Chotky, born on or about the 7 day of April, 1903

Name of Father: Chotky Tiger   a citizen of the Seminole   Nation.
Name of Mother: Lucy Deere   a citizen of the   Creek   Nation.
Okfuskee Canadian Town

Postoffice   Eufaula, I.T.

Applications for Enrollment of Creek Newborn
Act of 1905   Volume X

AFFIDAVIT OF ATTENDING PHYSICIAN OR MID-WIFE.

UNITED STATES OF AMERICA, Indian Territory, }
Western   DISTRICT.

we are personally acquainted with
~~I~~, We the undersigned , ~~a~~ *(blank)* , on oath state that ~~I attended on~~ Mrs. Lucy Deere , wife of Chotky Tiger ~~on the   day of   , 1   ~~; that there was born to her on ~~said date~~ or about the 7" day of April 1903 a male child; that said child was living March 4, 1905, and is said to have been named William Chotky

Witnesses To Mark:
{

John Brook
Jeannette A Brook

Subscribed and sworn to before me 30 day of Sept, 1905.

Drennan C Skaggs
Notary Public.

Dustin, Indian Territory, June 3, 1905.

Commission to the Five Civilized Tribes,
    Muskogee, Indian Territory.

Gentlemen:

I return herewith copies of testimony taken in the following cases, as I find it impossible to secure further evidence:

Sarty, Enrollment No. 520.
Chepe and Folle Homahta, Creek Indian Card Field No. 2871.
Katy and Nicey Gano, No. 2465 B.
✔ William Tiger, No. _____ B.
Amy Kelly, No. 2467 B.
Heliswa and Kaska Beaver, No. 2466 B.
Lena Bear, No. _____ B.
Setepake Scott, No. 2447 B.
Mahlahsee Mitchell, No. 2447 B.
Susanna and Onate Johnson, No. 2468 B.

Respectfully,
(Signed) Alex Posey,
Clerk in Charge Creek Field Party.

Applications for Enrollment of Creek Newborn
Act of 1905 Volume X

NC-791.

Muskogee, Indian Territory, October 18, 1905.

Clerk in Charge,
    Chickasaw Enrollment Division.

Dear Sir:

    On April 11, 1905, application was made to the Commission to the Five Civilized Tribes for the enrollment of William Chotky, born on or about April 7, 1903, child of Lucy Deere, a citizen by blood of the Creek Nation, and Chotky, deceased, a citizen by blood of the Chickasaw[sic] Nation.

    You are requested to advise the Creek Enrollment Division as to whether application was made for the enrollment of the said William Chotky as a citizen of the Chickasaw Nation and if so what disposition has been made of same.

                       Respectfully,
                                Commissioner.

REFER IN REPLY TO THE FOLLOWING:
NC 791

**DEPARTMENT OF THE INTERIOR,
COMMISSIONER TO THE FIVE CIVILIZED TRIBES.**

Muskogee, Indian Territory, October 31, 1905.

Chief Clerk,
    Creek Enrollment Division,

Dear Sir:

    Replying to your letter of October 18, 1905, in which you ask if application has been made for the enrollment as a citizen of the Chickasaw Nation of William Chotky, child of Lucy Deere, a citizen by blood of the Creek Nation and Chotky, deceased, a citizen by blood of the Chickasaw Nation, you are advised that it does not appear from the records of this office that application has been made for the enrollment of William Chotky as a citizen of the Chickasaw Nation.

                       Respectfully,
                       Tams Bixby Commissioner.

Applications for Enrollment of Creek Newborn
Act of 1905   Volume X

REFER IN REPLY TO THE FOLLOWING:

DEPARTMENT OF THE INTERIOR,
COMMISSIONER TO THE FIVE CIVILIZED TRIBES.

Muskogee, Indian Territory, March 30, 1906.

Mr. D. C. Skaggs,
    c/o Alex Posey,
        Creek Enrollment Field Party,
            Wetumka, Indian Territory.

Dear Sir:

    There is inclosed herewith original and carbon copies of testimony taken at Eufaula, Indian Territory, May 18, 1905, in the matter of the application for the enrollment of William Tiger, as a citizen by blood of the Creek Nation.

    You are requested to affix your signature to the affidavit attached to said testimony, have same properly executed before a Notary and return to this office at the earliest practicable date.

                Respectfully,
                          Wm. O. Beall
HEA-8   Acting Commissioner.

Cr. En. 791.

Muskogee, Indian Territory, June 29, 1906.

M. L. Mott,
    Attorney for Creek Nation,
        Muskogee, Indian Territory.

Sir:

    There is enclosed herewith a copy of the decision of the Commissioner to the Five Civilized Tribes in the matter of the application for the enrollment of William Chotky, as a citizen by blood of the Creek Nation.

    You are hereby notified that the Creek Nation will be allowed fifteen days from the date hereof within which to protest against said decision, and if at the expiration of that time no such protest has been made said William Chotky will be regularly listed for enrollment as a citizen by blood of the Creek Nation.

                Respectfully,
                          Commissioner.
Enc. LM- 678.

Applications for Enrollment of Creek Newborn
Act of 1905   Volume X

N C 791

Muskogee, Indian Territory, March 1, 1907.

Lucy Deere,
    Eufaula, Indian Territory.

Dear Madam :--

    You are hereby advised that on February 15, 1907, the Secretary of the Interior approved the enrollment of your minor child, William Chotky, as a citizen by blood of the Creek Nation, and that the name of said child appears upon the roll of New Born citizens by blood of the Creek Nation, enrolled under the Act of Congress approved March 3, 1905, as number 1171.

    This child is now entitled to allotment and application therefor should be made without delay at the Creek Land Office, Muskogee, Indian Territory.

                         Respectfully,

                                    Commissioner.

BIRTH AFFIDAVIT.

DEPARTMENT OF THE INTERIOR.
COMMISSION TO THE FIVE CIVILIZED TRIBES.

    IN RE APPLICATION FOR ENROLLMENT, as a citizen of the Creek Nation, of Beatrice Day, born on the 6 day of January, 1902

Name of Father: Robert Day   a citizen of the United States Nation.
Name of Mother: Vinita Day   a citizen of the   Creek   Nation.
Tuckabatche Town
                      Postoffice   Eufaula, Ind. Terr.

                            Child present
                    AFFIDAVIT OF MOTHER.

UNITED STATES OF AMERICA, Indian Territory, ⎫
    Western   DISTRICT. ⎭

    I, Vinita Day, on oath state that I am 27 years of age and a citizen by blood, of the Creek Nation; that I am the lawful wife of Robert Day, who is a citizen, by *(blank)* of the United States ~~Nation~~; that a female child was born to me on 6 day of

Applications for Enrollment of Creek Newborn
Act of 1905   Volume X

January , 1902 , that said child has been named Beatrice Day , and was living March 4, 1905.

Vinita Day

Witnesses To Mark:
{

Subscribed and sworn to before me this 7 day of April , 1905.

Drennan C Skaggs
Notary Public.

AFFIDAVIT OF ATTENDING PHYSICIAN OR MID-WIFE.

UNITED STATES OF AMERICA, Indian Territory,
  Western   **DISTRICT.** }

assisted the physician who I, Maud Matoy , a———, on oath state that I ^ attended on Mrs. Vinita Day , wife of Robert Day on the 6 day of January , 1902 ; that there was born to her on said date a *(blank)* child; that said child was living March 4, 1905, and is said to have been named Beatrice Day

Maud Matoy

Witnesses To Mark:
{

Subscribed and sworn to before me 7 day of April, 1905.

Drennan C Skaggs
Notary Public.

BIRTH AFFIDAVIT.

DEPARTMENT OF THE INTERIOR.

COMMISSION TO THE FIVE CIVILIZED TRIBES.

IN RE APPLICATION FOR ENROLLMENT, as a citizen of the Creek Nation, of Robert Day, Jr. , born on the 15 day of February , 1903

Name of Father: Robert Day , Sr.   a citizen of the United States Nation.
Name of Mother: Vinita Day   a citizen of the   Creek   Nation.
   Tuckabatche Town

Postoffice   Eufaula, Ind. Terr.

Applications for Enrollment of Creek Newborn
Act of 1905   Volume X

Child present
AFFIDAVIT OF MOTHER.

UNITED STATES OF AMERICA, Indian Territory, }
Western   DISTRICT.

I, Vinita Day , on oath state that I am 27 years of age and a citizen by blood , of the Creek Nation; that I am the lawful wife of Robert Day Sr. , who is a citizen, by blood of the Creek[sic]   Nation; that a male child was born to me on 15 day of February , 1903 , that said child has been named Robert Day, Jr. , and was living March 4, 1905.

Vinita Day

Witnesses To Mark:
{

Subscribed and sworn to before me this 7 day of April , 1905.

Drennan C Skaggs
Notary Public.

AFFIDAVIT OF ATTENDING PHYSICIAN OR MID-WIFE.

UNITED STATES OF AMERICA, Indian Territory, }
Western   DISTRICT.

assisted the physician who
I, Maud Matoy , a——— , on oath state that I ^ attended on Mrs. Vinita Day , wife of Robert Day, Sr. on the 15 day of February , 1903 ; that there was born to her on said date a male child; that said child was living March 4, 1905, and is said to have been named Robert Day, Jr.

Maud Matoy

Witnesses To Mark:
{

Subscribed and sworn to before me 7 day of April, 1905.

Drennan C Skaggs
Notary Public.

Applications for Enrollment of Creek Newborn
Act of 1905   Volume X

NC-793.

Muskogee, Indian Territory, October 18, 1905.

Jennie Harley,
    c/o Samson[sic] Harley,
        Eufaula, Indian Territory.

Dear Madam:

    In the matter of the application for the enrollment of your minor child, Joseph Harley, born August 11, 1904, as a citizen by blood of the Creek Nation, this office desires the affidavit of the attending physician or midwife at the birth of said child and a blank for that purpose is inclosed herewith.

    In the event that there was no attending physician or midwife in attendance at the birth of the said Joseph Harley it will be necessary for you to furnish this office with the affidavits of two disinterested persons relative to the birth of said child. Said affidavits must set forth said child's name, the date of his birth, the names of his parents and whether or not he was living on March 4, 1905.

                Respectfully,

                            Commissioner.

B C
Env.

HGH

REFER IN REPLY TO THE FOLLOWING:

DEPARTMENT OF THE INTERIOR,
COMMISSIONER TO THE FIVE CIVILIZED TRIBES.

Muskogee, Indian Territory, October 23, 1906.

Jennie Harley,
    c/o Sampson Harley,
        Eufaula, Indian Territory.

Dear Madam:

    You are hereby advised that the name of your minor child, Joseph Harley, is contained in the partial list of citizens by blood of the Creek Nation, approved by the Secretary of the Interior October 15, 1906, and that a selection of land in the Creek Nation may now be made for said child at the Creek Land Office in Muskogee, Indian Territory.

    This matter should receive your prompt attention.

Applications for Enrollment of Creek Newborn
Act of 1905   Volume X

Respectfully,
Tams Bixby   Commissioner.

BIRTH AFFIDAVIT.

DEPARTMENT OF THE INTERIOR.
COMMISSION TO THE FIVE CIVILIZED TRIBES.

IN RE APPLICATION FOR ENROLLMENT, as a citizen of the Creek Nation, of Joseph Harley, born on the 11th day of August, 1904

Name of Father: Sampson Harley   a citizen of the   Creek   Nation.
Name of Mother: Jennie Harley   a citizen of the   Creek   Nation.

Postoffice   Eufaula, Indian Territory

AFFIDAVIT OF MOTHER.

UNITED STATES OF AMERICA, Indian Territory,
Western   DISTRICT.

I, Jennie Harley, on oath state that I am about 30 years of age and a citizen by blood, of the Creek Nation; that I am the lawful wife of Sampson Harley, who is a citizen, by blood of the Creek Nation; that a male child was born to me on 11th day of August, 1904, that said child has been named Joseph Harley, and is now living.

Jennie Harley

Witnesses To Mark:
{

Subscribed and sworn to before me this 12th day of April, 1906.

My Commission expires July 8, 1906   *(Illegible)* Sampson
Notary Public.

AFFIDAVIT OF ATTENDING PHYSICIAN OR MID-WIFE.

UNITED STATES OF AMERICA, Indian Territory,
Western   DISTRICT.

I, Chotka Smith, a midwife, on oath state that I attended on Mrs. Jennie Harley, wife of Sampson Harley on the 11th day of August, 1906; that there was born to her on said date a male child; that said child is now living and is said to have been named Joseph Harley

Applications for Enrollment of Creek Newborn
Act of 1905   Volume X

Witnesses To Mark:
{ William C. *(Illegible)*
  Jessie Smith

            her
           Chotka x Smith
            mark

  Subscribed and sworn to before me this 12$^{\underline{th}}$ day of April, 1906.

My Commission expires July 8, 1906   *(Illegible)* Sampson
              Notary Public.

BIRTH AFFIDAVIT.

DEPARTMENT OF THE INTERIOR.
COMMISSION TO THE FIVE CIVILIZED TRIBES.

  IN RE APPLICATION FOR ENROLLMENT, as a citizen of the Creek Nation, of Joseph Harley, born on the 11 day of August, 1904

Name of Father: Sampson Harley a citizen of the Creek Nation. Tulmochussee Town
Name of Mother: Jennie Harley (nee McGilbra) a citizen of the Creek Nation. Tulmochussee Town
        Postoffice Eufaula, Indian Territory

AFFIDAVIT OF MOTHER.

UNITED STATES OF AMERICA, Indian Territory, } Child is present
  Western   DISTRICT.

  I, Jennie Harley, on oath state that I am about 25 years of age and a citizen by blood, of the Creek Nation; that I am the lawful wife of Sampson Harley, who is a citizen, by blood of the Creek Nation; that a male child was born to me on 11 day of August, 1904, that said child has been named Joseph Harley, and was living March 4, 1905.

           her
         Jennie x Harley
Witnesses To Mark: mark
{ Alex Posey
  DC Skaggs

  Subscribed and sworn to before me this 7 day of April, 1905.

          Drennan C Skaggs
          Notary Public.

Applications for Enrollment of Creek Newborn
Act of 1905 Volume X

AFFIDAVIT OF ATTENDING PHYSICIAN OR MID-WIFE.

UNITED STATES OF AMERICA, Indian Territory,
    Western DISTRICT.

    I, Sampson Harley, ~~a (blank)~~, on oath state that I attended on ^ my wife Mrs. Jennie Harley, ~~wife of~~ *(blank)* on the 11 day of August, 1904 ; that there was born to her on said date a *(blank)* child; that said child was living March 4, 1905, and ~~is said to have~~ has been named Joseph Harley

                                               his
                                    Sampson x Harley
Witnesses To Mark: mark
    Alex Posey
    DC Skaggs

    Subscribed and sworn to before me this 7 day of April, 1905.

                                    Drennan C Skaggs
                                    Notary Public.

                                                                     HGH

REFER IN REPLY TO THE FOLLOWING:
NC 794.

                       DEPARTMENT OF THE INTERIOR,
                COMMISSIONER TO THE FIVE CIVILIZED TRIBES.

                      Muskogee, Indian Territory, January 19, 1907.

Emma White,
    c/o Craft White,
        Bristow, Indian Territory.

Dear Madam:

    There is herewith enclosed one copy of the statement and order of the Commissioner to the Five Civilized Tribes, dated January 18, 1907, dismissing the application made by you for the enrollment of your minor child Myrtle Izona White, deceased, as a citizen of the Creek Nation.

                      Respectfully,
                      Tams Bixby Commissioner.

Register.
LM-23.

Applications for Enrollment of Creek Newborn
Act of 1905 Volume X

BIRTH AFFIDAVIT.

DEPARTMENT OF THE INTERIOR.
COMMISSION TO THE FIVE CIVILIZED TRIBES.

IN RE APPLICATION FOR ENROLLMENT, as a citizen of the Creek Nation, of Myrtle Izona White, born on the 6 day of Sept, 1903

Name of Father: Craft White   a citizen of the   U.S.   Nation.
Name of Mother: Emma " (nee Ellis)   a citizen of the   Creek   Nation.
     Tuskegee

                Postoffice   Bristow

AFFIDAVIT OF MOTHER.

UNITED STATES OF AMERICA, Indian Territory,
    Western   DISTRICT.

     I, Emma White, on oath state that I am 20 years of age and a citizen by blood, of the Creek Nation; that I am the lawful wife of Craft White, who is a citizen, by ~~(blank)~~ of the U. S. Nation; that a female child was born to me on 6 day of Sept, 1903, that said child has been named Myrtle Izona White, and ~~is now living~~. died Oct 10 1903

                                     Emma White

Witnesses To Mark:
{

     Subscribed and sworn to before me this 19 day of April, 1905.

                                Edw C Griesel
                                   Notary Public.

AFFIDAVIT OF ATTENDING ~~PHYSICIAN~~ OR MID-WIFE.

UNITED STATES OF AMERICA, Indian Territory,
    Western   DISTRICT.

     I, Hannah Mann, a Midwife, on oath state that I attended on Mrs. Emma White, wife of Craft White on the 6 day of Sept, 1903; that there was born to her on said date a female child; that said child ~~is now living~~ died Oct 10, 1903 and is said to have been named Myrtle Izona White

                                 her
                            Hannah x Mann
Witnesses To Mark: mark
   { J F Mann
     EC Griesel

Applications for Enrollment of Creek Newborn
Act of 1905   Volume X

Subscribed and sworn to before me this 19 day of April, 1905.

> Edw C Griesel
> Notary Public.

N.C. 794.   J.L.De.

DEPARTMENT OF THE INTERIOR,
COMMISSIONER TO THE FIVE CIVILIZED TRIBES.

In the matter of the application for the enrollment of Myrtle Izona White, deceased, as a citizen by blood of the Creek Nation.

STATEMENT AND ORDER.

The record in this case shows that on April 24, 1905, application was made, in affidavit form, for the enrollment of Myrtle Izona White, deceased, as a citizen by blood of the Creek Nation, under the provisions of the act of Congress approved March 3, 1905.

It appears from the affidavit filed in this matter that said Myrtle Izona White was born September 6, 1903, and died October 10, 1903.

The act of Congress approved March 3, 1905, (33 Stats., 1048), in part provides:

"That the Commission to the Five Civilized Tribes is authorized for sixty days after the date of the approval of this act to receive and consider applications for enrollment, of children, born subsequent to May twenty-fifth, nineteen hundred and one, and prior to March fourth, nineteen hundred and five, and living on said latter date, to citizens of the Creek tribe of Indians whose enrollment has been approved by the Secretary of the Interior prior to the approval of this act; and to enroll and make allotments to such children."

It is, therefore, ordered that the application for the enrollment of Myrtle Izona White, deceased, as a citizen by blood of the Creek Nation, be, and the same is, hereby dismissed.

> Tams Bixby Commissioner.

Muskogee, Indian Territory.
JAN 18 1907

Applications for Enrollment of Creek Newborn
Act of 1905 Volume X

BIRTH AFFIDAVIT.

DEPARTMENT OF THE INTERIOR.
COMMISSION TO THE FIVE CIVILIZED TRIBES.

IN RE APPLICATION FOR ENROLLMENT, as a citizen of the Creek Nation, of Clara White, born on the 5 day of Nov, 1904

Name of Father: Craft White	a citizen of the U.S.	Nation.
Name of Mother: Emma " nee Ellis	a citizen of the Creek	Nation.
(Tuskegee)		

Postoffice   Bristow

AFFIDAVIT OF MOTHER.

UNITED STATES OF AMERICA, Indian Territory,
   Western   DISTRICT.   Child Present

I, Emma White, on oath state that I am 20 years of age and a citizen by blood, of the Creek Nation; that I am the lawful wife of Craft White, who is a citizen, by *(blank)* of the U.S. Nation; that a female child was born to me on 5 day of Nov, 1904, that said child has been named Clara White, and is now living.

Emma White

Witnesses To Mark:

Subscribed and sworn to before me this 19 day of April, 1905.

Edw C Griesel
Notary Public.

AFFIDAVIT OF ATTENDING PHYSICIAN OR MID-WIFE.

UNITED STATES OF AMERICA, Indian Territory,
   Western   DISTRICT.

I, Lula Craig, a Midwife, on oath state that I attended on Mrs. Emma White, wife of Craft White on the 5 day of Nov, 1904; that there was born to her on said date a female child; that said child is now living and is said to have been named Clara White

Lula Craig

Witnesses To Mark:

Applications for Enrollment of Creek Newborn
Act of 1905 Volume X

Subscribed and sworn to before me this 19 day of April, 1905.

>Edw C Griesel
>Notary Public.

BIRTH AFFIDAVIT.

DEPARTMENT OF THE INTERIOR.
COMMISSION TO THE FIVE CIVILIZED TRIBES.

IN RE APPLICATION FOR ENROLLMENT, as a citizen of the Creek Nation, of Malissa Christy Mcintosh, born on the 13th day of March, 1904

Name of Father: Amos Mcintosh	a citizen of the	Creek Nation.
Name of Mother: Louine Mcintosh	a citizen of the	Creek Nation.

>Postoffice   Senora, I. T.

AFFIDAVIT OF MOTHER.

UNITED STATES OF AMERICA, Indian Territory,
Western DISTRICT.

    I, Louine Mcintosh, on oath state that I am Thirty five years of age and a citizen by Blood, of the Creek Nation; that I am the lawful wife of Amos Mcintosh, who is a citizen, by Blood of the Creek Nation; that a Female child was born to me on 13th day of March, 1904, that said child has been named Malissa Christa[sic] Mcintosh, and was living March 4, 1905.

>Louine McIntosh

Witnesses To Mark:
{

    Subscribed and sworn to before me this 19th day of April, 1905.

MY COMMISSION EXPIRES JULY 13th, 1908.

>J W Fowler
>Notary Public.

Applications for Enrollment of Creek Newborn
Act of 1905   Volume X

AFFIDAVIT OF ATTENDING PHYSICIAN OR MID-WIFE.

UNITED STATES OF AMERICA, Indian Territory,
Western   DISTRICT.

I, Senora Likowski , a Midwife , on oath state that I attended on Mrs. Louine Mcintosh , wife of Amos Mcintosh on the 13th day of March , 1904 ; that there was born to her on said date a *(blank)* child; that said child was living March 4, 1905, and is said to have been named Malissa Christa Mcintosh

Senora Likowski

Witnesses To Mark:
{

Subscribed and sworn to before me this 19th day of April , 1905.

MY COMMISSION EXPIRES JULY 13th, 1908.

J W Fowler
Notary Public.

BIRTH AFFIDAVIT.

DEPARTMENT OF THE INTERIOR.
COMMISSION TO THE FIVE CIVILIZED TRIBES.

IN RE APPLICATION FOR ENROLLMENT, as a citizen of the Creek Nation, of Maudy Van Mcintosh , born on the 27th day of December, 1901

Name of Father: Amos Mcintosh   a citizen of the   Creek   Nation.
Name of Mother: Louine Mcintosh   a citizen of the   Creek   Nation.

Postoffice   Senora, I. T.

AFFIDAVIT OF MOTHER.

UNITED STATES OF AMERICA, Indian Territory,
Western   DISTRICT.

I, Louine Mcintosh , on oath state that I am Thirty Five years of age and a citizen by Blood , of the Creek Nation; that I am the lawful wife of Amos Mcintosh , who is a citizen, by Blood of the Creek Nation; that a Female child was born to me on 27th day of December , 1901 , that said child has been named Maudy Van Mcintosh , and was living March 4, 1905.

Louine McIntosh

Witnesses To Mark:
{

Applications for Enrollment of Creek Newborn
Act of 1905   Volume X

Subscribed and sworn to before me this 19th day of April, 1905.

MY COMMISSION EXPIRES JULY 13th, 1908. J W Fowler
Notary Public.

AFFIDAVIT OF ATTENDING PHYSICIAN OR MID-WIFE.

UNITED STATES OF AMERICA, Indian Territory, }
Western   DISTRICT.

I, Fannie Burgess, a Midwife, on oath state that I attended on Mrs. Louine Mcintosh, wife of Amos Mcintosh on the 27th day of December, 1901; that there was born to her on said date a female child; that said child was living March 4, 1905, and is said to have been named Maudy Van Mcintosh

Fannie Burgess

Witnesses To Mark:
{

Subscribed and sworn to before me this 19th day of April, 1905.

MY COMMISSION EXPIRES JULY 13th, 1908.   J W Fowler
Notary Public.

BIRTH AFFIDAVIT.

DEPARTMENT OF THE INTERIOR.
COMMISSION TO THE FIVE CIVILIZED TRIBES.

IN RE APPLICATION FOR ENROLLMENT, as a citizen of the Creek Nation, of James Ellis, born on the 15 day of Nov, 1902

Name of Father: James Ellis (d)   a citizen of the   U.S.   Nation.
Name of Mother: Hannah Mann (nee Ellis)   a citizen of the   Creek   Nation.
(Tuskegee)

Postoffice   Bristow

Applications for Enrollment of Creek Newborn
Act of 1905 Volume X

AFFIDAVIT OF MOTHER.   Child Present

UNITED STATES OF AMERICA, Indian Territory,
Western   DISTRICT.

I, Hannah Mann, on oath state that I am 36 years of age and a citizen by blood, of the Creek Nation; that I ~~am~~ was the lawful wife of James Ellis (dec'd.), who is a citizen, by ~~(blank)~~ of the U.S. Nation; that a male child was born to me on 15 day of Nov, 1902, that said child has been named James Ellis, and was living March 4, 1905.

                                          Her
Witnesses To Mark: Hannah x Mann
{ J F Mann   mark
{ EC Griesel

Subscribed and sworn to before me this 19 day of April, 1905.
(Seal)

                                          Edw C Griesel
                                              Notary Public.

AFFIDAVIT OF ATTENDING PHYSICIAN ~~OR MID-WIFE~~.

UNITED STATES OF AMERICA, Indian Territory,
Western   DISTRICT.

I, F.A. Henshaw, a Physician, on oath state that I attended on Mrs. Hannah Mann, wife of James Ellis (d) on the 15 day of November, 1902; that there was born to her on said date a male child; that said child was living March 4, 1905, and is said to have been named James Ellis

                                          F.A. Henshaw
Witnesses To Mark:
{

Subscribed and sworn to before me this 19 day of April, 1905.
(Seal)

                                          Edw C Griesel
                                            Notary Public.

Applications for Enrollment of Creek Newborn
Act of 1905   Volume X

(The Birth Affidavit below typed as given.)

Commission to the Five Civilized Tribes.

In Re Application for enrollment of Sue Washington, born on 1oth day April 19o3. Name of father Edward M Washington. Name of mother Catherine Washington, a citizen by blood of the Creek nation. Post Office Eufaula, Indian Territory.

Affidavit of mother

Indian Territory
Western District

Catherine Washington, being duly sworn on oath states; that I am 27 years of age; that I am a citizen by blood of the Creek Nation; that I am the lawful wife of Edward M Washington; that on 1oth. day April 19o3 there was born unto me a female child; that said child is now living and has been named Sue Washington.

Sworn and subscribed to before me this *(blank)* day March 19o5

Notary Public

Affidavit of Physician.

Indian Territory
Western District

R. M. Counterman, a physician, being duly sworn on oath, states that I attended on Mrs. Catherine Washington, wife of Edward M Washington on the 1oth. day of April 19o3; that there was born unto her on said date a female child; that said child is now living and has been named Sue Washington.

R.M. Counterman

Sworn and subscribed to before me this 7th day of March 19o5.

Edwin G. Bedford
Notary Public
My commission
expires May 15th 1907.

Applications for Enrollment of Creek Newborn
Act of 1905 Volume X

BIRTH AFFIDAVIT.

DEPARTMENT OF THE INTERIOR.
COMMISSION TO THE FIVE CIVILIZED TRIBES.

IN RE APPLICATION FOR ENROLLMENT, as a citizen of the Creek Nation, of Sue Washington, born on the 10 day of April, 1903

Name of Father: E. M. Washington   a citizen of the United States Nation.
(Simpson)
Name of Mother: Catherine Washington   a citizen of the Creek Nation.
Tuckabatche Town
Postoffice   Eufaula, I.T.

AFFIDAVIT OF MOTHER.

Child present.

UNITED STATES OF AMERICA, Indian Territory,
Western   DISTRICT.

I, Catherine Washington, on oath state that I am 26 years of age and a citizen by blood, of the Creek Nation; that I am the lawful wife of E. M. Washington, who is a citizen, by *(blank)* of the United States Nation; that a female child was born to me on 10 day of April, 1903, that said child has been named Sue Washington, and was living March 4, 1905.

Catherine Washington

Witnesses To Mark:

Subscribed and sworn to before me this 3 day of April, 1905.

Drennan C Skaggs
Notary Public.

Applications for Enrollment of Creek Newborn
Act of 1905   Volume X

BIRTH AFFIDAVIT.

Department of the Interior,
COMMISSION TO THE FIVE CIVILIZED TRIBES.

IN RE APPLICATION FOR ENROLLMENT, as a citizen of the Creek Nation, of Hattie Mukes, born on the 29 day of Dec , 1903

Name of Father: Thomas Mukes   a citizen of the   U.S.   ~~Nation~~.
Name of Mother: Alice   " (McNac)   a citizen of the   Creek Nation.

Post-Office: Depew I.T.

AFFIDAVIT OF MOTHER.   (Child Present)

UNITED STATES OF AMERICA, ⎫
   INDIAN TERRITORY,   ⎬
  Western   District.   ⎭

I, Alice Mukes , on oath state that I am 25 years of age and a citizen by blood , of the Creek Nation; that I am the lawful wife of Thomas Mukes , who is not a citizen, by *(blank)* of the Creek Nation; that a female child was born to me on 29" day of Dec , 1903 , that said child has been named Hattie Mukes , and is now living.

                              Alice Mukes

WITNESSES TO MARK:
{

Subscribed and sworn to before me this 19" day of April, 1905.

                              J McDermott
                              Notary Public.

AFFIDAVIT OF ATTENDING PHYSICIAN OR MID-WIFE.

UNITED STATES OF AMERICA, ⎫
   INDIAN TERRITORY,   ⎬
  Western   District.   ⎭

I, Caroline McNac , a midwife , on oath state that I attended on Mrs. Alice Mukes , wife of Thomas Mukes on the 29" day of Dec , 1903; that there was born to her on said date a female child; that said child is now living and is said to have been named Hattie Mukes   her
                              Caroline x McNac
WITNESSES TO MARK: mark
{ EC Griesel
  Jesse McDermott

Applications for Enrollment of Creek Newborn
Act of 1905 Volume X

Subscribed and sworn to before me this 19" *day of* April, *1905*.
(Seal)
           J McDermott
             Notary Public.

BIRTH AFFIDAVIT.

Department of the Interior,
COMMISSION TO THE FIVE CIVILIZED TRIBES.

  IN RE APPLICATION FOR ENROLLMENT, as a citizen of the Creek Nation, of Ada Mukes, born on the 9 day of January , 1905

Name of Father: Thomas Mukes	a citizen of the U.S.	~~Nation~~.
Name of Mother: Alice "	a citizen of the Creek	Nation.

      Post-Office: Depew I.Ty.

     AFFIDAVIT OF MOTHER. (Child Present)

UNITED STATES OF AMERICA,
  INDIAN TERRITORY,
 Western District.

  I, Alice Mukes , on oath state that I am 25   years of age and a citizen by blood , of the Creek   Nation; that I am the lawful wife of Thomas Mukes , who is not a citizen, ~~by~~ *(blank)* of the Creek Nation; that a female child was born to me on 9" day of January , 1905 , that said child has been named Ada Mukes , and is now living.

           Alice Mukes
WITNESSES TO MARK:
{

 Subscribed and sworn to before me this 19" *day of* April, *1905*.
(Seal)
          J McDermott
            Notary Public.

   AFFIDAVIT OF ATTENDING PHYSICIAN OR MID-WIFE.

UNITED STATES OF AMERICA,
  INDIAN TERRITORY,
 Western District.

  I, Caroline McNac , a midwife , on oath state that I attended on Mrs. Alice Mukes , wife of Thomas Mukes on the 9" day of January , 1905; that there was

Applications for Enrollment of Creek Newborn
Act of 1905 Volume X

born to her on said date a female child; that said child is now living and is said to have been named Ada Mukes

<small>WITNESSES TO MARK:</small>
{ EC Griesel
 Jesse McDermott

Caroline x McNac
her   mark

Subscribed and sworn to before me this 19" *day of* April, 1905.
(Seal)

J McDermott
Notary Public.

BIRTH AFFIDAVIT.

DEPARTMENT OF THE INTERIOR.
COMMISSION TO THE FIVE CIVILIZED TRIBES.

IN RE APPLICATION FOR ENROLLMENT, as a citizen of the Creek Nation, of Wiley Knight, born on the 3 day of Sept , 1904

Name of Father: David Knight   a citizen of the Creek Nation. Hutchechubbee
Name of Mother: Hannah " (nee Bear)   a citizen of the Creek Nation. Artussee

Postoffice   Tuskegee IT

AFFIDAVIT OF MOTHER.   (Child present)

UNITED STATES OF AMERICA, Indian Territory, ⎫
 Western   DISTRICT.   ⎭

I, Hannah Knight , on oath state that I am 22   years of age and a citizen by blood , of the Creek Nation; that I am the lawful wife of David Knight , who is a citizen, by blood of the Creek Nation; that a male   child was born to me on 3 day of Sept , 1904 , that said child has been named Wiley Knight , and was living March 4, 1905.

Hannah x Knight
her   mark

Witnesses To Mark:
{ Edw C Griesel
 Jesse McDermott

Applications for Enrollment of Creek Newborn
Act of 1905   Volume X

Subscribed and sworn to before me this 19 day of April , 1905.

(Seal)   J McDermott
                                Notary Public.

Assistant
AFFIDAVIT OF ~~ATTENDING PHYSICIAN~~ OR MID-WIFE.

UNITED STATES OF AMERICA, Indian Territory, ⎱
    Western   **DISTRICT.**   ⎰

                                                help to
I, Nettie Bear assistant a midwife , on oath state that I ^ attended on Mrs. Hannah Knight , wife of David Knight on the 3" day of Sept. , 1904 ; that there was born to her on said date a *(blank)* child; that said child was living March 4, 1905, and is said to have been named Wiley Knight

                                          her
                            Nettie x Bear
Witnesses To Mark: mark
    ⎧ Edw C Griesel
    ⎩ Jesse McDermott

Subscribed and sworn to before me 5 day of April, 1905.
(Seal)

                        J McDermott
                        Notary Public.

BIRTH AFFIDAVIT.
                            DEPARTMENT OF THE INTERIOR.
                 COMMISSION TO THE FIVE CIVILIZED TRIBES.

IN RE APPLICATION FOR ENROLLMENT, as a citizen of the Creek Nation, of Lola Bear , born on the 22 day of Aug , 1903

Name of Father: Morgie Bear   a citizen of the   Creek   Nation.
Name of Mother: Nettie Bear   a citizen of the   Creek   Nation.

                    Postoffice   Newby I.T.

Applications for Enrollment of Creek Newborn
Act of 1905   Volume X

AFFIDAVIT OF MOTHER.

UNITED STATES OF AMERICA, Indian Territory, ⎱
   (blank)   DISTRICT. ⎰

    I, Nettie Bear , on oath state that I am 24 years of age and a citizen by Birth , of the Creek Nation; that I am the lawful wife of Morgie Bear , who is a citizen, by Birth of the Creek Nation; that a male child was born to me on 22 day of Aug , 1903 , that said child has been named Lola Bear , and is now living.

                                        her
                              Nettie x Bear
Witnesses To Mark: mark
  ⎰ John Gooden
  ⎱ ?. W. Livingston

    Subscribed and sworn to before me this 20 day of Dec , 1905.

                              L H Evert
                                Notary Public.
                              My commission expires May 31, 1908

AFFIDAVIT OF ATTENDING PHYSICIAN OR MID-WIFE.

UNITED STATES OF AMERICA, Indian Territory, ⎱
   Western   DISTRICT. ⎰

    I, Silla Jacobs , a midwife , on oath state that I attended on Mrs. Nettie Bear , wife of Morgie Bear on the 22 day of Aug , 1903 ; that there was born to her on said date a male child; that said child is now living and is said to have been named Lola Bear

                                        her
                              Silla x Jacobs
Witnesses To Mark: mark
  ⎰ John Gooden
  ⎱ ?. M. Livingston

    Subscribed and sworn to before me this 20 day of Dec , 1905.

                              L H Evert
                                Notary Public.
                              My commission expires May 31, 1908

Applications for Enrollment of Creek Newborn
Act of 1905   Volume X

Copy

BIRTH AFFIDAVIT.

DEPARTMENT OF THE INTERIOR,
COMMISSION TO THE FIVE CIVILIZED TRIBES.

In Re Application for Enrollment, as a citizen of the Creek Nation, of Roley Bear, born on the 21 day of August, 1903

Name of Father: March Bear   a citizen of the   Creek   Nation. Artussee

Name of Father: Nettie Bear (nee Marshall)   a citizen of the   Creek   Nation. Okfuskee

Post-office   Newby I. T.

AFFIDAVIT OF MOTHER.   (Child present)

UNITED STATES OF AMERICA,
    INDIAN TERRITORY,
    Western   District.

I, Nettie Bear, on oath state that I am 26 years of age and a citizen by blood, of the Creek Nation; that I am the lawful wife of March Bear, who is a citizen, by blood of the Creek Nation; that a male child was born to me on 21 day of August, 1903, that said child has been named Roley Bear, and ~~is now~~ was living. March 4, 1905.

                                     her
                               Nettie x Bear

WITNESSES TO MARK: mark
     { Edw C Griesel
       Jesse McDermott

Subscribed and sworn to before me this 19 day of April, 1905.

                               J McDermott
                                     NOTARY PUBLIC.

                                 Father
AFFIDAVIT OF ~~ATTENDING PHYSICIAN OR MID-WIFE~~.

UNITED STATES OF AMERICA,
    INDIAN TERRITORY,
    Western   District.

I, March Bear, ~~a~~ *(blank)*, on oath state that I attended on ~~Mrs~~. my, wife ~~of~~ when on the 21 day of August, 1903; that there was born to her on said

Applications for Enrollment of Creek Newborn
Act of 1905   Volume X

date a male child; that said child is now living March 4 1905 and is said to have been named Roley Bear

                                                           his
                                              March x Bear

WITNESSES TO MARK: mark
{ Edw C Griesel
{ Jesse McDermott

Subscribed and sworn to before me this 19 day of April , 1905.

                                              J McDermott
                                                          NOTARY PUBLIC.
             (Midwife Dead)   (Father present)

BIRTH AFFIDAVIT.

DEPARTMENT OF THE INTERIOR,
COMMISSION TO THE FIVE CIVILIZED TRIBES.

In Re Application for Enrollment, as a citizen of the Creek Nation, of Joe Bear , born on the 4 day of June , 1902

Name of Father: March Bear   a citizen of the   Creek   Nation.
Name of Father: Nettie Bear   a citizen of the   Creek   Nation.

                                  Post-office   Newby I. T.

                                AFFIDAVIT OF MOTHER.

UNITED STATES OF AMERICA,
   INDIAN TERRITORY,
     Western   District.

    I, Nettie Bear , on oath state that I am 26 years of age and a citizen by blood , of the Creek   Nation; that I am the lawful wife of March Bear , who is a citizen, by blood of the Creek   Nation; that a male child was born to me on 4 day of June , 1902 , that said child has been named   Joe Bear , and ~~is now living~~. died about 2 mos after
                                               her
                                          Nettie x Bear
WITNESSES TO MARK: mark
{ E C Griesel
{ Jesse McDermott

Applications for Enrollment of Creek Newborn
Act of 1905   Volume X

Subscribed and sworn to before me this 19 day of   April , 1905.

J McDermott

NOTARY PUBLIC.

Father
AFFIDAVIT OF ~~ATTENDING PHYSICIAN OR MID-WIFE~~.

UNITED STATES OF AMERICA,
   INDIAN TERRITORY,
 Western   District.

    I, March Bear , ~~a~~ *(blank)* , on oath state that I attended on ~~Mrs~~. my , wife ~~of~~ when on the 4 day of June , 1902 ; that there was born to her on said date a male child; that said child ~~is now living and is said to have been~~ was named Joe Bear and died about 2 mos after birth   his
March x Bear
mark

WITNESSES TO MARK:
  { E C Griesel
    Jesse McDermott

Subscribed and sworn to before me this 19 day of   April , 1905.

Seal
J McDermott
NOTARY PUBLIC.

AFFIDAVIT OF DISINTERESTED WITNESS.

UNITED STATES OF AMERICA,
Western DISTRICT,   SS
INDIAN TERRITORY.

I am

    I, the undersigned, on oath state that ~~we are~~ personally acquainted with Nettie Bear   wife of   Marche[sic] Bear   ; that there was born to her a   male child on or about the   21   day of   August 1903   ; that the said child has been named Roley Bear   , and was living March 4, 1905.

    We further state that we have no interest in this case.
her
Cella x Larney
mark

Witnesses:
Jesse McDermott
J.B. McClanahan

Applications for Enrollment of Creek Newborn
Act of 1905   Volume X

Subscribed and sworn to before me this 6th day of Sept. 1906

                         J McDermott
                         Notary Public.

AFFIDAVIT OF DISINTERESTED WITNESS.

UNITED STATES OF AMERICA,
INDIAN TERRITORY,
Western DISTRICT.   SS

                    I am
I, the undersigned, on oath state that ~~we are~~ personally acquainted with Nettie Bear wife of Marche[sic] Bear ; that there was born to her a male child on or about the 21 day of August, 1903 ; that the said child has been named Roley Bear , and was living March 4, 1905.

We further state that we have no interest in this case.

                         Millie Davis
Witnesses: _____

_____

Subscribed and sworn to before me this 6th day of Sept. 1906

                         J McDermott
                         Notary Public.

BIRTH AFFIDAVIT.
                  DEPARTMENT OF THE INTERIOR.
          COMMISSION TO THE FIVE CIVILIZED TRIBES.

      IN RE APPLICATION FOR ENROLLMENT, as a citizen of the Creek Nation, of Roley Bear , born on the 2 day of Aug , 1903

Name of Father: March Bear   a citizen of the   Creek   Nation.
Artussee
Name of Mother: Nettie Bear (nee Marshall)   a citizen of the   Creek   Nation.
Okfuskee
                  Postoffice   Newby, I.T.

Applications for Enrollment of Creek Newborn
Act of 1905   Volume X

AFFIDAVIT OF MOTHER.

UNITED STATES OF AMERICA, Indian Territory, ⎫
    Western   DISTRICT. ⎬

I, Nettie Bear , on oath state that I am 26 years of age and a citizen by blood , of the Creek   Nation; that I am the lawful wife of March Bear , who is a citizen, by blood of the Creek Nation; that a male child was born to me on 21 day of August , 1903 , that said child has been named Roley Bear , and was living March 4, 1905.

                                            her
                                     Nettie x Bear
Witnesses To Mark: mark
  ⎰ Edw C Griesel
  ⎱ Jesse McDermott

Subscribed and sworn to before me this 19 day of April , 1905.

(Seal)   J McDermott
                                         Notary Public.

                               Father
AFFIDAVIT OF ~~ATTENDING PHYSICIAN OR MID-WIFE~~.

UNITED STATES OF AMERICA, Indian Territory, ⎫
    Western   DISTRICT. ⎬

I, March Bear , ~~a~~ *(blank)* , on oath state that I attended on ~~Mrs~~.   my , wife ~~of~~ when   on the 21 day of Aug , 1903 ; that there was born to her on said date a male child; that said child was living March 4, 1905, and is said to have been named Roley Bear
                                           his
                                   March x Bear
Witnesses To Mark: mark
  ⎰ Edw C Griesel
  ⎱ Jesse McDermott

Subscribed and sworn to before me this 19" day of April , 1905.

(Seal)   J McDermott
                                         Notary Public.
                (Midwife Dead)   (Father present)

Applications for Enrollment of Creek Newborn
Act of 1905 Volume X

BIRTH AFFIDAVIT.

DEPARTMENT OF THE INTERIOR.
COMMISSION TO THE FIVE CIVILIZED TRIBES.

IN RE APPLICATION FOR ENROLLMENT, as a citizen of the Creek Nation, of Joe Bear, born on the 4 day of June, 1902

Name of Father: March Bear   a citizen of the Creek Nation.
Name of Mother: Nettie "   a citizen of the Creek Nation.

Postoffice   Newby, I.T.

AFFIDAVIT OF MOTHER.

UNITED STATES OF AMERICA, Indian Territory, } Western DISTRICT.

I, Nettie Bear, on oath state that I am 26 years of age and a citizen by blood, of the Creek Nation; that I am the lawful wife of March Bear, who is a citizen, by blood of the Creek Nation; that a male child was born to me on 4" day of June, 1902, that said child has been named Joe Bear, and ~~was living March 4, 1905~~. died about 2 mos after her

Nettie x Bear
mark

Witnesses To Mark:
{ E C Griesel
{ Jesse McDermott

Subscribed and sworn to before me this 19" day of April, 1905.

(Seal)   J McDermott
Notary Public.

Father
AFFIDAVIT OF ~~ATTENDING PHYSICIAN OR MID-WIFE~~.

UNITED STATES OF AMERICA, Indian Territory, } Western DISTRICT.

I, March Bear, ~~a~~ *(blank)*, on oath state that I attended on ~~Mrs.~~ my, wife ~~of~~ when on the 4" day of June, 1902; that there was born to her on said date a male child; that said child was ~~living March 4, 1905, and is said to have been~~ named Joe Bear and died about 2 mos after birth

his
March x Bear
mark

Witnesses To Mark:
{ E C Griesel
{ Jesse McDermott

Applications for Enrollment of Creek Newborn
Act of 1905   Volume X

Subscribed and sworn to before me this 19 day of April , 1905.

(Seal)   J McDermott
                                              Notary Public.
              (Midwife Dead)   (Father present)

NC 800   JLD
DEPARTMENT OF THE INTERIOR,
COMMISSIONER TO THE FIVE CIVILIZED TRIBES.

In the matter of the application for the enrollment of Joe Bear, deceased, as a citizen by blood of the Creek Nation.

....

STATEMENT AND ORDER.

The record in this case shows that on April 24, 1905, application was made, in affidavit form, for the enrollment of Joe Bear, deceased, as a citizen by blood of the Creek Nation, under the provisions of the Act of Congress approved March 3, 1905.

It appears from the affidavit filed in this matter that said Joe Bear, deceased, was born June 4, 1902, and died about two months thereafter.

The Act of Congress approved March 3, 1905, (33 Stats., 1048), provides:

"That the Commission to the Five Civilized Tribes is authorized for sixty days after the date of the approval of this act to receive and consider applications for enrollment, of children, <u>born subsequent to May twenty-fifth, nineteen hundred and one, and prior to March fourth, nineteen hundred and five, and living on said latter date,</u> to citizens of the Creek tribe of Indians whose enrollment has been approved by the Secretary of the Interior prior to the approval of this act; and to enroll and make allotments to such children."

It is, therefore, ordered that the application for the enrollment of Joe Bear, deceased, as a citizen by blood of the Creek Nation be, and the same is, hereby dismissed.

                              (No Signature) Commissioner.

Muskogee, Indian Territory.
JAN 4 1907

Applications for Enrollment of Creek Newborn
Act of 1905   Volume X

NC 800

Muskogee, Indian Territory, October 19, 1905

Marche Bear,
    Newby, Indian Territory.

Dear Sir:

    In the matter of the application for the enrollment of your minor child Roley Bear, born August 21, 1903, as a citizen by blood of the Creek Nation, this office desires the affidavit of the physician or midwife who attended on your wife, Nettie Bear, at the birth of Roley Bear and a blank for that purpose is inclosed herewith.

    In the event that there was no attending physician or midwife in attendance at the birth of said child it will be necessary for you to furnish this office with the affidavits of two disinterested persons relative to the birth of said Roley Bear. Said affidavits must set forth said child's name, the date of his birth, the names of his parents, and whether or not said child was living on March 4, 1905.

                  Respectfully,
                  Commissioner

BC
Env

J.D.

REFER IN REPLY TO THE FOLLOWING:
NC. 955.

DEPARTMENT OF THE INTERIOR,
COMMISSIONER TO THE FIVE CIVILIZED TRIBES.

Muskogee, Indian Territory, June 22, 1905.

Nettie Bear,
    Newby, Indian Territory.

Dear Madam:

    In the matter of the application for the enrollment of your minor child, Lola Bear, as a citizen by blood of the Creek Nation, you are advised that it is required that you furnish this office with the affidavits of yourself and the midwife, who attended you at the birth of said child, said affidavits showing the name of the child, the names of its parents, the date of birth, and whether said child was living March 4, 1906, and for this purpose there is herewith enclosed a blank affidavit. This matter should receive your immediate attention.

    You are further advised that this office is unable to identify you and Margie Bear, the father of said child, upon its rolls of citizens by blood of the Creek Nation, and it will

Applications for Enrollment of Creek Newborn
Act of 1905 Volume X

be necessary that you furnish this office with your maiden name, the names of your parents and other members of your family, the Creek Indian Town to which you [sic] Margie Bear belong, the names and roll numbers as same appear on your deeds or allotment certificates to land in the Creek Nation, and any other information which will enable this office to identify you and Margie Bear on its records.

Respectfully,
Tams Bixby
Commissioner.

1 BA

N C 801   Fannie Mitchell

Her father is Mitchell Sarwanoke & her mother is Nancy Sarwanoke, the interpreter took the fathers[sic] first name Mitchell for his surname, & therefore the child was called Fannie Mitchell in the affidavits instead of Fannie Sarwanoke. She is living now & is about 4 years old. They are full blood Snake Indians.

P.P. Ewing

NC-801.

Muskogee, Indian Territory, October 19, 1905.

Mitchell Sar-wa-no-ke,
    Eufaula, Indian Territory.

Dear Sir:

    In the matter of the application for the enrollment of your minor child Fannie Mitchell, born March 25, 1903, as a citizen by blood of the Creek Nation, this office desires the affidavit of the mother of said child and a blank for that purpose is inclosed herewith.

    You state in your affidavit, relative to the birth of said child, that no one attended on your wife at the time said Fannie Mitchell was born and in lieu of the affidavit of the physician or midwife it will be necessary for you to furnish this office with the affidavits of two disinterested witnesses relative to the birth of said child. Said affidavits must set forth said child's name, the date of her birth, the names of her parents and whether or not she was living on March 4, 1905.

Applications for Enrollment of Creek Newborn
Act of 1905   Volume X

Inasmuch as your surname is Sar-wa-no-ke it necessarily follows that the surname of your child must be Sar-wa-no-ka[sic] instead of Mitchell. In having the above affidavits prepared be careful to see that they correctly state the name of said child.

                        Respectfully,

                                          Commissioner.

Env.

NC-801

                              Muskogee, Indian Territory, December 15, 1905.

Mitchell Sar-wa-no-ke,
    Eufaula, Indian Territory.

Dear Sir:

In the matter of the application for the enrollment of your minor child, Fannie Mitchell, born March 25, 1903, as a citizen by blood of the Creek Nation, this Office requires the affidavit of the mother of said child, and a blank for that purpose is herewith enclosed.

You state in your affidavit relative to the birth of said child that no one attended on your wife at the time said Fannie Mitchell was born. In lieu of the affidavit of a physician or midwife, it will be necessary for you to furnish this Office with the affidavits of two disinterested persons relative to said child's birth, and a blank for that purpose is herewith enclosed.

Inasmuch as your surname is Sar-wa-no-ke, it necessarily follows that the surname of your child is Sar-wa-no-ke instead of Mitchell. In having the affidavits prepared, be careful to see that they correctly state the name of said child.

                        Respectfully,

1 B A   Commissioner.
Dis

Applications for Enrollment of Creek Newborn
Act of 1905 Volume X

NC 801

Muskogee, Indian Territory, January 12, 1907.

Nancy Sarwanoke (or Mitchell),
    Care of Mitchell Sarwanoke,
        Eufaula, Indian Territory.

Dear Madam:

    In the matter of the application for the enrollment of your minor child, Fannie Mitchell, born March 25, 1903, as a citizen by blood of the Creek Nation, this office requires the affidavit of the mother of said child, and a blank for that purpose is herewith inclosed.

    It is stated in the affidavit of Mitchell Sarwanoke relative to the birth of said child that no one was in attendance at the time said Fannie Mitchell was born. In lieu of the affidavit of a physician or midwife, you will be allowed ten days within which to furnish this office with the affidavits of two disinterested persons relative to said child's birth, and a blank for that purpose is herewith inclosed.

    Inasmuch as your surname is Sarwanoke, it necessarily follows that the surname of your child is Sarwanoke instead of Mitchell. In having the affidavits prepared be careful to see that they correctly state the name of said child.

                            Respectfully,

1 B A   Commissioner.
Dis

N C 801

Muskogee, Indian Territory, March 9, 1907.

Nancy Sarwanokee[sic],
    % Mitchell Sarwanokee,
        Eufaula, Indian Territory.

Dear Madam :--

    You are hereby advised that on March 2, 1907, the Secretary of the Interior approved the enrollment of your minor child, Fannie Sarwanokee, as a citizen by blood of the Creek Nation, and that the name of said child appears upon the roll of new born citizens by blood of the Creek Nation, enrolled under the Act of Congress approved March 3, 1905, as number 1272.

    This child is now entitled to allotment and application therefor should be made without delay at the Creek Land Office, Muskogee, Indian Territory.

Applications for Enrollment of Creek Newborn
Act of 1905 Volume X

Respectfully,

Commissioner.

BIRTH AFFIDAVIT.

DEPARTMENT OF THE INTERIOR.
COMMISSION TO THE FIVE CIVILIZED TRIBES.

IN RE APPLICATION FOR ENROLLMENT, as a citizen of the Creek Nation, of Fannie Mitchell, born on the 25 day of March, 1903

Name of Father: Mitchell Sarwanokee   a citizen of the   Creek   Nation. Okfusky[sic] Canadian Town
Name of Mother: Nancy Sarwanokee   a citizen of the   Creek   Nation. Eufaula Canadian Town

Postoffice   Eufaula Ind. Ter.

AFFIDAVIT OF MOTHER.

UNITED STATES OF AMERICA, Indian Territory,
    Western   DISTRICT.   }   Child is not present

I, Mitchell Sarwanokee, on oath state that I am about 40 years of age and a citizen by blood, of the Creek Nation; that I am the lawful ~~wife~~ husband of Nancy Sarwanokee, who is a citizen, by blood of the Creek Nation; that a female child was born to ~~me~~ her on 25 day of March, 1903, that said child has been named Fannie Mitchell, and was living March 4, 1905. That the mother is unable to appear personally and make application for the enrollment of the child on account of illness; that no one attended on her as midwife or physician at the birth of the child except me.

                                    his
                        Mitchell x Sarwanokee
Witnesses To Mark: mark
{ DC Skaggs
{ Alex Posey

Subscribed and sworn to before me this 7 day of April, 1905.

Drennan C Skaggs
Notary Public.

Applications for Enrollment of Creek Newborn
Act of 1905   Volume X

NC 801

WSC
JCL

DEPARTMENT OF THE INTERIOR,
COMMISSIONER TO THE FIVE CIVILIZED TRIBES.

In the matter of the application for the enrollment of Fannie Sarwanokee, as a citizen by blood of the Creek Nation.

DECISION.

The record in this case shows that on April 11, 1905, application was made, in affidavit form, for the enrollment of Fannie Mitchell, under the provisions of the Act of Congress approved March 3, 1905 (33 Stats. 1048). A written report in this matter made by P. P. Ewing, is attached to and made a part of the record herein.

As it appears from the evidence that the proper name of the applicant herein is Fannie Sarwanokee, further reference will be made to her under that name.

It appears from the evidence and the records in the possession of this office that the applicant herein, is the minor child of Mitchell Sarwanokee and Nancy Sarwanokee, duly enrolled citizens of the Creek Nation, whose names appear on a partial schedule of citizens of the Creek Nation, approved by the Secretary of the Interior, March 28, 1902, opposite numbers 8707 and 8708, respectively. Diligent efforts have been made by this office to secure further information relative to this child, but without success, owing to the fact that the parents are full bloods and members of the so-called Snake faction.

However, from the weight of the evidence it appears that th applicant was born on the 25th. day of March, 1903, and was living on March 4, 1905.

It is therefore, ordered and adjudged that the applicant, Fannie Sarwanokee is entitled to be enrolled as a citizen by blood of the Creek Nation, under the provisions of the Act of Congress approved March 3, 1905, (33 Stats. 1048), and the application for her enrollment as such is accordingly granted.

Tams Bixby Commissioner.

Muskogee, Indian Territory.
FEB 19 1907

Applications for Enrollment of Creek Newborn
Act of 1905   Volume X

BIRTH AFFIDAVIT.

See Dup. aff. of father

DEPARTMENT OF THE INTERIOR.
COMMISSION TO THE FIVE CIVILIZED TRIBES.

IN RE APPLICATION FOR ENROLLMENT, as a citizen of the Creek Nation, of Gertrude Grayson , born on the 2 day of Mar , 1904

Name of Father: Pete Grayson   a citizen of the   Creek   Nation.
Name of Mother: Hattie " (nee Perryman)   a citizen of the   Creek   Nation.

Postoffice   Bristow, I.T.

AFFIDAVIT OF MOTHER.   (Child present)

UNITED STATES OF AMERICA, Indian Territory,
    Western   DISTRICT.

I, Hattie Grayson , on oath state that I am 20 years of age and a citizen by blood, of the Creek Nation; that I am the lawful wife of   Pete Grayson , who is a citizen, by blood of the Creek Nation; that a female child was born to me on 2 day of Mar , 1904 , that said child has been named Gertrude Grayson , and is now living.

                              Hattie Grayson
Witnesses To Mark:
{

Subscribed and sworn to before me this 20 day of Apr. , 1905.

(Seal)   J. McDermott
                                    Notary Public.

AFFIDAVIT OF ATTENDING PHYSICIAN OR MID-WIFE.

UNITED STATES OF AMERICA, Indian Territory,
    (blank)   DISTRICT.

I, Susanna Perryman , a Mid Wife , on oath state that I attended on Mrs. Hattie Grayson , wife of Pete Grayson on the 2 day of Mar , 1904 ; that there was born to her on said date a female child; that said child is now living and is said to have been named Gertrude Grayson
                                       her
                              Susanna x Perryman
Witnesses To Mark: mark
 { Pete Grayson
   Jesse McDermott

Applications for Enrollment of Creek Newborn
Act of 1905   Volume X

Subscribed and sworn to before me this 20" day of Apr. , 1905.

        J. McDermott
         Notary Public.

BIRTH AFFIDAVIT.

DEPARTMENT OF THE INTERIOR.
COMMISSION TO THE FIVE CIVILIZED TRIBES.

IN RE APPLICATION FOR ENROLLMENT, as a citizen of the Creek Nation, of Gertrude Grayson, born on the 2 day of March, 1904

Name of Father: Pete Grayson   a citizen of the   Creek   Nation.
(Lochoboker)
Name of Mother: Hattie " (nee Perryman)   a citizen of the   Creek   Nation.
(Lochopocha)
       Postoffice   Bristow

      AFFIDAVIT OF ~~MOTHER~~. Father

UNITED STATES OF AMERICA, Indian Territory,
  Western   DISTRICT.

  I, Pete Grayson, on oath state that I am 28 years of age and a citizen by blood, of the Creek Nation; that I am the lawful ~~wife~~ Husband of Hattie Grayson, who is a citizen, by blood of the Creek Nation; that a female child was born to me on 2 day of March , 1904 , that said child has been named Gertrude Grayson , and is now living.

         Pete Grayson

Witnesses To Mark:
{

Subscribed and sworn to before me this 19 day of April, 1905.

 (Seal)   Edw C Griesel
         Notary Public.

Applications for Enrollment of Creek Newborn
Act of 1905 Volume X

N.C. 803.

DEPARTMENT OF THE INTERIOR,
COMMISSIONER TO THE FIVE CIVILIZED TRIBES.
Near Eufaula, Indian Territory, February 12, 1907.

In the matter of the application for the enrollment of Bennie (Smith) Pahoseyahola, as a citizen by blood of the Creek Nation.

Josie Pahoseyahola, being duly sworn, by J. McDermott, a notary public, testified as follows through Jesse McDermott, official interpreter:

BY THE COMMISSIONER:

Q What is your name? A Josie Pahoseyahola is my right name but I am sometimes known as Joseph Smith.
Q What is your age? A About thirty.
Q What is your postoffice address? A Eufaula.
Q Are you a citizen of the Creek Nation? A I am.
Q Have you filed on your land? A Yes.
Q Have you the deeds to your allotment? A Yes.

The witness presents allotment deeds issued to Josie Pahoseyahola Creek Indian Roll No. 7399.

Q Have you a child for whom you made application for enrollment in the Creek Nation? A Yes, there he is. (Indicating a small boy).
Q What is his name? A Bennie.
Q When was he born? A January 4, 1904. He was three years last month.
Q What is the name of his mother? A Chotka is her Indian name but her name on the allotment certificate appears little different.

The witness presents an allotment certificate issued to Soatka Pahoseyahola and states that the allotment described therein is his wife's. She is identified on Creek Indian Card Field No. 2487.

Q Have you any other children enrolled older that the one about whom you are testifying? A Yes.
Q What are their names? A Lodie is the only one.

There is an affidavit on file at the office of the Commissioner to the Five Civilized Tribes executed by yourself and wife on April 7, 1905, in which the name of your child is given as Bennie Smith.

Q What caused you to make application for his enrollment under the name Bennie Smith when it should have been Bennie Pahoseyahola? A My wife, not knowing any better, had allready[sic] signed an affidavit giving the name Bennie Smith before I was called in

Applications for Enrollment of Creek Newborn
Act of 1905   Volume X

to sign it and I noticed that the name was a little different from my surname but I never said anything about it.
Q Under what surname do you desire your child Bennie enrolled? A Just the same as mine.
Q Bennie Pahoseyahola? A Yes.
Q Was there a midwife in attendance when Bennie was born? A No, my wife was alone when Bennie was born.
Q Can you furnish the Commissioner the names of your neighbors, not related to you, who might know about when Bennie was born? A No, I have some neighbors but they are all related to me.

      I, Jesse McDermott, on oath state that the above and foregoing is a full and true transcript of my notes as taken in said cause on said date.

Jesse McDermott

    Subscribed and sworn to before me, this 13 day of Feb, 1907.

F. L. Moss
Notary Public

My Commission expires Jan. 20th 1908.

BIRTH AFFIDAVIT.

Copy

DEPARTMENT OF THE INTERIOR.
COMMISSION TO THE FIVE CIVILIZED TRIBES.

    IN RE APPLICATION FOR ENROLLMENT, as a citizen of the Creek Nation, of Bennie Smith, born on the 4 day of Jan , 1904

Name of Father: Joseph Smith (Yahola)   a citizen of the   Creek   Nation.
Name of Mother: Chotka Smith (Yahola)   a citizen of the   Creek   Nation.

Postoffice   Eufaula Ind. Ter

AFFIDAVIT OF MOTHER.

UNITED STATES OF AMERICA, Indian Territory, }   Child is present
    Western   DISTRICT.

    I, Chotka Smith , on oath state that I am about 29 years of age and a citizen by blood , of the Creek Nation; that I am the lawful wife of Joseph Smith , who is a citizen, by blood of the Creek Nation; that a male child was born to me on 4 day of

Applications for Enrollment of Creek Newborn
Act of 1905   Volume X

January , 1904 , that said child has been named Bennie Smith , and was living March 4, 1905.

            her
          Chotka x Smith
Witnesses To Mark: mark
 { Alex Posey
   D.C. Skaggs

  Subscribed and sworn to before me this 7 day of April , 1905.

          Drennan C Skaggs
          Notary Public.

AFFIDAVIT OF ATTENDING PHYSICIAN OR MID-WIFE.

UNITED STATES OF AMERICA, Indian Territory,
  Western   DISTRICT.

                 my wife
 I, Joseph Smith , a~~~~ *(blank)* , on oath state that I attended on ^ Mrs. Chotka Smith , ~~wife of~~ *(blank)* on the 4 day of Jan , 1904 ; that there was born to her on said date a male child; that said child was living March 4, 1905, and ~~is said to have~~ has been named Bennie Smith   her[sic]
         Joseph x Smith
Witnesses To Mark: mark
 { Alex Posey
   D.C. Skaggs

  Subscribed and sworn to before me 7 day of April, 1905.

          Drennan C Skaggs
          Notary Public.

(The above Birth Affidavit given again.)

Applications for Enrollment of Creek Newborn
Act of 1905 Volume X

BIRTH AFFIDAVIT.

DEPARTMENT OF THE INTERIOR.
COMMISSION TO THE FIVE CIVILIZED TRIBES.

IN RE APPLICATION FOR ENROLLMENT, as a citizen of the Creek Nation, of Bennie Pahoseyahola, born on the 4 day of January, 1904

Name of Father: Josie Pa ho sey ahola   a citizen of the Creek Nation.
C I 7399
Name of Mother: Soatka Paho sey ahola   a citizen of the Creek Nation.
C C F 2487
                           Postoffice   Eufaula Ind. Ter

AFFIDAVIT OF MOTHER.

UNITED STATES OF AMERICA, Indian Territory, }   Child is present
    Western   DISTRICT.

I, Soatka Paho sey ahola, on oath state that I am about 30 years of age and a citizen by blood, of the Creek Nation; that I am the lawful wife of Josie Paho sey ahola, who is a citizen, by blood of the Creek Nation; that a male child was born to me on 4 day of January, 1904, that said child has been named Bennie Paho sey ahola, and was living March 4, 1905. and is now living

                                    her
                          Soatka x Paho sey ahola
Witnesses To Mark: mark
    { J McDermott
      (Name Illegible)

Subscribed and sworn to before me this 12" day of February, 1907.

My Com Expires   J McDermott
July 25" 1907   Notary Public.

Bennie Smith h. C 803

Bennie Smith is about 4 years old & is the son of Joseph Smith & Chotka who have been married to my knowledge for over fifteen years. Joseph Smith was away from home when I call & Chotka has a baby about 2 weeks old so it was impossible for me to het her to go to Eufaula to take her affidavit. They are full blood Snake Indians.

                                  P.P. Ewing

Applications for Enrollment of Creek Newborn
Act of 1905   Volume X

NC 803

      Muskogee I T Oct 19 05

Chotka Smith
    c/o Joseph Smith,
        Eufaula I T

Dear Madam:

    In the matter of the application for the enrollment of your minor child, Bennie Smith, born January 4, 1904, as a citizen by blood of the Creek Nation, this office requires the affidavits of two disinterested witnesses relative to the birth of said child. Said affidavits must set forth said child's name, the date of his birth, the names of his parents, and whether or not he was living on March 4, 1905.

    This office has been unable to identify you upon the final roll of citizens by blood of the Creek Nation. It is necessary that you be so identified and you are requested to state the name under which you are finally enrolled, the names of your parents and other members of your family, the Creek Indian town to which you belong and your final roll number as the same appears upon your allotment certificate and deeds.

                Resp
                      Comr

                                                          HGH

REFER IN REPLY TO THE FOLLOWING:
NC 803

DEPARTMENT OF THE INTERIOR,
COMMISSIONER TO THE FIVE CIVILIZED TRIBES.

            Muskogee, Indian Territory, January 12, 1907.

Chotka Smith (or Soatka Pahoseyahola),
    Care of Joseph Smith (or Josie Pahoseyahola),
        Eufaula, Indian Territory.

Dear Madam:

    In the matter of the application for the enrollment of your minor child Bennie Smith, born January 4, 1904, as a citizen by blood of the Creek Nation, this office requires the affidavit of the midwife or physician in attendance at its birth, or in lieu thereof the affidavit of two disinterested witnesses relative to its birth, said affidavits to set forth the child's name, the date of his birth, the names of his parents and whether or not he was living on March 4, 1905. Blank forms for this purpose are herewith inclosed and you will be allowed ten days to have the same properly executed and return to this office.

Applications for Enrollment of Creek Newborn
Act of 1905 Volume X

It is presumed that you are the identical Soatka Pahoseyahola and that Joseph Smith is identified as Josie Pahoseyahola, and you are requested to appear at this office within ten days with said Josie to give testimony relative to your identification on the Creek Rolls.

                                    Respectfully,
1 B A   Tams Bixby   Commissioner.
Dis.

REFER IN REPLY TO THE FOLLOWING:
N.C. 803

DEPARTMENT OF THE INTERIOR,
COMMISSIONER TO THE FIVE CIVILIZED TRIBES.

                        Muskogee, Indian Territory, February 13, 1907.

Commissioner to the Five Civilized Tribes,
    Muskogee, Indian Territory.

Sir:

There are herewith enclosed copies of record in the matter of the application for the enrollment of Bennie (Smith) Pahoseyahola as a citizen by blood of the Creek Nation, together with the affidavit of the mother and copies of testimony taken in said case. The Creek Enrollment Field Party is unable to secure the affidavits of two disinterested witnesses relative to the birth of said child.

                                Respectfully,
                                Jessie McDermott
                                  Clerk in Charge.

                                                                               JWH
N C 803
                        Muskogee, Indian Territory, March 9, 1907.

Soatka Pahoseyahola,
    % Josie Pahoseyahola,
        Eufaula, Indian Territory.

Dear Madam :--

You are hereby advised that on March 2, 1907, the Secretary of the Interior approved the enrollment of your minor child, Bennie Pahoseyahola, as a citizen by blood of the Creek Nation, and that the name of said child appears upon the roll of new born citizens by blood of the Creek Nation, enrolled under the Act of Congress approved March 3, 1905, as number 1273.

Applications for Enrollment of Creek Newborn
Act of 1905   Volume X

This child is now entitled to allotment and application therefor should be made without delay at the Creek Land Office, Muskogee, Indian Territory.

Respectfully,

Commissioner.

N.C. 803   SAM
                                                                                                                    AG

DEPARTMENT OF THE INTERIOR,
COMMISSIONER TO THE FIVE CIVILIZED TRIBES.

In the matter of the application for the enrollment of Bennie Pahoseyahola as a citizen by blood of the Creek Nation.

DECISION.

The record in this case shows that on April 11, 1905, application was made in affidavit form for the enrollment of Bennie Pahoseyahola, under the name of Bennie Smith, as a citizen by blood of the Creek Nation. A supplemental affidavit as filed and further proceedings were had on February 12, 1907.

It appears from the evidence and the records in possession of this office that the correct name of said applicant is Bennie Pahoseyahola and not Bennie Smith and that he is the minor child of Josie Pahoseyahola and Soatka Pahoseyahola, whose names appear on a partial schedule of citizens by blood of the Creek Nation, approved by the Secretary of the Interior March 28, 1902, opposite numbers 7399 and 7400 respectively.

The evidence shows that said child was born January 4, 1903 and was living March 4, 1905.

It is therefore, ordered and adjudged that the said Bennie Pahoseyahola is entitled to enrollment as a citizen by blood of the Creek Nation, under the provisions of the Act of Congress approved March 3, 1905 (33 Stat. L., 1048), and the application for his enrollment as such is accordingly granted.

Tams Bixby Commissioner.

Muskogee, Indian Territory.
FEB 18 1907

Applications for Enrollment of Creek Newborn
Act of 1905   Volume X

STATE OF OKLAHOMA
  SS
COUNTY OF OKMULGEE

RECEIVED
SUPT. 5 CIVIC TRIBES
NOV 15 1915
ENCLOSURE TO
No. 103453

    Lewis Robinson, being first duly sworn, on oath states that his post office address is Beggs, Oklahoma; that he was acquainted with Abe W. Foster during his life time; that during the winter of 1898 and 1899 he went and lived with said Abe W. Foster and wife Lucy Foster; that about April 19, 1899, he left the home of Abe W. Foster and went to his home near Beggs, Oklahoma, that on or about said date Abe W. Foster and his wife, Lucy Foster separated or were divorced in accordance with the Creek custom; that soon thereafter he, Lewis Robinson and the said Lucy Foster were married in accordance with the Creek Custom of Marriage; that they lived together as husband and wife until June or July, 1912, when the said Lucy Foster died; that about July 25th, 1903, while he and the said Lucy Foster were living together as husband and wife a child wa born; that this child was names Susie Mills; that said child was enrolled by its mother, Lucy Foster, opposite New Born Creek Roll #781 as of 7/8th Indian blood and under the name of Susie Mills Foster; that said Lucy Foster gave the name of father as Abe W. Foster; that said child should have been enrolled as Susie Mills Robinson and that the name of the father should have been given as Lewis Robinson; that said enrollment records should be changed to show said child's name to be Susie Mills Robinson; that said child is now living and in in my care and custody.

    Affiant further states that the said Abe W. Foster was impotent.

Lewis Robinson

    Subscribed and sworn to before me this sworn to before me this 9th day of November, 1915.

R. P. Harrison Clerk
James E. Bentley Deputy

STATE OF OKLAHOMA SS
COUNTY OF OKMULGEE

RECEIVED
SUPT. 5 CIVIC TRIBES
NOV 15 1915
ENCLOSURE TO
No. 103453

    Sallie Foster, being first duly sworn, on oath, states that she is the mother of Abe W. Foster enrolled opposite roll #2292 as a 7/8th blood Creek Indian; that Abe W. Foster and Lucy Bruner were married about 1893 or 1894 and lived together as husband and wife until about April 19, 1899; that during the winter of 1898 and 1899 one Louis Robinson lived at her son's home and when he left in April 1899 Lucy Foster nee Bruner went with him and she and the said Louis Robinson lived together as husband and wife until her death which was in June or July 1912; that Susie Mills Foster was the child of the said Louis Robinson and Lucy Foster nee Bruner; that her son Abe W. Foster was impotent and was not the father of Susie Mills Foster.

Sallie Foster

Applications for Enrollment of Creek Newborn
Act of 1905   Volume X

      Subscribed and sworn to before me this sworn to before me this 4th day of October, 1915.

                        R. P. Harrison Clerk,
                        By James E Bentley Deputy

      We the undersigned certify that the statements made by Sallie Foster above set forth are substantially true as we verily believe.

                        (Name Illegible)
                        F. H. Morton
                        Alfred May

Subscribed and sworn to before me this 4th day of October, 1915

                        R P Harrison   Clerk
                        Farnes E Bentley   Deputy

SUPPLEMENTAL PROOF

(Creek Equalization)

In re heirs of   Abe W. Foster   , deceased.
Creek   Indian   , Roll No. 2292 .

Sallie Foster   , of   *(Illegible)*   Oklahoma, Roll No. _____, of lawful age, being duly sworn according to law deposes and says that the answers made to the following interrogatories are true:
Question, who was the father of Susie Mills Foster, answer Ben McIntosh
Question, when did Abe W. Foster and Lucy Bruner seperate[sic], answer, April 19, 1898
Question, how long after they seperated[sic] untill[sic] Susie Mills Foster was born answer, 5 years, 3 months, 6 days
Question was Lucy Bruner the wife of some one else at the time this child was born, answer yes
Question if so, who was her husband answer Lewis Roberson
                                her
                        (Name) x *(Illegible)*
                              mark

Subscribed and sworn to before me this sworn to before me this 8th day of June 1915.

                        Roy Shick
                        Notary Public.

My commission expires   Apr. 26, 1917   P.O.   Okmulgee, Okla

Applications for Enrollment of Creek Newborn
Act of 1905 Volume X

We, the undersigned, of lawful age, being duly sworn according to law, depose and say that we have read the foregoing questions and answers and know that the answers are true.

Witnesses to mark of Will Dan:

(Name Illegible) Okmulgee Okla
(Name Illegible) Okmulgee Okla

(Name Illegible)
P.O. Morin, Okla
his
Will x Dan
mark
P.O. Okmulgee, Okla.

Subscribed and sworn to before me this 14th day of June 1915.

Roy Shick
Notary Public.

My commission expires   April 26, 1917   .

```
RECEIVED
SUPT. 5 CIVIC TRIBES
OCT 8 1915
ENCLOSURE TO
No.        87735
```

IN THE LOCAL FIELD CLERK'S OFFICE
OKMULGEE, OKLAHOMA

STATEMENT OF SALLIE FOSTER MADE UNDER OATH
IN RE PROOF OF HEIRSHIP.

Sallie Foster states that Lewie Robison came and lived with Abe W. Foster, her son, and his wife, Lucy Bruner; that when Lewie Robison left her son's home in the spring, Lucy Bruner went and lived with him as husband and wife until her death; that during the time they were living together, Susie Mills Foster was born. It is also reported that Ben McIntosh is the Father of Susie Mills Foster.

STATE OF OKLAHOMA
    SS
COUNTY OF OKMULGEE

```
RECEIVED
SUPT. 5 CIVIC TRIBES
NOV 15 1915
ENCLOSURE TO
No.   103453
```

Lewis Robinson, being first duly sworn, on oath states that his post office address is Beggs, Oklahoma; that he was acquainted with Abe W. Foster during his life time; that during the winter of 1898 and 1899 he went and lived with said Abe W. Foster and wife Lucy Foster; that about April 19, 1899, he left the home of Abe W. Foster and went to his home near Beggs, Oklahoma, that on or about said date Abe W. Foster and his wife, Lucy Foster separated or were divorced in accordance with the Creek custom; that soon thereafter he, Lewis Robinson and the said Lucy Foster were married in accordance with the Creek Custom of Marriage; that they lived together as husband and

Applications for Enrollment of Creek Newborn
Act of 1905 Volume X

wife until June or July, 1912, when the said Lucy Foster died; that about July 25th, 1903, while he and the said Lucy Foster were living together as husband and wife a child wa born; that this child was names Susie Mills; that said child was enrolled by its mother, Lucy Foster, opposite New Born Creek Roll #781 as of 7/8th Indian blood and under the name of Susie Mills Foster; that said Lucy Foster gave the name of father as Abe W. Foster; that said child should have been enrolled as Susie Mills Robinson and that the name of the father should have been given as Lewis Robinson; that said enrollment records should be changed to show said child's name to be Susie Mills Robinson; that said child is now living and in in my care and custody.

      Affiant further states that the said Abe W. Foster was impotent.

                        Lewis Robinson

      Subscribed and sworn to before me this sworn to before me this 9th day of November, 1915.

                    R. P. Harrison Clerk
                    James E. Bentley Deputy

STATE OF OKLAHOMA   103453
                        SS
COUNTY OF OKMULGEE

      Sallie Foster, being first duly sworn, on oath, states that she is the mother of Abe W. Foster enrolled opposite roll #2292 as a 7/8th blood Creek Indian; that Abe W. Foster and Lucy Bruner were married about 1893 or 1894 and lived together as husband and wife until about April 19, 1899; that during the winter of 1898 and 1899 one Louis Robinson lived at her son's home and when he left in April 1899 Lucy Foster nee Bruner went with him and she and the said Louis Robinson lived together as husband and wife until her death which was in June or July 1912; that Susie Mills Foster was the child of the said Louis Robinson and Lucy Foster nee Bruner; that her son Abe W. Foster was impotent and was not the father of Susie Mills Foster.

                        Sallie Foster

      Subscribed and sworn to before me this sworn to before me this 4th day of October, 1915.

                    R. P. Harrison Clerk,
                    By James E Bentley Deputy

      We the undersigned certify that the statements made by Sallie Foster above set forth are substantially true as we verily believe.

                    (Name Illegible)
                    F. H. Morton
                    Alfred May

Applications for Enrollment of Creek Newborn
Act of 1905 Volume X

Subscribed and sworn to before me this 4th day of October, 1915

> R P Harrison Clerk
> Farnes E Bentley Deputy

LAW
EM-NP-2-19-31
Re: Abe W. Foster,
Creek, Roll No. 2292.

February 19, 1931.

Miss Susie Mills Foster,
    Beggs, Oklahoma.

Dear Madam:

    Receipt is acknowledged of your letter of February 7, 1931, making inquiry as to what disposition has been made of the allotment of Abe W. Foster, Creek, Roll No. 2292, who, you say, is your father, your mother being Lucy Foster, Creek, Roll No. 6238.

    In reply, I have to say it appears from the records of this office that Abe W. Foster was enrolled as a 7/8 blood Creek, Roll No. 2292, whose age was 37 years as of August 16, 1899; that on August 16, 1899, there was allotted to said Abe W. Foster the NW¼ of Section 24, Township 14 North, Range 13 East, containing 160 acres, now situate in Okmulgee County, Oklahoma, the NW¼ of the NW¼ thereof being homestead, and that patents covering this land were duly issued in the name of said Abe W. Foster and later approved by the Secretary of the Interior.

    It would further appear from the records of this office that on February 6, 1920, there was filed with the office a proof of death and heirship, executed on January 10, 1920, by Annie D. Wisner, of Okmulgee, Oklahoma, from which proof it would appear that said Abe W. Foster died on November 9, 1910, intestate, resident of Okmulgee County, Oklahoma, leaving no issue, but did leave as his heirs him surviving a widow, Lucy Bruner, but who was dead at the time of the execution of this proof; his mother, Sallie Foster, a 3/4 blood Creek, Roll No. 2293, who died on October 8, 1919; his maternal half-brother, Ben J. Wisener, a 3/4 blood Creek, Roll No. 2294; his maternal half-sister, Annie D. Wisener, enrolled as a 1/4 blood Creek, Roll No. 341, and his nephew, Fred Saulsberry, identified on the rolls as Fred Saulsbury, a Creek Freedman, Roll No. 1703, a child of a predeceased maternal half-brother, Raiford Saulsberry, who died before enrollment. It will be noted that in this proof you are not shown as being the child of said Abe W. Foster.

    While it would appear from the birth affidavit filed with this office in the matter of your enrollment as a citizen of the Creek Nation and from the census card showing the names of your parents that you were the child of Abraham Foster and Lucy Foster (nee Bruner), yet it does appear from affidavits later filed with the office that you

Applications for Enrollment of Creek Newborn
Act of 1905   Volume X

were born more than four years after your mother and the said Abraham Foster (Abe W. Foster) separated, and that you were born on July 25, 1903, while your mother and one, Lewis Robinson, identified as Lewis Robison, a Creek Freedman, Roll No. 4856, were living together as wife and husband. Said Lewis Robinson, in his affidavit executed on November 9, 1915, and filed with the office on November 15, 1915, stated that he was your father, and that you should have been enrolled as Susie Mills Robinson instead of Susie Mills Foster.

In connection with this, it will be stated for your information that within the past year a colored man has appeared at this office several times, insisting that he is the identical person whose name appears upon the Creek Rolls as Abe W. Foster, a 7/8 blood Creek Indian, opposite approved Roll No. 2292. This man admits that he was for several years absent from the Creek Nation, and has learned since his return that the Abe W. Foster allotment has been sold by persons who claimed to be the heirs of this allottee.

This office has no record as to what disposition has been made of the Abe W. Foster allotment, and in order to ascertain this fact, the records of Okmulgee County, Oklahoma, should be examined. So far as the records of this office show, said Abe W. Foster, Creek, Roll No. 2292, died on November 7, 1910, leaving as his heirs the persons shown in proof as noted above.

Respectfully,

Superintendent.

BIRTH AFFIDAVIT.

DEPARTMENT OF THE INTERIOR.
COMMISSION TO THE FIVE CIVILIZED TRIBES.

IN RE APPLICATION FOR ENROLLMENT, as a citizen of the Creek Nation, of Susie Mills, born on the 25 day of July, 1903

Name of Father: Abraham Foster   a citizen of the   Creek   Nation.
Name of Mother: Lucy Foster   a citizen of the   Creek   Nation.

Postoffice   Okmulgee & Bristow, I.T. respectively

AFFIDAVIT OF MOTHER.

UNITED STATES OF AMERICA, Indian Territory, }
   Western   DISTRICT.

I, Lucy Foster, on oath state that I am 28 years of age and a citizen by blood, of the Creek Nation; that I am the lawful wife of Abraham Foster, who is a citizen, by blood of the Creek Nation; that a female child was born to me on the 25th day

Applications for Enrollment of Creek Newborn
Act of 1905   Volume X

of July, 1903, that said child has been named Susie Mills, and was living March 4, 1905.

Lucy Foster

Witnesses To Mark:
{

Subscribed and sworn to before me this 19th., day of April, 1905.

(Name Illegible)
Notary Public.

My Com Ex. 7/14-06.

AFFIDAVIT OF ATTENDING PHYSICIAN OR MID-WIFE.

UNITED STATES OF AMERICA, Indian Territory,
 Western   DISTRICT.

I, Louisa Gooden, a mid-wife, on oath state that I attended on Mrs. Lucy Foster, wife of Abraham Foster on the 25 day of July, 1903; that there was born to her on said date a female child; that said child was living March 4, 1905, and is said to have been named Susie Mills

Louisa Gooden

Witnesses To Mark:
{

Subscribed and sworn to before me this 19th., day of April, 1905.

(Name Illegible)
Notary Public.

My Com Ex. 7/14-06.

Applications for Enrollment of Creek Newborn
Act of 1905   Volume X

(Copy)
Olive, I. T. Oct. 12th, 1905.

Hon. Tams Bixby,
    Commissioner to the Five Civilized Tribes,
    Muskogee, I. T.

Dear Sir:

    My wife, a Creek citizen, enrolled under her maiden name, Ellen London, and myself appeared on the 17th day of April, 1905, at Bristow, I. T. before your representative, with our minor child, John Granville McIntosh, and made application for enrollment of our said child, John Granville McIntosh, as a citizen of the Creek Nation. Written application being delivered to your representative at Bristow, Indian Territory at the time. The said written application was returned to me for correction by you. The corrections were made promptly and papers returned to your office, but since that time, I have not heard further from you, and would like to be advised without delay if the said corrected application were[sic] received by you and if same are alright now. As soon as the bill passed Congress admitting minor children of Creek citizens to be enrolled as citizens of the Creek Nation on behalf of my minor child, John Granville McIntosh after application for enrollment was made for him, selected for him the West one half of the West one half of Section 34, Township 19 North, Range 7 East and placed thereon fencing and some other improvements in order to hold the above described land for the benefit of my minor child, John Granville McIntosh. I understand through here-say, that this the above described land has been filed on in behalf of another minor child, who claim there were no improvements on the land at the time of filing. The improvements were on the land at the time of filing, and I can furnish you absolute proof by any number of creditable witnesses to that effect. I would like to be advised if the improvements made by me in behalf of my minor child on the above described land will hold the land as the allotment to be filed by me and my wife for our child, John Granville McIntosh.

                Yours very truly, (S'gd) Wm. R. McINTOSH

NC-805

                Muskogee, Indian Territory, October 14, 1905.

William R. McIntosh,
    Olive, Indian Territory.

Dear Sir:

    Receipt is acknowledged of your communication of October 12, 1905, in which you state that you are unable to secure the affidavit of the midwife who attended your wife, Ellen McIntosh, at the birth of her minor child, John Granville McIntosh. You further state that you have selected for said child the west one-half of the west one-half of section 34, township eighteen north, range seven east, and that you heard that said land

Applications for Enrollment of Creek Newborn
Act of 1905   Volume X

has been filed upon by another. You desire to be advised what you should do in the premises.

In reply you are advised that it will be necessary for you to secure the affidavits of two disinterested persons relative to the birth of your said child, John Granville McIntosh. Said affidavits must set forth said child's name, the names of his parents, the date of his birth and whether or not he was living March 4, 1905.

You are further advised that the west one-half of the west one-half of section 34, township eighteen north, range 7 east has been filed upon, and that if you claim a prior right to said land for your child, Jihn[sic] Granville McIntosh, by reason of having placed improvements thereon, you may institute a contest for same, but that no action will be taken in the contest proceedings so instituted by you until the enrollment of said John Granville McIntosh has been approved by the Secretary of the Interior.

Respectfully,

Commissioner.

NC-805

Muskogee, Indian Territory, December 26, 1905.

William R. McIntosh,
    Bristow, Indian Territory.

Dear Sir:

Receipt is acknowledged of your letter of December 21, 1905, relative to the enrollment of your minor child, John Granville McIntosh, as a citizen of the Creek Nation.

You are again advised that in lieu of the affidavit of the midwife, which you state cannot be obtained, you should file with this Office the affidavits of two disinterested persons relative to said child's birth, and a blank for that purpose is herewith enclosed.

This matter should receive your prompt attention.

Respectfully,

Commissioner.

Dis.

Applications for Enrollment of Creek Newborn
Act of 1905   Volume X

AFFIDAVIT.

UNITED STATES OF AMERICA,)
)
WESTERN JUDICIAL DISTRICT,) S.S.
)
INDIAN TERRITORY.   )

    William L. Anderson and Nevada Anderson, first being duly sworn on their oath state: That they are of legal age and now reside in Section twenty seven (27), Township eighteen (18) North, Range seven (7) East, Creek Nation, Indian Territory, and are close neighbors of William R. McIntosh and Ellen London McIntosh, nee Ellen London, his wife, and also with John Granville McIntosh, the minor child of William R. McIntosh and Elllen[sic] London McIntosh. That John Granville McIntosh was born to William R. McIntosh and Ellen London McIntosh on the 20th day of July, 1902, on which date we were living near William R. McIntosh and Ellen London McIntosh and since which day, namely the 20th day of July 1902, we have continued to live near the said William R. McIntosh, Ellen London McIntosh and John Granville McIntosh. That the said John Granville McIntosh is this date alive and living with his parents, the said William R. McIntosh and Ellen London McIntosh in Section twenty seven (27), Township eighteen (18) North, Range seven (7) East, Creek Nation, Indian Territory. Affiants further state on their oath that they are disinterested persons and have no personal interest whatever in making this affidavit. And further affiants sayeth not.

                                                                                   His
                                       William L. x Anderson
                                                 mark
                                       Nevada Anderson

WITNESSES TO
SIGNATURES AND MARKS.
  B.B. Jones (Bristow IT)
  Sam Young (P.O. Cushing OT)

                                                       March
Subscribed and sworn to before me this 24th day of ~~February~~, 1906. at Residence of Wm. L. Anderson - Creek Nation, IT
(in Sec 27 - T 18 North - R 7 East)

                                                      B. B. Jones
                                                      Notary Public.
My commission expires March 20th - 1908 -

Applications for Enrollment of Creek Newborn
Act of 1905 Volume X

United States)
of America,)
Indian Territory,)ss.
Western District.)

AFFIDAVIT OF WM. R. McINTOSH.

I, William R. McINtosh[sic], on oath state that I am forty eight years of age, and a Citizen, by blood, of the Creek Nation; that I am the lawful husband of Ellen McIntosh (Nee Ellen London), who is a citizen, by blood, of the Creek Nation; that a male child was born to William R. McIntosh and Ellen McIntosh (Nee Ellen London) on the twentieth day of July, 1902 at Okmulgee, I.T.; that the said child has been named John Granville McIntosh, and is now living.

That my wife, Ellen McIntosh (Nee Ellen London) was attended by an old colored woman, acting in the capacity of midwife, known as Aunt Mary on the said twentieth day of July, 1902, at Okmulgee, I.T., when our said child John Granville McIntosh was born.

Affiant further says that on the eighteenth day of April, 1905, we went to Okmulgee, I.T. to secure the Affidavit of the said midwife, known as Aunt Mary", and found, after making diligent inquiry for the said midwife, that she had moved away from Okmulgee, I.T. to some unknown place that is in the state of Arkansas, and on that account was unable to secure the Affidavit.

Wm. R. McIntosh

Subscribed and sworn to before me this the twenty-first (21) day of April, 1905.

B. B. Jones
Notary Public.

My commission expires March 20th. 1908.

BIRTH AFFIDAVIT.

DEPARTMENT OF THE INTERIOR.
COMMISSION TO THE FIVE CIVILIZED TRIBES.

IN RE APPLICATION FOR ENROLLMENT, as a citizen of the CREEK Nation, of John Granville McIntosh, born on the 20 day of July, 1902

Name of Father: William R McIntosh   a citizen of the   Creek   Nation.
    (Coweta)   (nee Ellen London)
Name of Mother: Ellen McIntosh   a citizen of the   Creek   Nation.
    (Cussehta)
                        Postoffice   Olive, Indian Ter.

Applications for Enrollment of Creek Newborn
Act of 1905   Volume X

AFFIDAVIT OF MOTHER.

UNITED STATES OF AMERICA, Indian Territory, ⎫
WESTERN   DISTRICT.   ⎬
                                    ⎭

Child Brought in
5/21/05

I, Ellen McIntosh (nee Ellen London), on oath state that I am 20 years of age and a citizen by blood, of the Creek Nation; that I am the lawful wife of William R McIntosh, who is a citizen, by blood of the Creek Nation; that a male child was born to me on 20th day of July, 1902, that said child has been named John Granville McIntosh, and is now living.

                                          her
Witnesses To Mark: Ellen x McIntosh (nee Ellen London)
   { B. B. Jones Bristow I.T.   mark
   { RW Lovett   "   "

Subscribed and sworn to before me this 4th day of April, 1905.

My Com Expires March 20-1908   B. B. Jones
                                           Notary Public.

1863 B -

BA-81.

DEPARTMENT OF THE INTERIOR,
COMMISSION TO THE FIVE CIVILIZED TRIBES.

Muskogee, Indian Territory, March 20, 1905.

In the matter of the application for the enrollment of Jackson C. Self as a citizen by blood of the Creek Nation.

John R. Self, being duly sworn, testified as follows:

EXAMINATION BY THE COMMISSION:
Q What is your name? A John R. Self.
Q What is your age? A 50.
Q What is your postoffice? A Calvin.

The witness is identified as John R. Self, on Creek Indian card, field No. 1054, and his name is contained in partial roll of Creek citizens by blood approved by the Secretary of the Interior March 13, 1902, Roll No. 3405.

Applications for Enrollment of Creek Newborn
Act of 1905 Volume X

Q Have you a child named Jackson C. Self? A Yes sir.
Q When was Jackson born? A 14th of August, 1901.
Q You mean 1901? A Yes sir.
Q Is Jackson Self living? A Yes sir.
Q Who was present at his birth? A Dr. Beard was the attending physician. There was a lady there by the name of Parker.
Q Who is the mother of Jackson C. Self? A My wife, Sarah E.
Q She is not a citizen? A No sir.

INDIAN TERRITORY,) I, J. Y. Miller, a stenographer to the Commission
Western District.) to the Five Civilized Tribes, do hereby certify
) upon oath that the above and foregoing is a true and complete translation of my notes as same appear in my stenographic report of this case.

JY Miller

Sworn to and subscribed before me
this the 26 day of April, 1905.

Zera E Parrish
My Comm. expires April 11, 1909.   Notary Public.

AFFIDAVIT OF DISINTERESTED WITNESS.

United States of America)
Indian Territory   ) SS.
(blank) District   )

I, Forest Zevely on oath state that I am personally acquainted with Sarah E Self wife of John R Self that there was born to her on or about the 14 day of Aug 1901 a male child; that said child was living March 4, 1905 and is said to have been name Jackson C Self.

I further state that I have no interest in this case.

Forest Zevely

Witness to mark.

Subscribed and sworn to before me this 28 day of Oct 1905.

My commission expires
Sept 8, 1905

W.W. Holder
Notary Public.

Applications for Enrollment of Creek Newborn
Act of 1905   Volume X

AFFIDAVIT OF DISINTERESTED WITNESS.

United States of America)
Indian Territory) SS.
(blank) District)

I, James A Self on oath state that I am personally acquainted with Sarah E Self wife of John R Self that there was born to her on or about the 14 day of Aug 1901 a male child; that said child was living March 4, 1905 and is said to have been name Jackson C Self.

I further state that I have no interest in this case.

                                                    James A Self

Witness to mark.

_____

_____

Subscribed and sworn to before me this 28 day of Oct 1905.

My commission expires
    Sept 8, 1905   W.W. Holder
                                      Notary Public.

_____

DEPARTMENT OF THE INTERIOR,
COMMISSIONER TO THE FIVE CIVILIZED TRIBES.

In re application for enrollment, as a citizen of the Creek Nation, of Jackson C Self, born on the 14th day of August 1901

name of the father Jas R Self a citizen of the Creek Nation.
Name of the mother Sarah E Self a citizen of the Creek Nation.

                              Postoffice   Kellyville

Affidavit of Mother

United States of America Indian Territory
Western District

I, Sarah E Self on oath states that I am Thirty Nine years of age and a non citizen by .... of the Creek Nation that I am the lawful wife of John R Self who is a Citizen by Birth of the Creek Nation that a male child was born to me on day of , 190, that said child has been named , and was living March 4, 1905. was born to me on 14th day of

Applications for Enrollment of Creek Newborn
Act of 1905   Volume X

August, 1901 that said child has been named Jackson C Self and was living march[sic] 4th 1905.

Sarah E Self

Must be two   John W Overstreet
witnesses   C C Don Carlos

Subscribed and sworn to before me this 7th day of April 1905.

John W Overstreet
Notary Public.

BIRTH AFFIDAVIT.

DEPARTMENT OF THE INTERIOR,
COMMISSION TO THE FIVE CIVILIZED TRIBES.

IN RE Application for Enrollment, as a citizen of the Creek Nation, of Jackson C Self, born on the 14th day of August, 1901

Name of Father: John R Self   a citizen of the   Creek   Nation.
Name of Mother: Sarah E Self   a citizen of the   United States.

Post-office: Mounds, Ind. Ter.

AFFIDAVIT OF MOTHER.

UNITED STATES OF AMERICA,
   INDIAN TERRITORY.
Northern   District.

I, Sarah E Self, on oath state that I am 36 years of age and a citizen ~~by~~ *(blank)*, of the United States ~~Nation~~; that I am the lawful wife of John R Self, who is a citizen, by blood of the Creek Nation; that a male child was born to me on 14th day of August, 1901, that said child has been named Jackson C Self, and is now living.

Sarah E Self

WITNESSES TO MARK:

Subscribed and sworn to before me this 30th day of October, 1901.

W. T. Reedy
<small>NOTARY PUBLIC.</small>

Applications for Enrollment of Creek Newborn
Act of 1905 Volume X

AFFIDAVIT OF ATTENDING PHYSICIAN OR MID-WIFE.

UNITED STATES OF AMERICA,
    INDIAN TERRITORY.
Northern   District.

    I, G. W. Beard, a physician, on oath state that I attended on Mrs. Sarah E Self, wife of John R Self on the 14th day of August, 1901 ; that there was born to her on said date a male child; that said child is now living and is said to have been named Jackson C Self

                                G. W. Beard

WITNESSES TO MARK:

    Subscribed and sworn to before me this 1st *day of* Nov, 1901.

                                W. T. Reedy
                                  NOTARY PUBLIC.

NC-806.

                        Muskogee, Indian Territory, October 19, 1905.

Sarah E. Self,
    c/o John R. Self,
        Kellyville, Indian Territory.

Dear Madam:

    In the matter of the application for the enrollment of your minor child, Jackson C. Self, born August 14, 1901, as a citizen by blood of the Creek Nation, this Office requires the affidavit of the physician or midwife who attended at his birth, and a blank for that purpose is inclosed herewith.

    If there was no physician or midwife in attendance when said child was born it will be necessary for you to furnish this office with the affidavits of two disinterested persons witnesses relative to his birth. Said affidavits must set forth said child's name, the date of his birth, the names of his parents and whether or not he was living on March 4, 1905.

    This office has been unable to identify you upon the final roll of citizens by blood of the Creek Nation. It is necessary that you be so identified before the rights of said child can be finally determined. You are therefore requested to state the name under which you are finally enrolled, the names of your parents and other members of your family, the Creek Indian town to which you belong and your final roll number as the same appears upon your allotment certificate and deeds.

Applications for Enrollment of Creek Newborn
Act of 1905   Volume X

                    Respectfully,
                                        Commissioner.
BC
Env.

                                                                    HGH

REFER IN REPLY TO THE FOLLOWING: DEPARTMENT OF THE INTERIOR,
———————————   COMMISSIONER TO THE FIVE CIVILIZED TRIBES.

                         Muskogee, Indian Territory, June 29, 1906.

George Hughes
   Sapulpa, Indian Territory.

Dear Sir:

   Receipt is acknowledged of your letter without date relative to the enrollment of Thomas Robbins, son of Mack Robbins and Sefiye Behen. You ask if the parents can file for said child, and if further proof is necessary.

   You are advised that notice has been sent to Cheyargee Behen in care of Mack Robbins, at Mounds, Indian Territory, the post office given in the application for the enrollment of James Robbins, to the effect that the name of their child appears in the partial list of citizens by blood of the Creek Nation approved by the Secretary of the Interior November 27, 1905. You are requested to advise either or both of said parents, who have made no response to notice relative to filing, that an application for a selection of land in the Creek Nation for said child may now be made at the Creek land Office in Muskogee, Indian Territory.

                         Respectfully,
                              Tams Bixby   Commissioner.

Applications for Enrollment of Creek Newborn
Act of 1905 Volume X

BIRTH AFFIDAVIT.

Department of the Interior,
COMMISSION TO THE FIVE CIVILIZED TRIBES.

IN RE APPLICATION FOR ENROLLMENT, as a citizen of the Creek Nation, of Thomas Robins, born on the 24" day of Aug, 1902.

Name of Father: Mack Robins   a citizen of the   Creek   Nation.
North Fork
Name of Mother: Se-far-yes (Shoot)   a citizen of the   Creek   Nation.
Euchee Town

Post-Office: Mounds IT

AFFIDAVIT OF MOTHER.

UNITED STATES OF AMERICA,
    INDIAN TERRITORY,
    Western   District.

I, Se-fr-yes (Shoot), on oath state that I am 24 years of age and a citizen by blood, of the Creek Nation; that I am not the lawful wife of Mack Robins, who is a citizen, by ~~blood~~ adoption of the Creek Nation; that a male child was born to me on 24" day of Aug, 1902, that said child has been named Thomas Robins, and is now living.

                                                her
                                  Se-far-ye x (Shoot)
WITNESSES TO MARK: mark
    Edw C Griesel
    Jesse McDermott

Subscribed and sworn to before me this 21" day of August, 1902.

    Seal   J McDermott
                                             Notary Public.

AFFIDAVIT OF ATTENDING PHYSICIAN OR MID-WIFE.

UNITED STATES OF AMERICA,
    INDIAN TERRITORY,
    Western   District.

I, Nancy Bigpond, a midwife, on oath state that I attended on ~~Mrs~~. Se-far-ye, not wife of Mack Robins on the 24" day of Aug, 1902; that there was born to her on said date a male child; that said child is now living and is said to have been named Thomas Robins

                                      her
                               Nancy x Bigpond
                                        mark

Applications for Enrollment of Creek Newborn
Act of 1905 Volume X

WITNESSES TO MARK:
{ Edw C Griesel
  Jesse McDermott

Subscribed and sworn to before me this 21" *day of* August, *1902*.

Seal   J McDermott
                                                 Notary Public.

NC-808.

Muskogee, Indian Territory, October 19, 1905.

Lucy Dunson,
　　c/o Luna E. Dunson
　　　　Fentress, Indian Territory.

Dear Madam:

　　In the matter of the application for the enrollment of your minor child Raymand[sic] Dunson, born September 14, 1902, as a citizen by blood of the Creek Nation your name is signed to your affidavit, relative to the birth of said child, "Lucy Hale, nee Dunson" and you state that you are the lawful wife of Luna E. Dunson.

　　If you are the lawful wife of Luna E. Dunson your name must necessarily be Lucy Dunson. For the purpose of correcting the discrepancy as to name you are requested to have the inclosed affidavits properly executed and when so executed return to this office in the inclosed envelope. Be careful to sign your name to your affidavit as the same appears in the body thereof.

　　　　　　　　　Respectfully,

CTD-9　　　　　　　　　　　　　　　　　　　　　Commissioner.
Env.

Applications for Enrollment of Creek Newborn
Act of 1905   Volume X

BIRTH AFFIDAVIT.

DEPARTMENT OF THE INTERIOR.
COMMISSION TO THE FIVE CIVILIZED TRIBES.

IN RE APPLICATION FOR ENROLLMENT, as a citizen of the Creek Nation, of Raymand Dunson, born on the 16 day of September, 1902

Name of Father: Luna E Dunson   a citizen of the   Creek   Nation.
Name of Mother: Lucy Hale (nee) Dunson   a citizen of the   Creek   Nation.

Postoffice   Fentress I. T.

AFFIDAVIT OF MOTHER.

UNITED STATES OF AMERICA, Indian Territory,
Western   DISTRICT.

I, Lucy Hale(nee) Dunson, on oath state that I am 27 years of age and a citizen by blood, of the Creek Nation; that I am the lawful wife of Luna E. Dunson, who is a citizen, by blood of the Creek Nation; that a male child was born to me on 16 day of September, 1902, that said child has been named Raymand Dunson, and was living March 4, 1905.

Lucy Hale (nee) Dunson

Witnesses To Mark:

Subscribed and sworn to before me this 19 day of April, 1905.

my Com. Exp. Aug. 19-1908   Tupper Dunn
                                    Notary Public.

AFFIDAVIT OF ATTENDING PHYSICIAN OR MID-WIFE.

UNITED STATES OF AMERICA, Indian Territory,
Western   DISTRICT.

I, Millisie Bird, a midwife, on oath state that I attended on Mrs. Lucy Hale (nee) Dunson, wife of Luna E. Dunson on the 16 day of September, 1902; that there was born to her on said date a male child; that said child was living March 4, 1905, and is said to have been named Raymand Dunson

her
Millisie x Bird
mark

Applications for Enrollment of Creek Newborn
Act of 1905   Volume X

Witnesses To Mark:
{ Luna E Dunson
{ Lucy Hale (nee) Dunson

Subscribed and sworn to before me this 19 day of April, 1905.

my Com. Exp. Aug. 19-1908   Tupper Dunn
                                   Notary Public.

BIRTH AFFIDAVIT.

DEPARTMENT OF THE INTERIOR.
COMMISSION TO THE FIVE CIVILIZED TRIBES.

IN RE APPLICATION FOR ENROLLMENT, as a citizen of the Creek Nation, of Raymand Dunson, born on the 16 day of September, 1902

Name of Father:	Luna E Dunson	a citizen of the	Creek	Nation.
Name of Mother:	Lucy Dunson	a citizen of the	Creek	Nation.

Postoffice   Fentress, I. T.

AFFIDAVIT OF MOTHER.

UNITED STATES OF AMERICA, Indian Territory, }
   Western   DISTRICT.   }

I, Lucy Dunson, on oath state that I am 27 years of age and a citizen by blood, of the Creek Nation; that I am the lawful wife of Luna E. Dunson, who is a citizen, by blood of the Creek Nation; that a male child was born to me on 16 day of September, 1902, that said child has been named Raymand Dunson, and was living March 4, 1905.

                                   Lucy Dunson

Witnesses To Mark:
{ WC Cook
{ Tupper Dunn

Subscribed and sworn to before me this 4 day of Nov., 1905.

my Com. Exp. Aug. 19" 1908   Tupper Dunn
                                   Notary Public.

Applications for Enrollment of Creek Newborn
Act of 1905   Volume X

AFFIDAVIT OF ATTENDING PHYSICIAN OR MID-WIFE.

UNITED STATES OF AMERICA, Indian Territory, }
   Western   DISTRICT.

    I, Millisie Bird , a midwife , on oath state that I attended on Mrs. Lucy Dunson , wife of Luna E. Dunson on the 16 day of September , 1902 ; that there was born to her on said date a male child; that said child was living March 4, 1905, and is said to have been named Raymand Dunson

                                her
                            Millisie x Bird
                              mark

Witnesses To Mark:
  { WC Cook
    Tupper Dunn

    Subscribed and sworn to before me this 4 day of Nov. , 1905.

my Com. Exp. Aug. 19-1908   Tupper Dunn
                                        Notary Public.

NC-809.

                            Muskogee, Indian Territory, October 19, 1905.

Ella Clinton,
      c/o Willis R. Clinton,
            Wealaka, Indian Territory.

Dear Madam:

    In the matter of the application for the enrollment of your minor child Rachel Clinton, born February 27, 1903, as a citizen by blood of the Creek Nation, this office is unable to identify you upon the final roll of citizens by blood of the Creek Nation.

    It is necessary that you be so identified before the rights of said child can be finally determined. You are therefore requested to state the name under which you have been finally enrolled, the names of your parents and other members of your family, the Creek Indian town to which you belong and your final roll number as the same appears upon your allotment certificate and deeds.

                              Respectfully,
                                                  Commissioner.

Applications for Enrollment of Creek Newborn
Act of 1905 Volume X

BIRTH AFFIDAVIT.

DEPARTMENT OF THE INTERIOR.
COMMISSION TO THE FIVE CIVILIZED TRIBES.

IN RE APPLICATION FOR ENROLLMENT, as a citizen of the CREEK Nation, of Rachel Clinton, born on the 27th day of Feb, 1904

Name of Father: Willis E. Clinton	a citizen of the Creek	Nation.
Name of Mother: Ella Clinton	a citizen of the Creek	Nation.

Postoffice   Wealaka, I.T.

AFFIDAVIT OF MOTHER.

UNITED STATES OF AMERICA, Indian Territory,
WESTERN DISTRICT.

    I, Ella Clinton, on oath state that I am Twenty-four years of age and a citizen by blood, of the Creek Nation; that I am the lawful wife of Willis E. Clinton, who is a citizen, by blood of the Creek Nation; that a female child was born to me on 27th day of February, 1904, that said child has been named Rachel Clinton, and is now living.

                                                                                  her
                                                                                 Ella x Clinton
Witnesses To Mark: mark
    { Bob Oshea
    { J H *(Illegible)*

    Subscribed and sworn to before me this 20th day of April, 1905.

                                                       E. B. Harris
                                                             Notary Public.

AFFIDAVIT OF ATTENDING PHYSICIAN OR MID-WIFE.

UNITED STATES OF AMERICA, Indian Territory,
WESTERN DISTRICT.

    I, Malissa Pense, a Mid-wife, on oath state that I attended on Mrs. Ella Clinton, wife of Willis E. Clinton on the 27th day of February, 1904 ; that there was born to her on said date a female child; that said child is now living and is said to have been named Rachel Clinton

                                                                  Malissa Pense

Applications for Enrollment of Creek Newborn
Act of 1905 Volume X

Witnesses To Mark:

{

    Subscribed and sworn to before me this 20<u>th</u> day of April, 1905.

                                          E. B. Harris
                                               Notary Public.

Ella Clinton, mother, identified as Ella Brown, Cr #792
(Nov 18-05) Griesel   from Deeds presented by father W.E.C.

N.C. 810   I.D.
DEPARTMENT OF THE INTERIOR,
COMMISSIONER TO THE FIVE CIVILIZED TRIBES.

In the matter of the application for the enrollment of William K. March as a citizen by blood of the Creek Nation.

ORDER

The record in this case shows that on April 12, 1905, there was filed with the Commission to the Five Civilized Tribes at Muskogee, Indian Territory, the application of Estella March for the enrollment of her minor child, William K. March, as a citizen by blood of the Creek Nation.

The evidence shows that said William K. March was born in the month of September, 1904, and that he was living March 4, 1905.

The evidence further shows that said William K. March is the minor child of Willie H. March and Estella March; and an examination of the records of this Office shows that the name of said Willie H. March and Estella March are not contained in the lists of citizens by blood of the Creek Nation whose enrollment has been approved by the Secretary of the Interior prior to March 3, 1905.

The Act of Congress approved March 3, 1905, (Public No. 212), provides:

> "That the Commission to the Five Civilized Tribes is authorized for sixty days after the date of the approval of this act to receive and consider applications for enrollment, of children, born subsequent to May twenty-fifth, nineteen hundred and one, and prior to March fourth, nineteen hundred and five, and living on said latter date, to citizens of the Creek tribe of Indians whose enrollment has been approved by the Secretary of the Interior prior to the approval of this act; and to enroll and make allotments to such children."

Applications for Enrollment of Creek Newborn
Act of 1905   Volume X

It is, therefore, ordered that there is no authority of law for the enrollment of said William K. March as a citizen by blood of the Creek Nation, and that the application for his enrollment as such should be and the same is hereby dismissed.

                                                           Commissioner.

Muskogee, Indian Territory.

BIRTH AFFIDAVIT.

DEPARTMENT OF THE INTERIOR.
COMMISSION TO THE FIVE CIVILIZED TRIBES.

IN RE APPLICATION FOR ENROLLMENT, as a citizen of the Creek Nation, of William K. March, born on the 25th day of September, 1904

Name of Father: Willie H. March   a citizen of the Creek   Nation.
Name of Mother: Estella March   a citizen of the Creek   Nation.

                        Postoffice   *(blank)*

AFFIDAVIT OF MOTHER.

UNITED STATES OF AMERICA, Indian Territory,
   (blank)   **DISTRICT.**

I, Estella March, on oath state that I am 27 years of age and a citizen by marriage, of the Greek[sic] Nation; that I am the lawful wife of Willie H March, who is a citizen, by birth of the Greek[sic] Nation; that a male child was born to me on 25th day of September, 1904, that said child has been named William K March, and is now living.

                                      Estella March

Witnesses To Mark:
  { Wm Crome

Subscribed and sworn to before me this 25th day of March, 1905.

                                      William Crome
                                          Notary Public.
                                    Salt Lake City, Utah

Applications for Enrollment of Creek Newborn
Act of 1905   Volume X

AFFIDAVIT OF ATTENDING PHYSICIAN OR MID-WIFE.

UNITED STATES OF AMERICA, Indian Territory,
   (blank)   DISTRICT.

    I,   Joseph Millieon , a   Physician   , on oath state that I attended on Mrs. Estella March , wife of   Willie H March   on the   25   day of   September   , 1904 ; that there was born to her on said date a   male   child; that said child is now living and is said to have been named William K March

Joseph Millieon M.D.

Witnesses To Mark:
{   Wm Crome

    Subscribed and sworn to before me this 25 day of March, 1905.

William Crome
Notary Public.

NC-811.

Muskogee, Indian Territory, October 19, 1905.

Mahala Leader,
    c/o Joshua Leader,
        Bixby, Indian Territory.

Dear Madam:

    In the matter of the application for the enrollment of your minor children, Absalom Leader, born March 21, 1902, and Edward Leader, born July 18, 1904, as citizens by blood of the Creek Nation, this office is unable to identify you upon the final roll of citizens by blood of the Creek Nation. It is necessary that you be so identified before the rights of said child can be finally determined.

    You are therefore requested to state the name under which you are finally enrolled, the names of your parents and other members of your family, the Creek Indian town to which you belong and your final roll number as the same appears upon your allotment certificate and deeds.

Respectfully,

Commissioner.

Applications for Enrollment of Creek Newborn
Act of 1905   Volume X

(The letter below typed as given.)

Bixby Ind Ter Oct 23, 1905

Reply refer to N C 811

Commission to the Five Civilized Tribes
        Muskogee, I.T.

Dear Sir:

    Replying to yours of the 9 Inst in regard to the matter of application for enrollment of my minor children Absolom Leader and Elwood Leader and that you wishes my identification will say that you will find my name on the Tuskegee Town roll If I am not mistaken with my mothers name Mrs Tewahley Vors and my name appear on the 1895 roll as Mahala Wilson and two of my children's names Noonley Wilson and one named Simeon J. Wilson my name was before marriage Mahala Tiger and I am sure you will find that name on the 189o roll but if you want further identification apply to Isom Peters of Bixby I T
When you write please address Mahala Leader C/O Isom Peters
                Box 77 Bixby I T

Muskogee, Indian Territory, October 26, 1905.

Mahala Leader,
    Box 77,
        Bixby, Indian Territory.

Dear Madam:

    Receipt is acknowledged of your letter of October 22, 1905, containing information which enables this office to identify you on its roll of citizens of the Creek Nation.

                Respectfully,

                              Commissioner.

Indian Territory } SS.
Western Dist.

I, Mahala Leader, a duly enrolled Creek citizen make oath that a male child was born to me on the 18th day of July 1904, and has been named Edward Leader and is now living on this date: April 19th 1905
                                      her
                        signed   Mahala x Leader
Witness to mark: mark
    Joshua Leader

Applications for Enrollment of Creek Newborn
Act of 1905   Volume X

Indian Territory ⎫
Western Dist.   ⎭ SS.

    Subscribed and sworn to before me this 19th day of April 1905.

                         J.F. Panther
                         Notary Public
                         My commission exp. July 2-1906

Indian Territory   ⎫
Western District ⎭ SS

We, Joshua Leader and Tewahley Vore, each for himself and herself swear that we (acting as midwifes) were present and bear witness that a male child was born to Mahala Leader on the 18th day of July 1904 and said child is now living at this date: April 19th 1905 and we are informed has been named Edward Leader.

Witness to mark   Joshua Leader
J. F. Panther   her
                               Tewahley x Vore
                                   mark

Indian Territory   ⎫
Western District ⎭ SS

Subscribed and sworn to before me this 19th day of April 1905.

                         J.F. Panther
                         Notary Public
                         My com. exp. July 2-1906.

Indian Territory ⎫
Western Dist.   ⎭ SS.

I, Mahala Leader, a duly enrolled Creek citizen make oath that a male child was born to me on the 21st day of March 1902, and has been named Absalom Leader and is now living on this date: April 19th 1905   her
                              signed   Mahala x Leader
Witness to mark: Joshua Leader   mark

Indian Territory   ⎫
Western District ⎭ SS

    Subscribed and sworn to before me this 19th day of April 1905.
                         J.F. Panther
                         Notary Public
                         My commission exp. July 2-1906

Applications for Enrollment of Creek Newborn
Act of 1905 Volume X

Indian Territory
Western District } SS

We, Joshua Leader and Tewahley Vore, each for himself and herself swear that we (acting as midwifes) were present and bear witness that a male child was born to Mahala Leader on the 21st day of March 1902 and said child is now living at this date: April 19th 1905 and we are informed has been named Absalom Leader.

Witness to mark   Joshua Leader
J. F. Panther   her
                                         Tewahley x Vore
                                                   mark

Indian Territory
Western District } SS

Subscribed and sworn to before me this 19th day of April 1905.

                        J.F. Panther
                        Notary Public
                        My com. exp. July 2-1906.

Cr NC-812

                      Muskogee, Indian Territory, July 19, 1905.

Rosanna Harry,
    Beggs, Indian Territory.

Dear Madam:

    In the matter of the application for the enrollment of your minor children, William and Jessie Harry, as citizens by blood of the Creek Nation, you are advised that without further information it is impossible for this office to identify you as a citizen of aid nation.

    You are requested to furnish this office with your maiden name, the names of your parents, the Creek Indian Town to which you belong, and, if possible, the roll number as same appears on your deeds to land in the Creek Nation, which will help identify you as a citizen of said Nation.

                      Respectfully,
                                    Commissioner.

Applications for Enrollment of Creek Newborn
Act of 1905 Volume X

BIRTH AFFIDAVIT.

DEPARTMENT OF THE INTERIOR.
COMMISSION TO THE FIVE CIVILIZED TRIBES.

IN RE APPLICATION FOR ENROLLMENT, as a citizen of the Creek Nation, of Jessie Harry, born on the 19th day of August, 1904

Name of Father: Jackson Harry   a citizen of the Creek Nation.
Name of Mother: Rosanna Harry   a citizen of the Creek Nation.

Postoffice   Beggs, IT

AFFIDAVIT OF MOTHER.

UNITED STATES OF AMERICA, Indian Territory, ⎫
     Western   DISTRICT. ⎭

     I, Rosanna Harry, on oath state that I am 21 years of age and a citizen by blood, of the Creek Nation; that I am the lawful wife of Jackson Harry, who is a citizen, by blood of the Creek Nation; that a male child was born to me on nineteenth day of August, 1904, that said child has been named Jessie Harry, and was living March 4, 1905.

                                           Rosanna Harry

Witnesses To Mark:
   { W^{m}FA Gierkes
   { DH Watson

     Subscribed and sworn to before me this Eight day of April, 1905.

                                       W^{m}FA Gierkes
                            NOTARY PUBLIC Notary Public.
                               My Commission Expires June 29, 1908

AFFIDAVIT OF ATTENDING PHYSICIAN OR MID-WIFE.

UNITED STATES OF AMERICA, Indian Territory, ⎫
     Western   DISTRICT. ⎭

     I, Caroline McNack, a midwife, on oath state that I attended on Mrs. Rosanna Harry, wife of Jackson Harry on the 19th day of August, 1904; that there was born to her on said date a male child; that said child was living March 4, 1905, and is said to have been named Jessie Harry

Applications for Enrollment of Creek Newborn
Act of 1905   Volume X

                                   her
                          Caroline x McNack
Witnesses To Mark: mark
{ W^{m}FA Gierkes
  DH Watson

Subscribed and sworn to before me this Eight day of April, 1905.

                                 W^{m}FA Gierkes
                         NOTARY PUBLIC Notary Public.
                            My Commission Expires June 29, 1908

BIRTH AFFIDAVIT.

DEPARTMENT OF THE INTERIOR.
COMMISSION TO THE FIVE CIVILIZED TRIBES.

    IN RE APPLICATION FOR ENROLLMENT, as a citizen of the Creek Nation, of Wilson Harry, born on the 10th day of March, 1902

Name of Father: Jackson Harry   a citizen of the   Creek   Nation.
Name of Mother: Rosanna Harry   a citizen of the   Creek   Nation.

                     Postoffice   Beggs, IT

AFFIDAVIT OF MOTHER.

UNITED STATES OF AMERICA, Indian Territory, ⎫
     Western   DISTRICT.   ⎬

    I, Rosanna Harry, on oath state that I am 21 years of age and a citizen by blood, of the Creek Nation; that I am the lawful wife of Jackson Harry, who is a citizen, by blood of the Creek Nation; that a male child was born to me on Tenth day of March, 1902, that said child has been named Wilson Harry, and was living March 4, 1905.

                                Rosanna Harry
Witnesses To Mark:
  { W^{m}FA Gierkes
    DH Watson

Subscribed and sworn to before me this Eight day of April, 1905.

                               W^{m}FA Gierkes
                     NOTARY PUBLIC Notary Public.
                        My Commission Expires June 29, 1908

Applications for Enrollment of Creek Newborn
Act of 1905   Volume X

AFFIDAVIT OF ATTENDING PHYSICIAN OR MID-WIFE.

UNITED STATES OF AMERICA, Indian Territory, }
Western   DISTRICT.

I, Caroline McNack , a midwife , on oath state that I attended on Mrs. Rosanna Harry , wife of Jackson Harry on the Tenth day of March , 1902 ; that there was born to her on said date a male child; that said child was living March 4, 1905, and is said to have been named Wilson Harry

             her
           Caroline x McNack
Witnesses To Mark: mark
{ W^{m}FA Gierkes
{ DH Watson

Subscribed and sworn to before me this Eight day of April , 1905.

          W^{m}FA Gierkes
       NOTARY PUBLIC Notary Public.
        My Commission Expires June 29, 1908

                N.C. 813
DEPARTMENT OF THE INTERIOR,
COMMISSIONER TO THE FIVE CIVILIZED TRIBES.
Muskogee, Indian Territory, November 6, 1905.

In the matter of the application for the enrollment of Jesse Sims as a citizen of the Creek Nation.

Bunner Sims being duly sworn testified as follows:

Q What is your name? A Bunner Sims.
Q Do you know how to spell your name? A Yes, sir
Q You are enrolled as Bunner Sims, is that the way you want it now? A Yes, sir
Q What is the name of your father? A Mark Sims.
Q What is the name of your mother? A I dont[sic] remember
Q If you had a brother what was his name? A Maxey

The witness is identified as Bunner Sims, on Creek Indian card 70, opposite roll No. 267.

Q How old are you? A I dont[sic] know.
Q What is your post office address? A Beggs
Q Is that your baby there? A Yes, sir

Applications for Enrollment of Creek Newborn
Act of 1905   Volume X

Q What is its name? A Jesse Sims
Q Is it a boy? A Yes, sir
Q How old is it? A Eight months
Q When was it born? A March 3 or 4th
Q Were you there when it was born? A Yes, sir
Q Was it born in the day or night time? A In the evening
Q After supper? A Yes, sir
Q How long after supper was it born, before 12 o'clock at night? A I don't know what time it was.
Q Did you look at the clock when it was born? A No, sir
Q Was it born before midnight? A Born in the evening

(Question explained by the official interpreter)

A We didn't have a clock at home and I don't know what time it was It was a long about six o'clock in the evening, it was a short time before sundown
Q Was it the third or fourth of March? A I am not positive as to the date whether it was the 3rd or 4th and I don't know the week day
Q Did you write down anywhere in a book the date of its birth? [sic] No
Q Did you have any one else besides the midwife there at the time A Nancy Gooden and Bessie Gooden was there
Q What is the name of the mother of this child Jesse? A Mary
Q Is that the woman there? A Yes, sir
Q Are you married to her and were you when the child was born? A Yes, sir
Q What was the name of her father? A Jim Gooden
Q Is he dead? A Yes, sir
Q What is the name of her mother? A Louisa West

    Mother of the child is identified as Mary Gooden on Creek Indian card 1142, opposite roll No. 3692

Mary Sims being duly sworn testified as follows, through Jesse McDermott, official interpreter.

Q What is your name? A Mary Sims.
Q How old are you? A 25
Q What was the name of your father? A Jim Gooden
Q What [sic] the name of your mother? A Louisa West
Q What is your post office address? A Beggs
Q You made out an affidavit signed by mark before Richard Hill a notary public and your age there is given as 22 years? A He was mistaken when he put it down
Q Have you a child by Bunner Sims named Jesse? A Yes, sir
Q Do you know how to spell that name Jesse? A No, sir I am uneducated
Q Is that Jesse in your arms? A Yes, sir
Q When was Jesse born? A He was born in March but I dont[sic] know the exact date
Q Do you remember what you told the notary public, Hill, when this affidavit was made out? A Yes

Applications for Enrollment of Creek Newborn
Act of 1905   Volume X

Q What day did you tell him? A I wasn't positive and told him either 3rd or 4th of March.
Q And you don't know now which of the two it was? A No, sir

The applicant is advised that this office would like to have her being in some one who knows the exact date when this child was born

Q Ask her in her own language what part of the day or night it was born? A It was nearly sundown but I don't know the day of the week.
Q Was Nancy Gooden the midwife? A Yes, sir
Q Who else was there? A Bessie Gooden and Nancy Gooden were the only ones there, they are my sisters.
Q Wasn't your husband there? A Yes, he was there
Q Didn't write it down anywhere in a book or make a record of it? A No, sir

Bunner Sims recalled.

Q Can you read and write? A Yes a very little
Q How should the name of your child Jesse Sims be spelled? A Jesse
Q And Simms the way you are enrolled? A Yes, sir, Simms
Q The Notary Public wrote it Sims? A He didn't know
Q You want him enrolled like you are enrolled Simms? A Yes, sir
Q And Jesse, not Jessie? A Yes, sir

We would like to have you bring in a witness who can tell us which of these two dates, 3rd or 4th of March, this child was born.

I, Anna Garrigues, on oath state that the above and foregoing is a true and correct transcript of my stenographic notes as taken in said cause on said date.

Anna Garrigues

Subscribed and sworn to before me this 11 day of November 1905

J. McDermott
Notary Public.

DEPARTMENT OF THE INTERIOR,
COMMISSIONER TO THE FIVE CIVILIZED TRIBES.
Muskogee, Indian Territory, April 28, 1906.

N. C. 813

In the matter of the application for the enrollment of Jesse Simms as a citizen by blood of the Creek Nation.

Applications for Enrollment of Creek Newborn
Act of 1905   Volume X

Mary SIMMS, being duly sworn, testified as follows:

Q What is your name? A Mary Simms, used to be Mary Gooden.
Q What is your age? A Twenty five, about.
Q What is your post office address? A Beggs.
Q What is the name of your father? A Jim Gooden.
Q What is the name of your mother? A Louisa West.

Witness is identified on Creek Indian card 3692

Q Have you a child named Jesse Simms? A Yes
Q Boy or girl? A Boy.
Q What is the name of the father of this child? A Bunner Simms.
Q What is the name of his father? A Mark Simms.
Q What is the name of your[sic] mother? A Eliza Simms.

The father of said child is identified as Bunner Simms opposite Creek Indian roll No. 267.

Q Yes child's name should be spelled Simms like the father? A Yes
Q Are you married to Bunner Simms? A Yes
Q How long have you been his wife? A Two years.
Q When was this child born A March 4, 1905
Q Is it living? A He is dead.
Q When did he die [sic] February 1, 1906
Q How old when he died? A It was a year old. almost.
Q Do you know how much it lacked of being a year old when it died? A I don't know.
Q Are you sure that your child Jesse was born March 4th.? A yes
Q In some testimony and affidavit given here before you said it was born March 3rd have you looked it up since that time? A Richard Hill was mistaken when he said 3rd of March.
Q Are you sure this child died on the first of this past gone February? A Yes
Q What makes you remember that? A Just because I know.

I, Anna Garrigues, on oath state that the above and foregoing is a true and correct transcript of my stenographic notes as taken in said cause on said date.

Anna Garrigues

Subscribed and sworn to before me
this 28 day of April 1906.   H.S. Hawkins
Notary Public.

Applications for Enrollment of Creek Newborn
Act of 1905 Volume X

N.C. 813.

DEPARTMENT OF THE INTERIOR,
COMMISSIONER TO THE FIVE CIVILIZED TRIBES.

In the matter of the application for the enrollment of Jesse Simms, deceased, as a citizen by blood of the Creek Nation.

STATEMENT AND ORDER.

The record in this case shows that on April 24, 1905, there was filed with the Commission to the Five Civilized Tribes, at Muskogee, Indian Territory, an affidavit in the matter of the birth of Jesse Simms which affidavit is considered as an original application for his enrollment as a citizen of the Creek Nation. Further proceedings were had in this matter on November 6, 1905 and April 28, 1906. A second affidavit in the matter of the birth of said applicant filed with this office on said latter date is also attached to and made part of the record herein.

The weight of evidence in this case establishes the date of birth of said applicant as March 4, 1905 and the date of death as February 1, 1906.

The Act of Congress approved March 3, 1905, (Public No. 212), provides:
"That the Commission to the Five Civilized Tribes is authorized for sixty days after the date of the approval of this act to receive and consider applications for enrollment, of children, born subsequent to May twenty-fifth, nineteen hundred and one, and prior to March fourth, nineteen hundred and five, and living on said latter date, to citizens of the Creek tribe of Indians whose enrollment has been approved by the Secretary of the Interior prior to the approval of this act; and to enroll and make allotments to such children."

It is therefore ordered that there is no authority of law for the enrollment of said Jesse Simms, deceased, as a citizen of the Creek Nation and that the application for his enrollment as such should be and the same is hereby dismissed.

Tams Bixby   Commissioner.

Muskogee, Indian Territory
AUG 22 1906

BIRTH AFFIDAVIT.

DEPARTMENT OF THE INTERIOR.
COMMISSION TO THE FIVE CIVILIZED TRIBES.

IN RE APPLICATION FOR ENROLLMENT, as a citizen of the Creek Nation, of Jesse Simms, born on the 4" day of March, 1905

Name of Father: Bunner Simms   a citizen of the   Creek   Nation.
Name of Mother: Mary Simms   a citizen of the   Creek   Nation.

Applications for Enrollment of Creek Newborn
Act of 1905   Volume X

Postoffice   Beggs I.T.

AFFIDAVIT OF MOTHER.

UNITED STATES OF AMERICA, Indian Territory,
Western   DISTRICT.

I, Mary Simms , on oath state that I am about 25 years of age and a citizen by blood , of the Creek Nation; that I am the lawful wife of Bunner Simms , who is a citizen, by blood of the Creek Nation; that a male child was born to me on 4 day of March , 1905 , that said child has been named Jesse Simms , and ~~is now living~~. died Feb 1- 1906.

                                                  her
                              Mary x Simms
Witnesses To Mark: mark
  { HGHains
    Anna Garrigues

Subscribed and sworn to before me this 28 day of April , 1906.

                              H.G. Hains
                              Notary Public.

BIRTH AFFIDAVIT.

DEPARTMENT OF THE INTERIOR.
COMMISSION TO THE FIVE CIVILIZED TRIBES.

IN RE APPLICATION FOR ENROLLMENT, as a citizen of the Creek Nation, of Jessie Sims , born on the 3rd day of March , 1905

Name of Father: Bunner Sims	a citizen of the	Creek	Nation.
Name of Mother: Mary Sims	a citizen of the	Creek	Nation.

Postoffice   Beggs I.T.

AFFIDAVIT OF MOTHER.

UNITED STATES OF AMERICA, Indian Territory,
Western   DISTRICT.

I, Mary Sims , on oath state that I am 22 years of age and a citizen by blood , of the Creek Nation; that I am the lawful wife of Bunner Sims , who is a citizen, by blood of the Creek Nation; that a male child was born to me on 3rd day of March , 1905 , that said child has been named Jessie Sims , and was living March 4, 1905.

Applications for Enrollment of Creek Newborn
Act of 1905 Volume X

Witnesses To Mark:
{ Will Staton
 Andrew Fisher

her
Mary x Sims
mark

Subscribed and sworn to before me this 21st day of April, 1905.

Richard J Hill
Notary Public.

My commission expires March 29th 1909

AFFIDAVIT OF ATTENDING PHYSICIAN OR MID-WIFE.

UNITED STATES OF AMERICA, Indian Territory, }
    Western   DISTRICT.

I, Nancy Gooden, a Midwife, on oath state that I attended on Mrs. Mary Sims, wife of Bunner Sims on the 3rd day of March, 1905; that there was born to her on said date a male child; that said child was living March 4, 1905, and is said to have been named Jessie Sims

her
Nancy x Gooden
mark

Witnesses To Mark:
{ Will Staton
 Andrew Fisher

Subscribed and sworn to before me this 21st day of April, 1905.

Richard J Hill
Notary Public.

My commission expires March 29th 1909

(The letter below should be with the prior applicant's file and is typed as given.)

N C 812

COPY   August th 6.1905 Edna I. T,

Commissioner to the five Civilized tribe
Muskogee Indian Territory

i have receave you notes sum time aGo i ReGard of the enrollment of my cheldran William and Jessie Hary the ar my cheldran all so my first name youse Rosey McNack and it is change to Hary My town is Tabatch

(Signed) Rosanna Hary

Applications for Enrollment of Creek Newborn
Act of 1905   Volume X

NC-813.

Muskogee, Indian Territory, October 19, 1905.

May[sic] Sims,
   c/o Bunna[sic] Sims,
      Beggs, Indian Territory.

Dear Madam:

    In the matter of the application for the enrollment of your minor child, Jesse Sims, as a citizen by blood of the Creek Nation this office desires further testimony relative to the date of the birth of said child.

    You are hereby notified to appear at the office of the Commissioner to the Five Civilized Tribes within fifteen days from date with Nancy Gooden, the midwife who attended at the birth of said child and at least one other intelligent witness who knows the exact day and the exact time of day at which said Jesse Sims was born.

                     Respectfully,
                              Commissioner.

(The letter below typed as given)

                     (COPY)

                  Beggs I. T. Oct. 26, 1005

Commission to the Five Civilized tribes[sic]
   Muskogee I. T.

Dear Sir in reply will that we came almost not haveing our witness to come to town ever before, and now since you had requested of us to come and bring Nancy Gooden to give testimony, she will in no wise come which we can't make her come because all of the familie that could testife about Jesse Simms Brith are Chito Harjo or Snakis in facts they good two children which they ought to have had them enrolled   But they would not: Nancy Gooden got one her self has not been enrolled. The last time that we made out the application We just force her to come to Beggs, Indian Territory But she almost not coming. and now to come to Muskogee to give testimony is impossible as we could make her come. She is a Snake and will never come We want the child to be enrolled and file for him soon as possible But we dont know what to do, Because the midwife won't come to be our witness any more Therefore I ask information what must be done, as we are awful anxious to fix it right But we are not to blame. But the midwife who will not come. Or if the Commission would send of the things that are needed we may be able to fix it, But I state for fact that our witness will not come, as the would not have their own

Applications for Enrollment of Creek Newborn
Act of 1905   Volume X

children enrolled Soplease give me an immediate answer if possible. Very truly yours (Signed) Bruner Simms

---

N.C. 813   Muskogee, Indian Territory, November 2, 1905.

Bunner Sims,
    Beggs, Indian Territory.

Dear Sir:

   Receipt is acknowledge of your letter of October 26, 1905, in which you state that Nancy Gooden, the midwife who attended at the birth of your minor child, Jesse Sims, belongs to the Snake faction of Creek Indians and that she will not appear before this office as requested and ask what to do in the matter.

   In reply you are advised that the mother of said child and at least one intelligent person, who knows the exact day and exact time of day that said Jesse Sims was born, should appear at the office of the Commissioner to the Five Civilized Tribes, within fifteen days from date, for the purpose of being examined under oath.

                    Respectfully,
                                    Commissioner.

(The letter below typed as given)

                    Beggs Ind. Ter.
                    2/24   06

Commissioner to the Five Civilized Tribes
        Muskogee I.T.

Dear Sir, in replying to the last letter in the matter of Brunner Simms' child Jessie Simms It is a very hard thing for him to get the midwife to come to Muskogee to give any testimony. Because he has tried his best to get them to go with him so a he could have his child enrolled   But they could not go and will not go   as I know that myself that they wont go   That was why I wrote before asking information   The only trouble is that the midwife would'nt go   It is a fact that they belong to the Snake party and can't be force to go and also the same ~~party~~ parties got some minors which should have been enrolled but they would have nothing to do with it at all   If the Commission could fix it some way so as to end enrolled the child, it will be the only way but for the midwife she'll never come to give any testimony   And no doubt but what it will take more witness as the child is now deceased
It is a fact that the Commission will have to do some thing in regard of the mid wife. and it the Commission would depend on the midwife coming *(illegible)* ~~it~~ in a danger that the child may never be enrolled who is absolutly entitled to be enrolled

Applications for Enrollment of Creek Newborn
Act of 1905   Volume X

So I ask the Commission to kindly fix it some way for the child. The only hope
>Yours truly
>Mary Simms

NC 813.

Muskogee, Indian Territory, August 24, 1906.

Mary Simms,
>Beggs, Indian Territory.

Dear Madam:

    You are hereby advised that in the matter of the application for the enrollment of your minor child, Jesse Simms, deceased, as a citizen by blood of the Creek Nation, a statement and order was rendered by the Commissioner to the Five Civilized Tribes, under date of August 22, 1906, dismissing said application.

    A copy of said statement and order is enclosed herewith.

Respectfully,

Enc. LM-60.   Commissioner.
Register.

Cr BA-178
BA-140

Muskogee, Indian Territory, March 23, 1905.

Matilda Cat,
>Bristow, Indian Territory.

Dear Madam:

    The Commission is in receipt of your letter of March 3, in which you ask if you can file for Cicero and Stella Snapp, deceased children of Amanda Snapp (deceased).

    There is herewith enclosed blank form of birth affidavit, which should be properly filled out, giving the date of birth of Stella Snapp.

    This matter should receive your prompt attention.

Respectfully,

1 B A   Chairman.

Applications for Enrollment of Creek Newborn
Act of 1905 Volume X

Think record should show that David Dearsaw and David Derisaw are the same person.
J?B

NC-815 (Copy)

x----------------------------------x
: MARRIAGE-LICENSE :
x----------------------------------x

UNITED STATES OF AMERICA, : To Any Person Authorized
   Indian Territory,   ss. NO. 362 : by Law to Solemnize
First Judicial Division. : Marriage--
 : GREETING.
 :

You are hereby commanded to solemnize the Rite and publish the Banns of Matrimony between Mr. DAVID DEARSHAW[sic] of Tulsa, in the Indian Territory, aged 30 years, and Miss MAGGIE CHAMBERLAIN of Tulsa, in the Indian Territory, aged 18 years, according to law, and do you officially sign and return this LICENSE to the parties therein named.

    Witness my hand and Official Seal, this 26 day of May, A.D. 1894.

                        (signed)   JOS. W. PHILLIPS,
  (SEAL)   Clerk of the U. S. Court.
By Arthur Walcott,
    Deputy.

                CERTIFICATE OF MARRIAGE.

United States of America,
   Indian Territory,   ss.   I, Sylvester Morris, a Minister of the
First Judicial Division.   Gospel, do hereby certify that on the 29
                                        day of May, A. D. 1894, I did duly and according to law, as commanded in the foregoing License, solemnize the Rite and publish the Banns of Matrimony between the parties therein named.
    Witness my hand this the 30 day of May, A. D. 1894.
    My credentials are recorded in the Office of the Clerk of the United States Court, Indian Territory, First Judicial Division, Book A, Page 161.

                             (signed)   SYLVESTER MORRIS,
                                       a Minister of the Gospel.

Applications for Enrollment of Creek Newborn
Act of 1905   Volume X

Certificate of Record.

United States of America,
    Indian Territory,   ss.
1st Judicial Division.

    I, Joseph W. Phillips, Clerk of the United States Court in the Indian Territory, do hereby certify that the instrument hereto attached was filed for record in my office the 1st day of June, 1894, at . . . .M., and duly recorded in Book C Marriage Record, Page 350.

    Witness my hand and seal of said Court at Muscogee[sic] in said Territory, this 2" day of June, A. D. 1894.

                                              JOS. W. PHILLIPS, Clerk
By J. S. Dodson,
        Deputy.
(SEAL)

                          FILED
                       JUN 1, 1894
            JOSEPH W. PHILLIPS, Clerk

INDIAN TERRITORY, Western District.
    I, J. Y. Miller, a stenographer to the Commission to the Five Civilized Tribes, do hereby certify that the above and foregoing is a true and complete copy of its original as found in the files of the aforesaid Commissioner, in Muskogee, Indian Territory.

                                        JY Miller

Sworn to and subscribed before me
this the 28th day of October,
1905.   J McDermott
                                          Notary Public.

BIRTH AFFIDAVIT.
                    DEPARTMENT OF THE INTERIOR.
          COMMISSION TO THE FIVE CIVILIZED TRIBES.

    IN RE APPLICATION FOR ENROLLMENT, as a citizen of the Creek Nation, of Lila Dearsaw, born on the 25" day of Sept , 1902

Name of Father: David Dearsaw   a citizen of the   Creek   Nation.
Name of Mother: Maggie Dearsaw   a citizen of the   -----   Nation.

                              Postoffice   Okmulgee IT

Applications for Enrollment of Creek Newborn
Act of 1905 Volume X

AFFIDAVIT OF MOTHER.

UNITED STATES OF AMERICA, Indian Territory, }
Western DISTRICT.

I, Maggie Dearsaw , on oath state that I am 28 years of age and a non citizen by marriage , of the ----- Nation; that I am the lawful wife of David Dearsaw , who is a citizen, by blood of the Creek Nation; that a female child was born to me on 25th day of September , 1902 , that said child has been named Lila Dearsaw , and was living March 4, 1905.

Maggie Dearsaw

Witnesses To Mark:
{ W^{m}FA Gierke
  Lewis Adams

Subscribed and sworn to before me this 8th day of April , 1905.

W^{m}FA Gierkes
NOTARY PUBLIC Notary Public.
My Commission Expires June 29, 1908

AFFIDAVIT OF ATTENDING PHYSICIAN OR MID-WIFE.

UNITED STATES OF AMERICA, Indian Territory, }
Western DISTRICT.

I, Sarak[sic] Chamblen , a midwife , on oath state that I attended on Mrs. Maggie Dearsaw , wife of David Dearsaw on the 25th day of September , 1902 ; that there was born to her on said date a female child; that said child was living March 4, 1905, and is said to have been named Lila Dearsaw

Sarah Chamblen

Witnesses To Mark:
{ W^{m}FA Gierke
  Lewis Adams

Subscribed and sworn to before me this 8th day of April , 1905.

W^{m}FA Gierkes
NOTARY PUBLIC Notary Public.
My Commission Expires June 29, 1908

Applications for Enrollment of Creek Newborn
Act of 1905 Volume X

BIRTH AFFIDAVIT.

DEPARTMENT OF THE INTERIOR.
COMMISSION TO THE FIVE CIVILIZED TRIBES.

IN RE APPLICATION FOR ENROLLMENT, as a citizen of the Creek Nation, of Lila Derisaw, born on the 25 day of Sept, 1902

Name of Father: David Derisaw   a citizen of the   Creek   Nation.
Name of Mother: Maggie Derisaw   non citizen of the ~~Creek~~ Creek Nation.

Postoffice   Okmulgee I.T.

AFFIDAVIT OF MOTHER.

UNITED STATES OF AMERICA, Indian Territory,
Western   DISTRICT.

I, Maggie Derisaw, on oath state that I am about 31 years of age and a citizen ~~by~~ Non Citizen, of Creek Nation; that I am the lawful wife of David Derisaw, who is a citizen, by blood of the Creek Nation; that a female child was born to me on 25 day of Sept, 1902, that said child has been named Lila Derisaw, and is now living.

                                Maggie Derisaw

Witnesses To Mark:
{

Subscribed and sworn to before me this 11 day of Nov, 1905.

                                Fred Comstock
                                    Notary Public.

My Com Exp 7/2/06

AFFIDAVIT OF ATTENDING PHYSICIAN OR MID-WIFE.

UNITED STATES OF AMERICA, Indian Territory,
Western   DISTRICT.

I, Sarah Chamblin, a Mid-wife, on oath state that I attended on Mrs. Maggie Derisaw, wife of David Derisaw on the 25 day of Sept, 1902; that there was born to her on said date a female child; that said child is now living and is said to have been named Lila Derisaw

                                Sarah Chamblen

Witnesses To Mark:
{

Applications for Enrollment of Creek Newborn
Act of 1905 Volume X

Subscribed and sworn to before me this 11 day of Nov , 1905.

                                      Fred Comstock
                                      Notary Public.
My Com Exp 7/2/06

BIRTH AFFIDAVIT.

DEPARTMENT OF THE INTERIOR.
COMMISSION TO THE FIVE CIVILIZED TRIBES.

IN RE APPLICATION FOR ENROLLMENT, as a citizen of the Creek Nation, of Willie Dearsaw, born on the 2nd day of March , 1905

Name of Father: David Dearsaw	a citizen of the Creek	Nation.
Name of Mother: Maggie Dearsaw	non citizen of the -----	Nation.

                                Postoffice   Okmulgee, IT.

AFFIDAVIT OF MOTHER.

UNITED STATES OF AMERICA, Indian Territory, }
      Western   DISTRICT.

I, Maggie Dearsaw , on oath state that I am 28 years of age and a none citizen by ----- , of the ----- Nation; that I am the lawful wife of David Dearsaw , who is a citizen, by blood of the Creek Nation; that a male child was born to me on second day of March , 1905 , that said child has been named Willie Dearsaw , and was living March 4, 1905.

                                      Maggie Dearsaw

Witnesses To Mark:
   { W^{m}FA Gierke
     Lewis Adams

Subscribed and sworn to before me this 8th day of April , 1905.

                                      W^{m}FA Gierkes
                             NOTARY PUBLIC Notary Public.
                                My Commission Expires June 29, 1908

Applications for Enrollment of Creek Newborn
Act of 1905   Volume X

AFFIDAVIT OF ATTENDING PHYSICIAN OR MID-WIFE.

UNITED STATES OF AMERICA, Indian Territory,
Western   DISTRICT.

I, Sarah Chamblen , a midwife , on oath state that I attended on Mrs. Maggie Dearsaw , wife of David Dearsaw on the second day of March , 1905 ; that there was born to her on said date a male child; that said child was living March 4, 1905, and is said to have been named Willie Dearsaw

Sarah Chamblen

Witnesses To Mark:
{ W^{m}FA Gierke
  Lewis Adams

Subscribed and sworn to before me this 8th day of April , 1905.

W^{m}FA Gierkes
NOTARY PUBLIC Notary Public.
My Commission Expires June 29, 1908

BIRTH AFFIDAVIT.

DEPARTMENT OF THE INTERIOR.
COMMISSION TO THE FIVE CIVILIZED TRIBES.

IN RE APPLICATION FOR ENROLLMENT, as a citizen of the Creek Nation, of Willie Derisaw , born on the 2 day of March , 1905

Name of Father: David Derisaw   a citizen of the   Creek   Nation.
Name of Mother: Maggie Derisaw   non citizen of the   Creek   Nation.

Postoffice   Okmulgee I.T.

AFFIDAVIT OF MOTHER.

UNITED STATES OF AMERICA, Indian Territory,
Western   DISTRICT.

I, Maggie Derisaw , on oath state that I am about 31 years of age and a citizen ~~by~~ Non Citizen , of Creek Nation; that I am the lawful wife of David Derisaw , who is a citizen, by birth of the Creek Nation; that a male child was born to me on 2 day of March , 1905 , that said child has been named Willie Derisaw , and is now living.

Maggie Derisaw

Witnesses To Mark:
{

Applications for Enrollment of Creek Newborn
Act of 1905   Volume X

Subscribed and sworn to before me this 11 day of Nov , 1905.

Fred Comstock
Notary Public.

My Com Exp 7/2/06

AFFIDAVIT OF ATTENDING PHYSICIAN OR MID-WIFE.

UNITED STATES OF AMERICA, Indian Territory,
Western   **DISTRICT.**

I, Sarah Chamblin , a Mid-wife , on oath state that I attended on Mrs. Maggie Derisaw , wife of David Derisaw on the 2 day of March , 1905 ; that there was born to her on said date a male child; that said child is now living and is said to have been named Willie Derisaw

Sarah Chamblen

Witnesses To Mark:
{

Subscribed and sworn to before me this 11 day of Nov , 1905.

Fred Comstock
Notary Public.

My Com Exp 7/2/06

NC-615[sic].

Muskogee, Indian Territory, October 19, 1905.

Maggie Derisaw,
Okmulgee, Indian Territory.

Dear Madam:

In the matter of the application for the enrollment of your minor children Lila Derisaw, born September 25, 1902, and Willie Derisaw, born March 2, 1905, as citizens by blood of the Creek Nation, this office requires proof of marriage between yourself and David Derisaw, the father of said child.

Such evidence of marriage may consist of either the original or a certified copy of your marriage license and certificate.

Respectfully,

Commissioner.

Applications for Enrollment of Creek Newborn
Act of 1905   Volume X

Muskogee, Indian Territory, October 28, 1905.

Maggie Dearshaw,
    Care David Dearshaw,
        Okmulgee, Indian Territory.

Dear Madam:

Receipt is acknowledged of your letter, without date, enclosing your marriage license and certificate of which a certified copy has been made and filed in the matter of the application for the enrollment of your minor children, Lila and Willie Dearshaw, as citizens by blood of the Creek Nation.

In accordance with your request there is herewith returned to you the original license and certificate.

Respectfully,

Commissioner.

N.C. 815

Muskogee, Indian Territory, November 2, 1905.

David Dearsaw,
    Okmulgee, Indian Territory.

Dear Sir:

In the matter of the application for the enrollment of your minor children, Lila Dearsaw, born September 25, 1902 and Willie Dearsaw, born March 2, 1905, as citizens by blood of the Creek Nation; this office is unable to identify you on its final roll of citizens by blood of the Creek Nation, under the name Dearsaw; you are requested to state the names of your parents, the Creek Indian town to which you belong and your roll number as the same appears on your deeds and allotment certificate.

You are requested to advise this office whether you were ever known by the name of Derisaw.

You are advised that if your name is in fact Derisaw and not Dearsaw, it will be necessary for your wife to execute a new affidavit in the case, giving your correct surname, the correct name of said children and of herself.

Respectfully,

Commissioner.

2 B A

Applications for Enrollment of Creek Newborn
Act of 1905   Volume X

NC 815

C O P Y.

Beggs, I. T. 11/11 1905

Gents

My selection No. 5197 is where my land is alloted[sic].

If these papers are not O.K. please advise.

Yours truly

David Derisaw
C[sic]

Copy

Filed Jan. 15, 1900
Chas A. Davidson Clerk
No 434

Marriage License

United States of America }
Indian Territory   } S S.
Northern District   }

To Any Person Authorized by Law
To Solemnize Marriage - Greeting

You are Hereby Commanded to Solemnize[sic] the Rite and publish the Banns of matrimony between Mr. Lewis Adams of Sapulpa, in the Indian Territory, aged 27 years, and Miss Anna Chamblin of Sapulpa, in the Indian Territory, aged 23 years, according to law; and do you officially sign and return this License to the parties therein names.

Witness my hand and official seal, at Muscogee[sic], Indian Territory, this 14 day of December, A.D. 1899.

(Seal)
Jas. A. Winston
Clerk of the U. S. Court
By N. S. Young Deputy

Applications for Enrollment of Creek Newborn
Act of 1905 Volume X

Certificate of Marriage

United States of America }
    Indian Territory   } S S.
    Northern District }

I, J. M. Porter, a Minister of the Gospel, Do Hereby Certify, that on the 13th day of January A.D. 1900, I did duly and according to law as commanded in the foregoing License, solemize[sic] the Rite and publish the Banns of Matrimony between the parties therein named.
    Witness my hand this 13th day of January A.D. 1900.
    My credentials are recorded in the office of the Clerk of the United States Court in Indian Territory, Northern District, Book A, Page 251.

                              J. M. Porter
                              A Minister o the Gospel
                              Pastor M. E Church South

United States
    Indian Territory   Beggs IT 10/21/05
    Western District.

I hereby certify that the foregoing is a true and correct copy of original

                              Fred Comstock
My Com Exp 7/2/06   Notary Public.

BIRTH AFFIDAVIT.
DEPARTMENT OF THE INTERIOR.
COMMISSION TO THE FIVE CIVILIZED TRIBES.

    IN RE APPLICATION FOR ENROLLMENT, as a citizen of the Creek Nation, of Ethel Adams, born on the 28th day of February, 1905

Name of Father: Lewis Adams   a citizen of the   Creek   Nation.
Name of Mother: Annie Adams   non citizen of the   (blank)   ~~Nation~~.

                      Postoffice   Beggs, I.T.

Applications for Enrollment of Creek Newborn
Act of 1905   Volume X

AFFIDAVIT OF MOTHER.

UNITED STATES OF AMERICA, Indian Territory, }
Western DISTRICT.

I, Annie Adams , on oath state that I am 26 years of age and a non citizen ~~by~~ *(blank)* , of the ------ Nation; that I am the lawful wife of Lewis Adams , who is a citizen, by blood of the Creek Nation; that a female child was born to me on 28th day of February , 1905 , that said child has been named Ethel Adams , and was living March 4, 1905.

Annie Adams

Witnesses To Mark:
{

Subscribed and sworn to before me this 4th day of April , 1905.

W^{m}FA Gierkes
NOTARY PUBLIC Notary Public.
My Commission Expires June 29, 1908

AFFIDAVIT OF ATTENDING PHYSICIAN OR MID-WIFE.

UNITED STATES OF AMERICA, Indian Territory, }
Western DISTRICT.

I, Sarah Chamblen , a midwife , on oath state that I attended on Mrs. Annie Adams , wife of Lewis Adams on the 28th day of February , 1905 ; that there was born to her on said date a female child; that said child was living March 4, 1905, and is said to have been named Ethel Adams

Sarah Chamblen

Witnesses To Mark:
{

Subscribed and sworn to before me this 4th day of April , 1905.

W^{m}FA Gierkes
NOTARY PUBLIC Notary Public.
My Commission Expires June 29, 1908

Applications for Enrollment of Creek Newborn
Act of 1905   Volume X

BIRTH AFFIDAVIT.

DEPARTMENT OF THE INTERIOR.
COMMISSION TO THE FIVE CIVILIZED TRIBES.

IN RE APPLICATION FOR ENROLLMENT, as a citizen of the Creek Nation, of Andrew Adams, born on the 12 day of January, 1903

Name of Father: Lewis Adams	a citizen of the Creek	Nation.
Name of Mother: Annie Adams	non citizen of the *(blank)*	~~Nation.~~

Postoffice   Beggs, I.T.

AFFIDAVIT OF MOTHER.

UNITED STATES OF AMERICA, Indian Territory, ⎤
   Western   DISTRICT.   ⎦

I, Annie Adams, on oath state that I am 26 years of age and a non citizen ~~by~~ *(blank)*, of the ------ ~~Nation~~; that I am the lawful wife of Lewis Adams, who is a citizen, by blood of the Creek Nation; that a male child was born to me on 12th day of January, 1903, that said child has been named Andrew Adams, and was living March 4, 1905.

Annie Adams

Witnesses To Mark:
{

Subscribed and sworn to before me this 4th day of April, 1905.

W^{m}FA Gierkes
NOTARY PUBLIC Notary Public.
My Commission Expires June 29, 1908

AFFIDAVIT OF ATTENDING PHYSICIAN OR MID-WIFE.

UNITED STATES OF AMERICA, Indian Territory, ⎤
   Western   DISTRICT.   ⎦

I, Sarah Chamblen, a midwife, on oath state that I attended on Mrs. Annie Adams, wife of Lewis Adams on the 12th day of January, 1903; that there was born to her on said date a male child; that said child was living March 4, 1905, and is said to have been named Andrew Adams

Sarah Chamblen

Witnesses To Mark:
{

Applications for Enrollment of Creek Newborn
Act of 1905 Volume X

Subscribed and sworn to before me this 4th day of April, 1905.

W^{m}FA Gierkes
NOTARY PUBLIC Notary Public.
My Commission Expires June 29, 1908

NC-816.

Muskogee, Indian Territory, October 19, 1905.

Annie Adams,
    c/o Lewis Adams,
        Beggs, Indian Territory.

Dear Madam:

    In the matter of the application for the enrollment of your minor children, Andrew Adams, born January 12, 1903, and Ethel Adams, born February 28, 1905, as citizens by blood of the Creek Nation, You are advised that it will be necessary for you to furnish this office with proof of your marriage to Lewis Adams, the father of said children.

    Such evidence may consist of either the original or a certified copy of your marriage license or certificate.

        Respectfully,

                Commissioner.

Muskogee, Indian Territory, October 26, 1905.

Lewis Adams,
    Beggs, Indian Territory.

Dear Sir:

    Receipt is acknowledged of you letter of October 21, 1905, enclosing certified copy of your marriage license and certificate.

        Respectfully,

                Commissioner.

Applications for Enrollment of Creek Newborn
Act of 1905   Volume X

NC-817.

Muskogee, Indian Territory, October 19, 1905.

Naomi Pemberton,
    William T. Pemberton,
        Checotah, Indian Territory.

Dear Madam:

    In the matter of the application for the enrollment of your minor child, Reacy Adeline Pemberton, born October 6, 1902, as a citizen by blood of the Creek Nation, this office requires evidence of your marriage to William T. Pemberton, the father of said child.
    Such evidence may consist of either the original or a certified copy of your marriage license and certificate.

                Respectfully,

                          Commissioner.

N.C. 817

Muskogee, Indian Territory, October 31, 1905.

William T. Pemberton,
    Checotah, Indian Territory.

Dear Sir:

    Receipt is acknowledged of your communication, without date, enclosing your marriage license and certificate, a copy of which has been made and filed in the matter of the application for the enrollment of your minor child, Reacy Adaline Pemberton, as a Creek freedman.

    In compliance with your request the original marriage license and certificate are herewith returned to you.

                Respectfully,

                          Commissioner.

N.C. 817

(The letter below typed as given.)

                (Copy)

Mr daws   Please return this copy of licine When through With

                        (signed) William T. Pemberton

Checotah I T

Applications for Enrollment of Creek Newborn
Act of 1905 Volume X

(On reverse side of original letter)

this is our copy ouf our Mariage Naana Pemberton and William T. Puberton

yours truly

CERTIFICATE OF RECORD.

United States of America,
    Indian Territory,   ss.
    Northern District.

    I, Charles A. Davidson, Clerk of the United States Court in the Northern District, Indian Territory, do hereby certify that the instrument hereto attached was filed for record in my office the 2 day of December, 1901, at . . . . , and duly recorded in Book L, Marriage Record, Page 392.
    Witness my hand and seal of said Court at Muskogee, in said Territory, this 4 day of December, A. D. 1901.

(signed)   CHAS. A. DAVIDSON, Clerk.

Northern Dist. Ind. Ter.
FILED
DEC 2, 1901
CHAS. A. DAVIDSON,
Clerk of U.S. Courts

INDIAN TERRITORY, Western District.

    I, J. Y. Miller, a stenographer to the Commissioner to the Five Civilized Tribes, do hereby certify that the above and foregoing is a true and complete copy of its original.

JY Miller

Subscribed and sworn to before me
  this the 30th day of October,
1905.
                         Edw C Griesel
                              Notary Public.

Applications for Enrollment of Creek Newborn
Act of 1905 Volume X

NC-817 (Copy)

MARRIAGE LICENSE.

UNITED STATES OF AMERICA,
    Indian Territory,   ss.   NO. 416
    Northern District.

TO ANY PERSON AUTHORIZED BY LAW TO SOLEMNIZE MARRIAGE--GREETING.

    You are hereby commanded to solemnize the Rite and publish the Banns of Matrimony between Mr. William T. Pemberton of Eufaula, in the Indian Territory, aged 21 years, and Miss Naomi Millsaps, of Eufaula, in the Indian Territory, aged 21 years, according to law, and do you officially sign and return this License to the parties therein named.

    Witness my hand and official seal at Muskogee, Indian Territory, this 2nd day of November, A. D. 1901.
        (signed)   CHAS. A. DAVIDSON,
                Clerk of the U.S. Court.
(SEAL)
By Wm. R. Shackelford,
    Deputy.

CERTIFICATE OF MARRIAGE.

United States of America,
    Indian Territory,   ss.   I, A. R. Montgomery, a Minister of the
    Northern District.   Gospel, do hereby certify that on the 5
                                   day of November, A. D. 1901, I did duly and according to law as commanded in the foregoing license, solemnize the Rite and publish the Banns of Matrimony between the parties therein named.
    Witness my hand this the 5 day of November, A. D. 1901.
    My credentials are recorded in the office of the Clerk of the United States Court, Indian Territory, Northern District, Book B, Page 2?9.

        (signed)   A. R. MONTGOMERY,
                            A Minister of the Gospel.

Applications for Enrollment of Creek Newborn
Act of 1905   Volume X

BIRTH AFFIDAVIT.

DEPARTMENT OF THE INTERIOR.
COMMISSION TO THE FIVE CIVILIZED TRIBES.

IN RE APPLICATION FOR ENROLLMENT, as a citizen of the Creek Nation, of Reacy Adeline Pemberton , born on the 6th day of October , 1902

Name of Father: William T. Pemberton a citizen of the Creek Nation.
Name of Mother: Naomi Pemberton a citizen of the United States Nation.

Postoffice Checotah, Ind. Ter.

AFFIDAVIT OF MOTHER.

UNITED STATES OF AMERICA, Indian Territory,
Western DISTRICT.

I, Naomi Pemberton , on oath state that I am 25 years of age and a citizen xxxxxxxxxx , of the United States ~~Nation~~; that I am the lawful wife of William T. Pemberton , who is a citizen, by blood of the Creek Nation; that a female child was born to me on 6th day of October , 1902 , that said child has been named Reacy Adeline Pemberton , and was living March 4, 1905.

Naomi Pemberton

Witnesses To Mark:
{

Subscribed and sworn to before me this 17th day of March , 1905.

My commission expires July 3rd 1906. Charles Buford
Notary Public.

AFFIDAVIT OF ATTENDING PHYSICIAN OR MID-WIFE.

UNITED STATES OF AMERICA, Indian Territory,
Western DISTRICT.

I, Sarah C. Millsap , a mid-wife , on oath state that I attended on Mrs. Naomi Pemberton , wife of William T. Pemberton on the 6th day of October , 1902 ; that there was born to her on said date a female child; that said child was living March 4, 1905, and is said to have been named Reacy Adeline Pemberton

Sarah C. Millsap

Witnesses To Mark:
{

Applications for Enrollment of Creek Newborn
Act of 1905   Volume X

Subscribed and sworn to before me this 17th day of March, 1905.

My commission expires July 3rd 1906.   Charles Buford
                                          Notary Public.

BA-26-138.
DEPARTMENT OF THE INTERIOR,
COMMISSIONER TO THE FIVE CIVILIZED TRIBES.

Muskogee, Indian Territory, March 14, 1905.

In the matter of the application for the enrollment of Leo Bennett Escoe (or Ferdinand DeSoto Escoe) as a citizen by blood of the Creek Nation.

Chas. J. Escoe, being duly sworn, testified as follows:

EXAMINATION BY THE COMMISSION:
Q What is your name? A Charles J. Escoe.
Q What is your age? A 49.
Q What is your postoffice? A Checotah.

The witness is identified as Charlie J. Escoe, on Creek Indian card, field No. 274, and his name is contained in partial list of Creek citizens by blood approved by the Secretary of the Interior March 13, 1902, Roll No. 908.

Q Have you a child named Ferdinand Escoe? A Yes, sir, I have.
Q Sometimes called Ferdinand DeSoto Escoe? A Yes sir.
Q Did you have a child called Leo Bennett Escoe? A Yes, sir; we have changed the names.
Q These two children are the same? A Yes sir. They are one child with two different names.
Q He was formerly called Leo Bennett Escoe and now called Ferdinand DeSoto Escoe? A No sir; was formerly called Ferdinand DeSoto Escoe and now called Leo Bennett Escoe.
Q When was that child born? A October 1, 1902.
Q Now living? A Yes sir.
Q Now living? A Yes sir.

Affidavits filed in this case November 4, 1902, September 15, 1903 and March 14, 1905, are made a part of the record herein.

Applications for Enrollment of Creek Newborn
Act of 1905   Volume X

INDIAN TERRITORY,   )
Western District.   )   I, J. Y. Miller, a stenographer to the Commission
)   to the Five Civilized Tribes, do hereby certify
)   that the above and foregoing is a true and
complete translation of my notes as same appear in my stenographic report of this case.

JY Miller

Sworn to and subscribed before me
this the 24 day of April, 1905.

Zera E Parrish

My Comm. expires April 11, 1909.   Notary Public.

NC-818

DEPARTMENT OF THE INTERIOR,
COMMISSIONER TO THE FIVE CIVILIZED TRIBES.

Muskogee, Indian Territory, November 1, 1905.

In the matter of the enrollment of Leo Bennett Escoe as a citizen by blood of the Creek Nation.

Charlie J. Escoe, being duly sworn, testified as follows:

EXAMINATION BY THE COMMISSIONER:
Q What is your name? A Charlie J. Escoe.
Q We have an affidavit signed by you, Charlie J. Escoe; is that your name? A Yes, Charlie.
Q Have you a child named Leo Bennett Escoe? A Yes sir.
Q You testified here that that child--you first called it Ferdinand DeSoto Escoe and changed its name to what its correct name now is, Leo Bennet[sic] Escoe[sic]--is that right? A Yes, sir; that is right.
Q You are a citizen of the Creek Nation? A Yes, sir.
Q Is the mother of this child a citizen of any tribe in Indian Territory? A Cherokee Freedman.
Q Cherokee Freedman? A Yes sir.
Q Did she get her land? a No sir; attending for her right now; it isn't settled.
Q She is an applicant for enrollment as a Cherokee Freedman? A Yes sir.
Q Has any application ever been made for this child--to have this child, Leo Bennett Escoe, enrolled as a citizen of the Cherokee Nation? A To the best of my knowledge it has not been; it might have been. I was wanting to get the child on the roll. And I might have made one for the Cherokee Nation. I don't remember it.
Q Well now, Mr. Escoe, if it should be found that this child has rights in either the Cherokee or the Creek Nation, in which Nation do you elect to have it enrolled to have a chance to take its land? A With me, myself.
Q In which Nation? A In the Creek Nation, with myself.

Applications for Enrollment of Creek Newborn
Act of 1905   Volume X

Q When was that child born, Charlie? A To the best of my knowledge--it has been so long since I spoke about it--it seems to be the first of October, 1902, to the best of my knowledge. I have forgotten all about it, friends.
Q Is the child living now? A Yes, living.
Q With you or with the mother? A With me--both, it is my wife.

THE COMMISSIONER (to the applicant for his child): You may send in your wife's affidavit, selecting in which Nation she wants to have her child enrolled.

INDIAN TERRITORY, Western District.
I, J. Y. Miller, a stenographer to the Commissioner to the Five Civilized Tribes, do hereby certify that the above and foregoing is a true and complete translation of my notes as same appear in my stenographic report of this case.

JY Miller

Sworn to and subscribed before me
this the 4th day of November,
1905.   Edw C Griesel   Notary Public

N.C. 818

Muskogee, Indian Territory, November 1, 1905.

Chief Clerk,
    Cherokee Enrollment Division.

Dear Sir:

March 13, 1905, application was made to the Commission to the Five Civilized Tribes for the enrollment as a citizen by blood of the Creek Nation of Leo Bennett Escoe, formerly known as Ferdinand De Soto Escoe, born October 1, 1902, child of Charlie J. Escoe, a citizen of the Creek Nation, and Dora Escoe, said to be a citizen of the Cherokee Nation.

You are requested to advise the Creek Enrollment Division, whether or not application has been made for the enrollment of said Leo Bennett Escoe, as a citizen of the Cherokee Nation and if so what disposition has been made of same.

Respectfully,
Commissioner.

Applications for Enrollment of Creek Newborn
Act of 1905   Volume X

REFER IN REPLY TO THE FOLLOWING:

DEPARTMENT OF THE INTERIOR,
COMMISSIONER TO THE FIVE CIVILIZED TRIBES.

Muskogee, Indian Territory, November 10, 1905.

Chief Clerk,
    Creek Enrollment Division.

Dear Sir:

    In reply to your letter of November 1, (NC 818), asking to be advised if application has ever been made for the enrollment, as a citizen of the Cherokee Nation, of Leo Bennett Escoe, formerly known as Ferdinand De Soto Escoe, born October 1, 1902, child of Charlie J.. Escoe, a citizen of the Creek Nation, and Dora Escoe, an alleged citizen of the Cherokee Nation, you are advised that it does not appear from an examination of the records of the Cherokee Enrollment Division that any application has ever been made for the enrollment of said child as a citizen of the Cherokee Nation.

                      Respectfully,
                      Tams Bixby   Commissioner.

LS

BIRTH AFFIDAVIT.

DEPARTMENT OF THE INTERIOR,
COMMISSION TO THE FIVE CIVILIZED TRIBES.

    IN RE *Application for Enrollment*, as a citizen of the Creek Nation, of Ferdinand Escoe , born on the 1st day of October , 1902

Name of Father: Charles J. Escoe   a citizen of the   Creek   Nation.
                                                          Freedman
Name of Mother: Dora Escoe   a citizen of the Cherokee   Nation.

                    Post-office: Checotah, I. T.

AFFIDAVIT OF MOTHER.

UNITED STATES OF AMERICA, ⎫
    INDIAN TERRITORY.   ⎬
    Western   District. ⎭

    I, Dora Escoe , on oath state that I am 23 years of age and a citizen Freedman , of the   Cherokee   Nation; that I am the lawful wife of   Charles J. Escoe , who is a citizen, by

Applications for Enrollment of Creek Newborn
Act of 1905 Volume X

Blood of the Creek Nation; that a Male child was born to me on 1st day of October, 1902, that said child has been named Ferdinand Escoe, and is now living.

                      her
             Dora Escoe x

WITNESSES TO MARK: mark
{ A A Smith
  Lizzie Lewis

Subscribed and sworn to before me this 1st *day of* November, 1902.

             J.B. Morrow
My Commission Expires July 1, 1908.   *NOTARY PUBLIC.*

AFFIDAVIT OF ATTENDING PHYSICIAN OR MID-WIFE.

UNITED STATES OF AMERICA,
   INDIAN TERRITORY.
  Western   District.

I, Dorcas Love, a Midwife, on oath state that I attended on Mrs. Dora Escoe, wife of Charles J. Escoe on the 1st day of October, 1902; that there was born to her on said date a male child; that said child is now living and is said to have been named Ferdinand Escoe

                    her
           Dorcas Love x

WITNESSES TO MARK: mark
{ A A Smith
  Lizzie Lewis

Subscribed and sworn to before me this 1st *day of* November, 1902.

             J.B. Morrow
My Commission Expires July 1, 1908.   *NOTARY PUBLIC.*

BIRTH AFFIDAVIT.

DEPARTMENT OF THE INTERIOR.
COMMISSION TO THE FIVE CIVILIZED TRIBES.

IN RE APPLICATION FOR ENROLLMENT, as a citizen of the Creek Nation, of Leo Bennett Escoe, born on the 1st day of October, 1902

Name of Father: Charlie J. Escoe   a citizen of the   Creek   Nation.
Name of Mother: Dora Escoe   a citizen of the   Cherokee Nation.

            Postoffice   Checotah Ind. Ter.

Applications for Enrollment of Creek Newborn
Act of 1905   Volume X

AFFIDAVIT OF MOTHER.

UNITED STATES OF AMERICA, Indian Territory, ⎱
   Western   DISTRICT. ⎰

    I, Dora Escoe , on oath state that I am 24   years of age and a citizen by blood , of the Creek   Nation; that I am the lawful wife of , who is a Freedman citizen, by *(blank)* of the Creek[sic] Nation; that a male   child was born to me on   1$^{\underline{st}}$ day of October , 1902 , that said child has been named   Leo Bennett Escoe , and was living March 4, 1905.

                                                her
                                         Dora x Escoe

Witnesses To Mark: mark
{ A A Smith
  W^m A Reid

    Subscribed and sworn to before me this 13$^{\underline{th}}$ day of March , 1905.

                                        J.B. Morrow
My Commission Expires July 1, 1908.   Notary Public.

AFFIDAVIT OF ATTENDING PHYSICIAN OR MID-WIFE.

UNITED STATES OF AMERICA, Indian Territory, ⎱
   Western   DISTRICT. ⎰

    I, Dorcas Love , a Mid-wife , on oath state that I attended on Mrs. Dora Escoe , wife of Charlie J. Escoe on the 1$^{\underline{st}}$ day of October , 1902 ; that there was born to her on said date a male child; that said child was living March 4, 1905, and is said to have been named Leo Bennett Escoe

                                                her
                                       Dorcas x Love
Witnesses To Mark: mark
{ A A Smith
  W^m A Reid

    Subscribed and sworn to before me this 13$^{\underline{th}}$ day of March , 1905.

                                        J.B. Morrow
My Commission Expires July 1, 1908.   Notary Public.

Applications for Enrollment of Creek Newborn
Act of 1905   Volume X

CHECOTAH, IND. TER., March 13 - 1905.

Indian Territory }
Western District.

This certifies that application for enrollment was made to the Commission of The Five Civilized for Ferdinand DeSoto Escoe previous to September first 1903. That the said child was not enrolled. That the application hereto attached, for the enrollment of Leo Bennett Escoe is for the same identical child except that we the parents of said child have decided to change its name from Ferdinand Desoto, to Leo Bennett Escoe.

Witnesses to mark   Charlie J. Escoe
W^m A Reid   her
A A Smith   Dora x Escoe
                                                   mark

Subscribed and sworn to before me this 13$^{\underline{th}}$ day of March 1905.

                                    J.B. Morrow
My Commission Expires July 1, 1908.   Notary Public

United States of America   )
)
Indian Territory   ) ss
)
Western District   )

Personally appeared before me this 2nd day of November 1905, Dora Escoe well known to me as the party whose name is hereto subscribed, who makes oath and says that she is enrolled as a Cherokee Freedman, that she is the mother of Leo Bennett Escoe, and that it is her desire that the said Leo Bennett Escoe be enrolled with his father Charlie J. Escoe, as a Creek Citizen by blood.   her
Witness   Dora x Escoe   SEAL
A.A. Smith   mark
J.D. Faulkner

Subscribed to and sworn to before me this 2nd day of November 1905

                                    J.D. Faulkner
                          Notary Public for the Western District

My commission expires Feb 19th 1907

Applications for Enrollment of Creek Newborn
Act of 1905   Volume X

BIRTH AFFIDAVIT.

DEPARTMENT OF THE INTERIOR,
COMMISSION TO THE FIVE CIVILIZED TRIBES.

Leo Bennett

IN RE APPLICATION FOR ENROLLMENT, as a citizen of the Cherokee Nation, of ~~Dora~~ Escoe, born on the 1 day of October, 1902

Name of Father: Charles J Escoe   a citizen of the Creek Nation.
Name of Father: Dora Escoe   a citizen of the Cherokee Nation.

Post-Office: Checotah Ind. Ter

AFFIDAVIT OF MOTHER.

UNITED STATES OF AMERICA,
INDIAN TERRITORY,
Western   District.

I, Dora Escoe, on oath state that I am 23 years of age and a citizen by Birth, of the Cherokee Nation; that I am the lawful wife of Charles J Escoe, who is a citizen, by Birth of the Creek Nation; that a Male child was born to me on the 1 day of October, 1902, that said child has been named Leo Bennett, and is now living.

         her
Dora x Escoe
         mark

WITNESSES TO MARK:
{ W.A. Plummer
{ J. H. McLean

Subscribed and sworn to before me this 14 day of September, 1903.

W.A. Plummer

My Commission expires   NOTARY PUBLIC.
July 3rd 1907

AFFIDAVIT OF ATTENDING PHYSICIAN OR MID-WIFE.

UNITED STATES OF AMERICA,
INDIAN TERRITORY,
Western   District.

I, Dorcas Love, a midwife, on oath state that I attended on Mrs. Dora Escoe, wife of Charles J Escoe on the 1 day of October, 1902; that there was born to her on said date a male child; that said child is now living and is said to have been named Leo Bennett

         her
Dorcas x Love
         mark

Applications for Enrollment of Creek Newborn
Act of 1905   Volume X

WITNESSES TO MARK:
{ W.A. Plummer
{ J. H. McLean

Subscribed and sworn to before me this 14 day of September , 1903.

My Commission expires
July 3rd 1907

W.A. Plummer
NOTARY PUBLIC.

BA-52-53.

DEPARTMENT OF THE INTERIOR,
COMMISSIONER TO THE FIVE CIVILIZED TRIBES.

Muskogee, Indian Territory, April 26, 1905.

In the matter of the application for the enrollment of Elizabeth Francis and Amos Francis as citizens by blood of the Creek Nation.

Annie Francis, being duly sworn, testified as follows:

EXAMINATION BY THE COMMISSION:
Q What is your name? A Annie Francis.
Q How old are you? A 25.
Q What is your postoffice? A Muskogee.
Q You are a citizen of the Creek Nation, are you? A Yes sir.

The witness is identified as Annie Francs, and her name is contained in the partial list of Creek citizens by blood, approved by the Secretary of the Interior, March 28, 1902, Roll No. 8304.

Q Have you a child named Elizabeth Francis? A Yes sir.
Q How old is Elizabeth? A Four years old.
Q Is Elizabeth Francis living? A Yes sir.
Q She is here; is she? A Yes sir.
Q In what year was Elizabeth Francis born? A I don't recollect now.
Q You say you don't recollect? A No sir
Q Have you a child named Amos Francis? A Yes sir.
Q How old is Amos? A About eight years old.
Q Is Amos here with you today? A Yes sir.
Q Is he living? A Yes sir.

Applications for Enrollment of Creek Newborn
Act of 1905   Volume X

Q Who was present with you when Amos Francis was born? A My grandma; she is dead.
Q Who was with you when Elizabeth was born? A Dinah Williams.
Q She is living? A Yes sir.
Q She is here today? A She didn't come today.
Q Does she live in Muskogee? A Yes sir.
Q You filed an affidavit here in January, 1902, and you said in that affidavit that Elizabeth Francis was born on the second day of November, 1899; is that correct? A Yes sir.
Q That ~~don't~~ would make Elizabeth a little more than five years old now; is that right? A Yes sir.
Q Who is the father of Elizabeth and Amos Francis? A William Francis.

William Francis is identified on Creek Indian card, field No. 127, and his name is contained in the partial list of Creek citizens by blood, approved by the Secretary of the Interior March 13, 1902.

The children are present and appear to be about the ages indicated.

INDIAN TERRITORY, Western District.
I, J. Y. Miller, a stenographer to the Commissioner to the Five Civilized Tribes, do hereby certify that the above and foregoing is a true and complete translation of my notes as same appear in my stenographic report of this case.

JY Miller

Sworn to and subscribed before me
this the 29 day of April, 1905.

Zera E Parrish
Notary Public.

N.C. 819

DEPARTMENT OF THE INTERIOR,
COMMISSIONER TO THE FIVE CIVILIZED TRIBES.
MUSKOGEE, Indian Territory, August 30, 1905.

In the matter of the application for the enrollment of Elizabeth Francis as a citizen by blood of the Creek Nation.

Annie Francis being duly sworn testified as follows:

Q What is your name? A Annie Francis.
Q Ever known by any other name? A When I went to school I was known as Annie White

Witness is identified as Annie White on Creek Indian card 3057 opposite roll No. 8304.

Applications for Enrollment of Creek Newborn
Act of 1905   Volume X

Q What is the name of your father? A I dont[sic] know. William McComb could tell you.
Q What was the name of your father? A I dont[sic] know. William McComb knows all about my family
Q You testified before in this case? A Yes, sir
Q When was your child Elizabeth born? A On the second day of November, I couldn't tell you what year but he[sic] will be five years old this November.
Q You are sure of that? A Yes, sir, will be five years old this coming November.

Q You testified before and you said she was over five years, and you also made an affidavit three years ago here and stated Elizabeth was born in 1899, second f November. A I made a mistake about it, he[sic] will be five years old this next November
Q And the midwife Dinah Williams swore that the child was born in November 1901 that would make it four years old? A Yes, sir
Q Now we would like to know whether this child is three, four or five years old--Dinah Williams in her affidavit called the child Lizzie she meant Elizabeth did she? A Yes, sir.
Q Do you think she knows how old the child is? A I don't know whether she would or not, she aint[sic] got good sense. He[sic] is nearly five years old, I know that.
Q When you say "he" you mean Elizabeth? A Yes, sir
Q Is she living? A Yes, sir, she is right here
Q Is Amos living? A Yes
Q He is going on eight? A Yes, sir
Q Is your child Freeland Francis living? A No, dead
Q When did he die? A June 22, 1905
Q What is your post office address? A Muskogee
Q Did you ever have Freeland here in this office? A Yes, sir
Q And you are sure Elizabeth is going on five years old? A Yes, sir

----

I, Anna Garrigues, state that the above and foregoing is a true and correct copy of my stenographic notes as taken in said cause on said date.

                                              Anna Garrigues

Subscribed and sworn to before
me this 30th day of August 1905.

                                              Henry G. Hains
                                              Notary Public.

Applications for Enrollment of Creek Newborn
Act of 1905 Volume X

(The letter below belongs with application for Jesse Simms, NC 813)

N.C. 813

Beggs, I.T.

Commission to the Five Civilized Tribes,
    Muskogee, I.T.

Sir:

    Please give me an information what Bunner Simms must do and how to get his child enrolled who was born March fourth. He has ask me to write and find it and as he could not find it out himself and I also will come and file soon as I can Let me hear from you soon.

    Maxcy Simms

BIRTH AFFIDAVIT.

DEPARTMENT OF THE INTERIOR.
COMMISSION TO THE FIVE CIVILIZED TRIBES.

    IN RE APPLICATION FOR ENROLLMENT, as a citizen of the Creek Nation, of Freeland Francis, born on the 30 day of April, 1903

Name of Father: William Francis	a citizen of the Creek Nation.
Name of Mother: Annie Francis	a citizen of the Creek Nation.

                      Postoffice   *(blank)*

AFFIDAVIT OF MOTHER.

UNITED STATES OF AMERICA, Indian Territory,
    Western   **DISTRICT.**

    I, Annie Francis, on oath state that I am 25 years of age and a citizen by blood, of the Creek Nation; that I am the lawful wife of William Francis (deceased), who is a citizen, by blood of the Creek Nation; that a male child was born to me on 30 day of April, 1903, that said child has been named Freeland Francis, and was living March 4, 1905.

                            her
                       Annie x Francis
Witnesses To Mark: mark
   { Irwin Donovan
     Edward Merrick

    Subscribed and sworn to before me this 26th day of April, 1905.

Applications for Enrollment of Creek Newborn
Act of 1905 Volume X

Edward Merrick
Notary Public.

AFFIDAVIT OF ATTENDING PHYSICIAN OR MID-WIFE.

UNITED STATES OF AMERICA, Indian Territory, }
Western DISTRICT.

I, Dinah Williams , a midwife , on oath state that I attended on Mrs. Annie Francis , wife of William Francis on the 30 day of April , 1903 ; that there was born to her on said date a male child; that said child was living March 4, 1905, and is said to have been named Freeland Francis
                                                        her
                                      Dinah x Williams
Witnesses To Mark: mark
{ Zera E Parrish
  Lona Merrick

Subscribed and sworn to before me 1st day of May, 1905.

Zera E Parrish
Notary Public.

DEPARTMENT OF THE INTERIOR.
COMMISSION TO THE FIVE CIVILIZED TRIBES.

In the matter of the death of Freeland Francis a citizen of the Creek Nation, who formerly resided at or near Muskogee , Ind. Ter., and died on the 22" day of June , 1905

AFFIDAVIT OF RELATIVE.

UNITED STATES OF AMERICA, Indian Territory, }
Western DISTRICT.

I, Annie Francis , on oath state that I am 25 years of age and a citizen by blood , of the Creek Nation; that my postoffice address is Muskogee , Ind. Ter.; that I am the Mother of Freeland Francis who was a citizen, by blood , of the Creek Nation and that said Freeland Francis died on the 22" day of June , 1905
                                        her
                                  Annie x Francis
Witnesses To Mark: mark
{ H.G. Hains
  Jesse McDermott

Applications for Enrollment of Creek Newborn
Act of 1905   Volume X

Subscribed and sworn to before me this 30" day of Aug, 1905.

J McDermott
Notary Public.

B. A. 52.

J.J.B.

Muskogee, Indian Territory, September 29, 1903.

Annie Francis,
Muskogee, Indian Territory.

Dear Madam:

There is on file with the Commission an affidavit executed by you relative to the birth of your minor child, Elizabeth Francis, who, it is claimed, is entitled to enrollment as a citizen of the Creek Nation. It is desired that further testimony be submitted in the case.

You are therefore required to appear before the Commission at its office in Muskogee, Indian Territory, with two witnesses who know the date of the birth of said child, for the purpose of being examined under oath.

Respectfully,

Chairman.

J.J.B.

B. A. 52 & 53

Muskogee, Indian Territory, December 13, 1904.

William Francis,
Muskogee, Indian Territory.

Dear Sir:

There are on file with the Commission affidavits executed by Annie Francis relative to the birth of the minor children, Amos and Elizabeth Francis, who, it is claimed, are entitled to enrollment as citizens of the Creek Nation. It is desired that further evidence be submitted in the case.

Applications for Enrollment of Creek Newborn
Act of 1905   Volume X

You are therefore required to appear before the Commission at its office in Muskogee, Indian Territory, with two witnesses who know the dates of birth of said children, for the purpose of being examined under oath.

                        Respectfully,

                                              Chairman.

NC-819.

                                        Muskogee, Indian Territory, October 19, 1905.

Annie Francis,
    Muskogee, Indian Territory.

Dear Madam:

    In the matter of the application for the enrollment of your minor child, Freeland Francis, as a citizen by blood of the Creek Nation, it is stated in your affidavit that said Freeland Francis was born April 30, 1903, and in the affidavit of Dinah Williams, the midwife who attended at his birth, that he was born April 30, 1904.

    In order to correct this discrepancy there is herewith inclosed a form of birth affidavit which has been partially filled out. You are requested to fill in the correct date of the birth of Freeland Francis and have the same executed, taking care to see that the notary public, before whom said affidavits are executed, affixes both his name and seal to each affidavit. In case any signature is by mark the same must be attested by two disinterested witnesses.

                        Respectfully,

CTD-11   Commissioner.
Env.

N.C. 819.

                                        Muskogee, Indian Territory, December 20, 1905.

Annie Francis,
    Muskogee, Indian Territory.

Dear Madam:

    In the matter of the application for the enrollment of your minor child, Freeland Francis, you state in your affidavit on file in said case that said Freeland Francis was born April 30, 1903 and Dinah Williams who attended at the birth of said child, states he was born April 30, 1904. In order that this discrepancy may be corrected, there is herewith enclosed blank form of birth affidavit; if the date given by you is the correct one, it will be necessary for the midwife to execute a new affidavit. If the date given by Dinah

Applications for Enrollment of Creek Newborn
Act of 1905 Volume X

Williams is correct, it will be necessary for you to execute a new affidavit giving the correct date of the birth of said child.

This matter should be attended to at once and the affidavit returned to this office in the enclosed envelope.

Respectfully,

BA Env.   Commissioner.

BIRTH AFFIDAVIT.

DEPARTMENT OF THE INTERIOR.
COMMISSION TO THE FIVE CIVILIZED TRIBES.

    IN RE APPLICATION FOR ENROLLMENT, as a citizen of the Creek Nation, of Clarence Selvidge, born on the 21 day of August, 1901

Name of Father: R. B. Selvidge   a citizen of the United States Nation.
Name of Mother: Susie Selvidge (nee Tiger)   a citizen of the   Creek   Nation.
  Hillabee Town
                                  Postoffice   Henryetta, Ind. Terr.

AFFIDAVIT OF MOTHER.

                                        Child present.

UNITED STATES OF AMERICA, Indian Territory, ⎫
    Western   DISTRICT.   ⎬

    I, Susie Selvidge, on oath state that I am 23 years of age and a citizen by blood, of the Creek Nation; that I am the lawful wife of R. B. Selvidge, who is a citizen, by *(blank)* of the United States Nation; that a male child was born to me on 21 day of August, 1901, that said child has been named Clarence Selvidge, and was living March 4, 1905.

                                        Susie Selvidge
Witnesses To Mark:
  {

    Subscribed and sworn to before me this 10 day of April, 1905.

                                        Drennan C Skaggs
                                          Notary Public.

Applications for Enrollment of Creek Newborn
Act of 1905 Volume X

AFFIDAVIT OF ATTENDING PHYSICIAN OR MID-WIFE.

UNITED STATES OF AMERICA, Indian Territory,

United States of America)
                               (ss
Western Judicial District)

Dr G.W. West, being duly sworn says he was the attending physician at the birth of a son on the 21st, day of August 1901. That said child was born to Susan Selvidge nee Tiger and is living at this date, and said child is now known Clarence Selvidge.

                               Geo. W. West, M.D.

Subscribed and sworn to before me a Notary Public this _____ day of March 1905. My Commission expires July 8th 1906

                               (Name Illegible)
                               Notary Public.

                                                                                          HGH
                                                                                          E.G.

REFER IN REPLY TO THE FOLLOWING: **DEPARTMENT OF THE INTERIOR,**
NC-821.   **COMMISSIONER TO THE FIVE CIVILIZED TRIBES.**

                                     Muskogee, Indian Territory, October 19, 1905.

Hattie Barnett,
     c/o George Barnett,
          Haskell, Indian Territory.

Dear Madam:

    In the matter of the application for the enrollment of your minor child Clifford Marion Barnett, born October 25, 1902, as a citizen by blood of the Creek Nation, you are advised that this office requires evidence of the marriage between you and George Barnett, the father of said child.

    Such evidence may consist of either the original or a certified copy of your marriage license and certificate.

                                Respectfully,
                                Tams Bixby
                                        Commissioner.

Applications for Enrollment of Creek Newborn
Act of 1905 Volume X

N. C.

Muskogee, Indian Territory, December 15, 1905.

Hattie Barnett,
 Care George Barnett,
  Haskell, Indian Territory.

Dear Madam:

 In the matter of the application for the enrollment of your minor child, Clifford Marion Barnett, born October 25, 1902, as a citizen by blood of the Creek Nation; you are again advised that this office requires evidence of your marriage to George Barnett, the father of said child. Said evidence may consist of either the original or a certified copy of your marriage license and certificate.

    Respectfully,
        Commissioner.

JWH

N C 821

Muskogee, Indian Territory, March 1, 1907.

George Barnett,
 Haskell, Indian Territory.

Dear Sir :--

 You are hereby advised that on February 15, 1907, the Secretary of the Interior approved the enrollment of your minor child, Clifford Marion Barnett, as a citizen by blood of the Creek Nation, and that the name of said child appears upon the roll of New Born citizens by blood of the Creek Nation, enrolled under the Act of Congress approved March 3, 1905, as number 1173.

 This child is now entitled to allotment and application therefor should be made without delay at the Creek Land Office, Muskogee, Indian Territory.

    Respectfully,
        Commissioner.

Applications for Enrollment of Creek Newborn
Act of 1905   Volume X

N C 821

JWH

Muskogee, Indian Territory, March 1, 1907.

Hattie Pruett,
    Coweta, Indian Territory.

Dear Madam :--

    You are hereby advised that on February 15, 1907, the Secretary of the Interior approved the enrollment of Clifford Marion Barnett as a citizen by blood of the Creek Nation, and that the name of said child appears upon the roll of New Born citizens by blood of the Creek Nation, enrolled under the Act of Congress approved March 3, 1905, as number 1173.

    This child is now entitled to allotment and application therefor should be made without delay at the Creek Land Office, Muskogee, Indian Territory.

                  Respectfully,

                              Commissioner.

N C 821

JWH

Muskogee, Indian Territory, March 1, 1907.

A. L. Routh,
    Broken Arrow, Indian Territory.

Dear Sir :--

    You are hereby advised that on February 15, 1907, the Secretary of the Interior approved the enrollment of Clifford Marion Barnett as a citizen by blood of the Creek Nation, and that the name of said child appears upon the roll of New Born citizens by blood of the Creek Nation, enrolled under the Act of Congress approved March 3, 1905, as number 1173.

    This child is now entitled to allotment and application therefor should be made without delay at the Creek Land Office, Muskogee, Indian Territory.

                    Respectfully,

                              Commissioner.

Applications for Enrollment of Creek Newborn
Act of 1905   Volume X

CERTIFICATE OF RECORD.

United States of America,
  INDIAN TERRITORY,   } ss.
  Northern District.

    I, JAMES A. WINSTON, Clerk of the United States Court in the Northern District, Indian Territory, do hereby certify that the instrument hereto attached was filed for record in my office the   2   day of   Oct   1897 at ………. M., and duly recorded in Book   F , Marriage Record, Page   111

                  WITNESS my hand and seal of said Court at Muscogee, in said Territory, this   4   day of   Oct   A. D. 1897

                                            Jas. A. Winston   Clerk.
                  By   Deputy.

MARRIAGE LICENSE

United States of America,
  INDIAN TERRITORY,   } ss.
  Northern District.

To Any Person Authorized by Law to Solemnize Marriage--Greeting:

    You are Hereby Commanded to Solemnize the Rite and publish the Banns of Matrimony between Mr.   Geo. S. Barnett   of   Chaska , in the Indian Territory, aged   20   years and Miss Hattie B. Webber   of   Chaska   in the Indian Territory aged   17   years according to law, and do you officially sign and return this License to the parties therein named.

    WITNESS my hand and official seal at Muscogee Indian Territory this   28"   day of   Sept   A.D. 189 7

                                          J. A. Winston
                                          Clerk of the U.S. Court

By   ------------------   Deputy

Applications for Enrollment of Creek Newborn
Act of 1905   Volume X

CERTIFICATE OF MARRIAGE.

United States of America,
INDIAN TERRITORY,   } ss.
Northern District.

I, J. R. Rowell   , *a Minister of the Gospel, DO HEREBY CERTIFY that on the* 20 *day of* September *A. D.* 1897, *I did duly and according to law as commanded in the foregoing License, solemnize the Rite and publish the Banns of Matrimony between the parties therein named.*

WITNESS my hand this 30 *day of* September   *A. D. 1897*

My credentials are recorded in the office of the Clerk of the United States Court, Indian Territory, Northern District, Book A *, Page* 189   .

J R Rowell
A Minister of the Gospel

Note—This License and Certificate of Marriage must be returned to the Office of the Clerk of the United States Court in the Northern District, Indian Territory, from whence it was issued, within sixty days from the date thereof, or the party to whom the license was issued will be liable in the amount of the One Hundred Dollars ($100.00)

See dup. aff.

BIRTH AFFIDAVIT.

DEPARTMENT OF THE INTERIOR.
COMMISSION TO THE FIVE CIVILIZED TRIBES.

IN RE APPLICATION FOR ENROLLMENT, as a citizen of the Creek Nation, of Clifton Barnett , born ~~on the day of~~ during the year, 1903

Name of Father: George Barnett   a citizen of the   Creek   Nation.
Euchee
Name of Mother: Hattie   "   a citizen of the   U.S.   Nation.
              (white)

Postoffice   Broken Arrow
              Fry

Applications for Enrollment of Creek Newborn
Act of 1905   Volume X

Child now with a Mr. Craig, a white man at Fry
abandoned by parents   AFFIDAVIT OF ~~MOTHER~~.
                                                  (Gregory)   Acquaintance
UNITED STATES OF AMERICA, **Indian Territory,** ⎫
    Western   DISTRICT.   ⎭

I, Noah Gregory , on oath state that I am 44 years of age and a citizen by blood, of the Creek   Nation; that I am ~~the lawful wife of~~ acquainted with George and Hattie Barnett , who ~~is a~~ are citizen s, by blood of the Creek   Nation; that a male child was born to ~~me~~ them ~~on~~ during ~~day of~~ the year , 1903 , that said child has been named Clifton Barnett , and was living March 4, 1905.

             Noah E. Gregory
Witnesses To Mark:
  {

Subscribed and sworn to before me this 1 day of May , 1905.

             Edward C. Griesel.
             Notary Public.

(The above Birth Affidavit given again)

BIRTH AFFIDAVIT.
DEPARTMENT OF THE INTERIOR,
COMMISSION TO THE FIVE CIVILIZED TRIBES.

In Re Application for Enrollment, as a citizen of the Creek Nation, Clifford Marion Barnett , born on the 25" day of October , 1902

Name of Father: George Barnett   a citizen of the   Creek   Nation.
Name of Father: Hattie Barnett   a citizen of the   Creek   Nation.

        Post-office   Haskell, I.T.

AFFIDAVIT OF MOTHER.

UNITED STATES OF AMERICA, ⎫
  INDIAN TERRITORY,   ⎬
 Western   District.   ⎭
                 non
I, Hattie Barnett , on oath state that I am 25 years of age and a ^ citizen by ----- , of the ------- Nation; that I am the lawful wife of George Barnett , who is a

248

Applications for Enrollment of Creek Newborn
Act of 1905 Volume X

citizen, by Indian Roll of the Creek Nation; that a Male child was born to me on 25" day of October , 1902 , that said child has been named Clifford Marion Barnett, and is now living.

(signed) Hattie Barnett

WITNESSES TO MARK:
{ H. L. Wineland
John J. Jefferson Jr

Subscribed and sworn to before me this 29" day of March , 1905.

My Commission Expires   H. L. Wineland
    January 13^{th,} 1907   **NOTARY PUBLIC.**

AFFIDAVIT OF ATTENDING PHYSICIAN OR MID-WIFE.

UNITED STATES OF AMERICA,
    INDIAN TERRITORY,
  Western   District.

    I, Emma Litchlyter , a midwife , on oath state that I attended on Mrs. Hattie Barnett , wife of George Barnett on the 25" day of October , 1902 ; that there was born to her on said date a *(blank)* child; that said child is now living and is said to have been named Clifford Marion Barnett

(signed) Emma Litchlyter

WITNESSES TO MARK:
{ H. L. Wineland
John J. Jefferson Jr

Subscribed and sworn to before me this 29" day of March , 1905.

My Commission Expires   H. L. Wineland
    January 13^{th,} 1907   **NOTARY PUBLIC.**

(The above Birth Affidavit given again.)

Applications for Enrollment of Creek Newborn
Act of 1905   Volume X

BIRTH AFFIDAVIT.

DEPARTMENT OF THE INTERIOR.
COMMISSION TO THE FIVE CIVILIZED TRIBES.

IN RE APPLICATION FOR ENROLLMENT, as a citizen of the Creek Nation, of Kizzie Staley, born on the 6 day of Feb, 1905

Name of Father: John Staley   a citizen of the   Creek   Nation.
(Euchee)
Name of Mother: Sak-co-ta "   a citizen of the   "   Nation.
(Euchee)
                                   Postoffice   Mounds

AFFIDAVIT OF MOTHER.
                                                        Child Present

UNITED STATES OF AMERICA, Indian Territory, ⎫
      Western   DISTRICT.   ⎭

I, Sak-co-ta Staley, on oath state that I am 34 years of age and a citizen by blood, of the Creek Nation; that I am the lawful wife of John Staley, who is a citizen, by blood of the Creek Nation; that a female child was born to me on 6 day of Feb, 1905, that said child has been named Kizzie Staley, and was living March 4, 1905.
                                                her
                              Sak-co-ta x Staley
Witnesses To Mark: mark
  ⎰ David Shelby
  ⎱ Jesse McDermott

Subscribed and sworn to before me this 27 day of April, 1905.

(Seal)   Edw C Griesel
                                         Notary Public.

AFFIDAVIT OF ATTENDING ~~PHYSICIAN~~ OR MID-WIFE.

UNITED STATES OF AMERICA, Indian Territory, ⎫
      Western   DISTRICT.   ⎭

I, Lizzie Tiger, a Midwife, on oath state that I attended on Mrs. Sak-co-ta Staley, wife of John Staley on the 6 day of Feb, 1905; that there was born to her on said date a female child; that said child was living March 4, 1905, and is said to have been named Kizzie Staley
                              Lizzie Tiger
Witnesses To Mark:
  ⎰
  ⎱

Applications for Enrollment of Creek Newborn
Act of 1905 Volume X

Subscribed and sworn to before me this 27 day of April, 1905.

(Seal)
                        Edw C Griesel
                        Notary Public.

BIRTH AFFIDAVIT.

DEPARTMENT OF THE INTERIOR.
COMMISSION TO THE FIVE CIVILIZED TRIBES.

IN RE APPLICATION FOR ENROLLMENT, as a citizen of the Creek Nation, of Kissie Staley, born on the 6th day of February, 1905

Name of Father: John Staley   a citizen of the   Creek   Nation.
Name of Mother: Sa-Co-Ta "   a citizen of the   Creek   Nation.

                    Postoffice   Mounds, Indian Territory.

AFFIDAVIT OF MOTHER.

UNITED STATES OF AMERICA, Indian Territory, }
    Western   DISTRICT.

    I, Sa-Co-Ta Staley, on oath state that I am Thirty four years of age and a citizen by blood, of the Creek Nation; that I am the lawful wife of John Staley, who is a citizen, by blood of the Creek Nation; that a female child was born to me on Sixth day of February, 1905, that said child has been named Kissie Staley, and was living March 4, 1905.

                                her
                          Sa-co-ta x Staley
Witnesses To Mark: mark
{ Stand Waity Tiger
  D J Red

Subscribed and sworn to before me this 8th day of April, 1905.

                        D J Red
                        Notary Public.

AFFIDAVIT OF ATTENDING PHYSICIAN OR MID-WIFE.

UNITED STATES OF AMERICA, Indian Territory, }
    Western   DISTRICT.

    I, Lizzie Thomas Tiger, a *(blank)*, on oath state that I attended on Mrs. Sa-Co-Ta Staley, wife of John Staley on the Sixth day of February, 1905; that there

Applications for Enrollment of Creek Newborn
Act of 1905   Volume X

was born to her on said date a female child; that said child was living March 4, 1905, and is said to have been named Kissie Staley

Lizzie Thomas Tiger

Witnesses To Mark:
{

Subscribed and sworn to before me this 8th day of April, 1905.

D J Red
Notary Public.

BIRTH AFFIDAVIT.

DEPARTMENT OF THE INTERIOR.
COMMISSION TO THE FIVE CIVILIZED TRIBES.

IN RE APPLICATION FOR ENROLLMENT, as a citizen of the Creek Nation, of Nellie Staley, born on the 4 day of Nov, 1902

Name of Father: John Staley   a citizen of the   Creek   Nation.
Euchee
Name of Mother: Sak-co-ta "   a citizen of the   "   Nation.
(Euchee)

Postoffice   Mounds

AFFIDAVIT OF MOTHER.

Child Present

UNITED STATES OF AMERICA, Indian Territory, }
       Western   DISTRICT.

I, Sak-co-ta Staley, on oath state that I am 34 years of age and a citizen by blood, of the Creek Nation; that I am the lawful wife of John Staley, who is a citizen, by blood of the Creek Nation; that a female child was born to me on 4 day of Nov, 1902, that said child has been named Nellie Staley, and was living March 4, 1905.

                                                               her
                                     Sa-co-ta x Staley

Witnesses To Mark: mark
{ David Shelby
{ Jesse McDermott

Subscribed and sworn to before me this 27 day of April, 1905.

(Seal)   Edw C Griesel
                                Notary Public.

Applications for Enrollment of Creek Newborn
Act of 1905 Volume X

AFFIDAVIT OF ATTENDING PHYSICIAN OR MID-WIFE.

UNITED STATES OF AMERICA, Indian Territory, }
    Western   DISTRICT.

    I, Lizzie Tiger , a Mid wife , on oath state that I attended on Mrs. Sak-co-ta Staley , wife of John Staley on the 4 day of Nov , 1902 ; that there was born to her on said date a female child; that said child was living March 4, 1905, and is said to have been named Nellie Staley

                                    Lizzie Tiger

Witnesses To Mark:
{

    Subscribed and sworn to before me this 27 day of April , 1905.

(Seal)   Edw C Griesel
                                        Notary Public.

BIRTH AFFIDAVIT.

DEPARTMENT OF THE INTERIOR.
COMMISSION TO THE FIVE CIVILIZED TRIBES.

    IN RE APPLICATION FOR ENROLLMENT, as a citizen of the Creek Nation, of Nellie Staley, born on the 4th day of November , 1902

Name of Father: John Staley   a citizen of the   Creek   Nation.
Name of Mother: Sa-Co-Ta Staley   a citizen of the   Creek   Nation.

                        Postoffice   Mounds, Indian Territory.

AFFIDAVIT OF MOTHER.

UNITED STATES OF AMERICA, Indian Territory, }
    Western   DISTRICT.

    I, Sa-Co-Ta Staley , on oath state that I am Thirty four years of age and a citizen by blood , of the Creek Nation; that I am the lawful wife of John Staley , who is a citizen, by blood of the Creek Nation; that a female child was born to me on 4th day of November , 1902 , that said child has been named Nellie Staley , and was living March 4, 1905.

                                            her
                                  Sa-co-ta x Staley

Witnesses To Mark: mark
{ Stand Waity Tiger
  D J Red

Applications for Enrollment of Creek Newborn
Act of 1905   Volume X

Subscribed and sworn to before me this 8th day of April, 1905.

D J Red
Notary Public.

AFFIDAVIT OF ATTENDING PHYSICIAN OR MID-WIFE.

UNITED STATES OF AMERICA, Indian Territory, }
    Western   DISTRICT.

I, Lizzie Thomas Tiger, a *(blank)*, on oath state that I attended on Mrs. Sa-Co-Ta Staley, wife of John Staley on the 4th day of November, 1902; that there was born to her on said date a female child; that said child was living March 4, 1905, and is said to have been named Nellie Staley

Lizzie Thomas Tiger

Witnesses To Mark:
{

Subscribed and sworn to before me this 8th day of April, 1905.

D J Red
Notary Public.

NC-822.

Muskogee, Indian Territory, October 19, 1905.

Sak-co-ta Staley,
    c/o John Staley,
        Mounds, Indian Territory.

Dear Madam:

In the matter of the application for the enrollment of your minor child, born February 6, 1905, as a citizen by blood of the Creek Nation, the given name of said child is spelled in your affidavit of April 8, 1905 Kissie, and in your affidavit of April 27, 1905 the name of said child is spelled Kizzie.

You are requested to advise this office, at an early date, as to which of the above names is the correct name of said child.

Respectfully,

Commissioner.

Applications for Enrollment of Creek Newborn
Act of 1905   Volume X

OFFICE OF

Real Estate
Insurance...

D. J. RED.

Farm Loans and
Conveyancing.....

Mounds, I. T.   July 7th,   *190* 6

Hon. Tams Bixby, Commissioner,
        Muskogee, I. T.

Dear Sir :

    Replying to your favor of the 28th of June last in which you say " You are again advised that there were filed in this office " affidavits of the mother of said child and the midwife, in which " affidavits the name of the child is spelled " Kissie" and "Kizzie " Staley, and this office desires to know which, if either, of said " names is correctly spelled " I desire tos ay the name if spelled Kissie. This in reference to the enrolling of the child of Sak-co-ta Staley as a citizen of the Creek Nation.
Should it be necessary to file additional affidavits or proof, kindly inform me of the fact and I will comply with your requirement.

                                            Very respectfully,

                            John Staley

                    By S.W. Tiger

BIRTH AFFIDAVIT.

DEPARTMENT OF THE INTERIOR,
COMMISSION TO THE FIVE CIVILIZED TRIBES.

IN RE Application for Enrollment, as a citizen of the Creek Nation, of   Joseph A. Hengst, born on the 6th. day of   December , 1901

Name of Father: William C. Hengst,   a citizen of the non-citizen   Nation.
Name of Mother: Emma J. Hengst,   a citizen of the   Creek   Nation.
  (Cussehta)

                        Post-office: Sapulpa, I.T.

Applications for Enrollment of Creek Newborn
Act of 1905   Volume X

AFFIDAVIT OF MOTHER.

Child Brought in
5/25/05 - Gr

UNITED STATES OF AMERICA, ⎫
INDIAN TERRITORY. ⎬
Western- - - - - - - - District. ⎭

    I, Emma J. Hengst, - - - - - - - - - , on oath state that I am ---35----- years of age and a citizen by blood------- , of the Creek - - - - - - - -- Nation; that I am the lawful wife of William C. Hengst,- - - - - - - - , who is a citizen, by a non-citizen- of the Creek - - - - - Nation; that a male child was born to me on 6th.--- day of December, A.D.1901.- -1-- , that said child has been named Joseph A. Hengst,- - - - - - - - - , and is now living.

                                              Emma J. Hengst

WITNESSES TO MARK:

    Subscribed and sworn to before me this 14th. day of   March,A.D. , 1905.

        My commission expires May 7, 1908.   James J. Mars
                                                    NOTARY PUBLIC.

AFFIDAVIT OF ATTENDING PHYSICIAN OR MID-WIFE.

UNITED STATES OF AMERICA, ⎫
INDIAN TERRITORY. ⎬
Western- - - -   District. ⎭

    I, Mrs. Cathren Wall, - - - - - - - - - , a Midwife, - - - - , on oath state that I attended on Mrs. Emma J. Hengst, - - - - -- , wife of William C. Hengst, - - - - - on the 6th.- - day of December, A.D.1901.- - - - , 1- -- ; that there was born to her on said date a male - - - - - - child; that said child is now living and is said to have been named Joseph A. Hengst, - - - - - - - -

                                            her
                                   Cathren x Wall

WITNESSES TO MARK: mark
    Lucy J Speer
    William C. Hengst

    Subscribed and sworn to before me this 14th. day of   March,A.D. , 1905.

        My commission expires May 7, 1908.   James J. Mars
                                                    NOTARY PUBLIC.

Applications for Enrollment of Creek Newborn
Act of 1905   Volume X

BIRTH AFFIDAVIT.

DEPARTMENT OF THE INTERIOR,
COMMISSION TO THE FIVE CIVILIZED TRIBES.

IN RE Application for Enrollment, as a citizen of the ------------Creek---------Nation, of Charles A. Hengst.-------- born on the 23rd. day of September,----- , 1904

Name of Father: William C. Hengst,--------------- a citizen of the non-citizen---- Nation.
Name of Mother: Emma J. Hengst,---------------- a citizen of the Creek-----------Nation.
(Cussehta)
Post-office: Sapulpa, I.T.-------------------------

AFFIDAVIT OF MOTHER.
Child Brought in
5/25/05 - Gr

UNITED STATES OF AMERICA,
    INDIAN TERRITORY.
-------Western---------District.

I, Emma J. Hengst, - - - - - - - - - , on oath state that I am ---35--------- years of age and a citizen by ------blood-------- , of the ----------Creek - - - - - - - -- Nation; that I am the lawful wife of William C. Hengst,- - - - - - - - - , who is a citizen, by a non-citizen--- of the ----Creek - - - - - Nation; that a male----- child was born to me on ---23rd.--- day of September, -----------1904 , that said child has been named Charles Augustus Hengst,- - - - - - - - - , and is now living.

Emma J. Hengst

WITNESSES TO MARK:
{

Subscribed and sworn to before me this --14th.-- *day of* March,-A.D.------------ , 1905.

My commission expires July 11, 1906.   F. L. Mars
NOTARY PUBLIC.

AFFIDAVIT OF ATTENDING PHYSICIAN OR MID-WIFE.

UNITED STATES OF AMERICA,
    INDIAN TERRITORY.
----Western-----------District.

I, Mrs. Lucy J. Speer,------------- , a midwife---------, on oath state that I attended on Mrs. Emma J. Hengst, ----------, wife of William C. Hengst, -------- on the -23rd.-- day of September, A. D.-------- , 1904 ; that there was born to her on said date a------ male ---------- child; that said child is now living and is said to have been named Charles Augustus Hengst, ------------

Lucy J Speer

Applications for Enrollment of Creek Newborn
Act of 1905   Volume X

WITNESSES TO MARK:
{

Subscribed and sworn to before me this 14th. day of   March, A. D.------------, 1905.

My commission expires July 11, 1906.   F. L. Mars
                                                                           NOTARY PUBLIC.

BIRTH AFFIDAVIT.

DEPARTMENT OF THE INTERIOR.
COMMISSION TO THE FIVE CIVILIZED TRIBES.

IN RE APPLICATION FOR ENROLLMENT, as a citizen of the Creek Nation, of Porter Tiger, born on the 21st day of August, 1902

Name of Father: Stand Waity Tiger   a citizen of the   Creek   Nation.
Name of Mother: Lizzie Thomas Tiger   a citizen of the   Creek   Nation.

Postoffice   Mounds, Indian Territory

AFFIDAVIT OF MOTHER.

UNITED STATES OF AMERICA, Indian Territory, }
   Western   DISTRICT.

I, Lizzie Thomas Tiger, on oath state that I am twenty four years of age and a citizen by blood, of the Creek Nation; that I am the lawful wife of Stand Waity Tiger, who is a citizen, by blood of the Creek Nation; that a male child was born to me on 21st day of August, 1902, that said child has been named Porter Tiger, and was living March 4, 1905.

                                             Lizzie Thomas Tiger
Witnesses To Mark:
{

Subscribed and sworn to before me this 8th day of April, 1905.

                                             D J Red
                                                   Notary Public.

258

Applications for Enrollment of Creek Newborn
Act of 1905 Volume X

AFFIDAVIT OF ATTENDING PHYSICIAN OR MID-WIFE.

UNITED STATES OF AMERICA, Indian Territory,
Western DISTRICT.

I, Sa-Co-Ta Staley, a *(blank)*, on oath state that I attended on Mrs. Lizzie Thomas Tiger, wife of Stand Waity Tiger on the 21st day of August, 1902 ; that there was born to her on said date a male child; that said child was living March 4, 1905, and is said to have been named Porter Tiger

            her
         Sa-Co-ta x Staley
Witnesses To Mark: mark
 { DJ Red
  Stand Waity Tiger

Subscribed and sworn to before me 8th day of April, 1905.

        D. J. Red
         Notary Public.

BIRTH AFFIDAVIT.
DEPARTMENT OF THE INTERIOR.
COMMISSION TO THE FIVE CIVILIZED TRIBES.

IN RE APPLICATION FOR ENROLLMENT, as a citizen of the Creek Nation, of Porter Tiger, born on the 21 day of Aug, 1902

Name of Father: Stanwaitie Tiger   a citizen of the   Creek   Nation.
(Euchee)
Name of Mother: Lizzie Tiger nee Thomas   a citizen of the   Creek   Nation.
(Euchee)
        Postoffice   Mounds

AFFIDAVIT OF MOTHER.
          Child Present
UNITED STATES OF AMERICA, Indian Territory,
Western DISTRICT.

I, Lizzie Tiger, on oath state that I am 24 years of age and a citizen by blood, of the Creek Nation; that I am the lawful wife of Stanwaitie Tiger, who is a citizen, by blood of the Creek Nation; that a male child was born to me on 21 day of Aug, 1902, that said child has been named Porter Tiger, and was living March 4, 1905.

        Lizzie Tiger
Witnesses To Mark:
 {

Applications for Enrollment of Creek Newborn
Act of 1905 Volume X

Subscribed and sworn to before me this 27 day of April, 1905.

(Seal)   Edw C Griesel
                                   Notary Public.

AFFIDAVIT OF ATTENDING PHYSICIAN OR MID-WIFE.

UNITED STATES OF AMERICA, Indian Territory, ⎫
     Western   DISTRICT.   ⎭

I, Sak-co-ta Staley, a Midwife, on oath state that I attended on Mrs. Lizzie Tiger, wife of Stanwaitie Tiger on the 21 day of Aug, 1902; that there was born to her on said date a male child; that said child was living March 4, 1905, and is said to have been named Porter Tiger

                                           her
                              Sak-co-ta Staley x
Witnesses To Mark: mark
  ⎰ David Shelby
  ⎱ Jesse McDermott

Subscribed and sworn to before me this 27 day of April, 1905.

(Seal)   Edw C Griesel
                                   Notary Public.

BIRTH AFFIDAVIT.

DEPARTMENT OF THE INTERIOR.
COMMISSION TO THE FIVE CIVILIZED TRIBES.

IN RE APPLICATION FOR ENROLLMENT, as a citizen of the Creek Nation, of Fletcher Raymond Gregory, born on the 22^d day of July, 1903

Name of Father: Noah Gregory   a citizen of the   Creek   Nation.
Euchee
Name of Mother: Carrie Gregory   a citizen of the   Creek   Nation.
Euchee
                            Postoffice   Sapulpa I.T.

Applications for Enrollment of Creek Newborn
Act of 1905 Volume X

AFFIDAVIT OF MOTHER.

UNITED STATES OF AMERICA, Indian Territory, ⎱
    Western   DISTRICT.   ⎰

    I, Carrie Gregory , on oath state that I am 37 years of age and a citizen by blood , of the Creek Nation; that I am the lawful wife of Noah Gregory , who is a citizen, by blood of the Creek Nation; that a male child was born to me on 22^d day of July , 1903 , that said child has been named Fletcher Raymond Gregory , and was living March 4, 1905.

                                                Carrie Gregory

Witnesses To Mark:
{

    Subscribed and sworn to before me this 25 day of April , 1905.

                                                J McDermott
                                                     Notary Public.

AFFIDAVIT OF ATTENDING PHYSICIAN OR MID-WIFE.

UNITED STATES OF AMERICA, Indian Territory, ⎱
    Western   DISTRICT.   ⎰

    I, Mat H Morrow , a midwife , on oath state that I attended on Mrs. Carrie Gregory , wife of Noah Gregory on the 22 day of July , 1903 ; that there was born to her on said date a male child; that said child was living March 4, 1905, and is said to have been named Fletcher Raymond Gregory

                                                her
                                          Mat H x Morrow
Witnesses To Mark: mark
   { David Shelby
     ECGriesel

Subscribed and sworn to before me 22^d day of April, 1905.

                                                J McDermott
                                                Notary Public.

Applications for Enrollment of Creek Newborn
Act of 1905 Volume X

J.D.

DEPARTMENT OF THE INTERIOR,
COMMISSIONER TO THE FIVE CIVILIZED TRIBES.

In the matter of the application for the enrollment of Josephine (Posey) Boston as a citizen by blood of the Creek Nation.

DECISION.

The record in this case shows that on May 5, 1903, Josephine (Posey) Boston appeared before the Commission to the Five Civilized Tribes at Muskogee, Indian Territory, and made application for the enrollment of herself, her adult daughter, Lizzie Perkins, her minor children, Ella Boston and Don Boston and her minor grandchild Muggy Perkins as citizens by blood of the Creek Nation; that on July 13, 1903 said Commission rendered a decision denying said application, and that on September 28, 1903, the Department affirmed said decision.

The record further shows that on June 20, 1905, the Department, on motion of the attorneys for the applicants, rescinded its action of September 28, 1903 and remanded the record in the case for a readjudication[sic] upon its merits after a hearing had to determine whether the name of Joseph Bosey, appearing upon the 1890 authenticated tribal roll of the Creek Nation, was identical with Josephine (Posey) Boston, the principal applicant herein, and if found that she is identical with said Joseph Bosey, to determine whether or not said applicant ha, since said enrollment, expatriated herself from the Creek Nation.

By agreement of the parties in interest a hearing was had in the case July 8, 1905. Further proceedings were had July 10, July 12, July 14, August 1, August 2, August 9, and August 11, 1905.

All the applicants herein claim their right to enrollment as citizens by blood of the Creek Nation blood of the Creek Nation through the principal applicant, said Josephine (Posey) Boston. Said Josephine (Posey) Boston claims that the name Joseph Bosey which appears upon the 1890 authenticated tribal roll of the Creek Nation was intended for her maiden name, Josephine Posey. Said applicant also claims to have been admitted to citizenship in the Creek Nation by the National Council of said nation.

The evidence shows that the name Bosey on said 1890 roll was intended for the name Posey, and no witness could be found who was acquainted with or who had ever heard of a person named Joseph Posey. Many of the witnesses, in reply to hypothetical questions, testified that the name Joseph might have been written when it was the intention of the person placing the name on the roll to write Josie or Josephine. There is also much evidence purporting to corroborate or verify the supposition that the name Joseph was intended for Josephine. It appears from the testimony of several of the witnesses that at the time the principal applicant herein attempted to have her name placed upon the Creek roll, one Joe Mingo was the king of Broken Arrow town, to which town said applicant claims to belong; that Mrs. Boston had presented to him her claim to citizenship in the Creek Nation and that he had promised to place her name on the roll; that he subsequently told several persons that he had placed her name on the roll; that he was uneducated, that he wrote and spelled very poorly, if at all, and that he might have written or caused to be written, the name Joseph because of his unfamiliarity with the

Applications for Enrollment of Creek Newborn
Act of 1905   Volume X

name Josephine. The testimony on this point further shows, however, that all the conversations or dealings with Joe Mingo, to which the testimony relates occurred during the years 1894 to 1896 inclusive, or from four to six years subsequent to the date of the 1890 roll on which the name Joseph Bosey appears. No testimony was submitted to the effect that the applicant ever made an attempt, prior to 1890, to have her name placed upon the Creek roll.

The name Joseph Bosey appears upon the 1890 roll in the family of one T. B. Posey, whose surname, together with the surnames of all the family, is spelled thereon Bosey. Walter Posey and John M. Posey whose names appear in the same family testified that they had never heard of the applicant before they were summoned to give testimony in this case. James Posey, a member of the same family, testified that he had never heard of the applicant before. James Posey also testified that money was drawn for him at the 1890 payment. Mrs. Eliza Allen Posey at the 1890 payment; that she had never heard of the applicant in this case and that she drew money at that payment for James Posey when she drew for the balance of the family. The name James Posey does not appear on the 1890 roll. There is his own testimony and the testimony of his brothers that he received the money and of Mrs. Eliza Allen that she drew it for him. The enrollment of Walter, James and John M. Posey does not depend on their names appearing on the 1890 roll (their right to citizenship have been questioned subsequent to that time they were admitted by the Commission to the Five Civilized Tribes under the act of Congress June 10, 1890 (29 Stats., 321) and their testimony may be presumed to be disinterested. The applicant does not claim to have received the 1890 payment. It is, therefore, certainly more reasonable to assume that the name Joseph resulted from an error in transcribing the abbreviation Jas. as Jos. then writing it in full from the latter abbreviation; Joseph, than it is to assume that the name Joseph was intended for a person named Josephine, who makes no claim to having received the payment nor to having taken steps to have her name placed on the roll until from four to six years after the roll was made.

George Tiger and Temiye Kernals, both members of the House of Kings, or upper house, of the Creek National Council, during the period when Mrs. Boston claims to have been making efforts to have her name placed on the Creek rolls, testify that she was admitted to citizenship by the council. Legus Perryman, who was principal chief, at the time, has no recollection of her alleged admission. The minutes of the House of Kings for the years 1894 to 1896 inclusive show that no application for the admission of the applicant herein to citizenship in the Creek Nation was considered by that house during the period within which her application is allege to have been made; nor was any resolution introduced nor any action taken in said house in any manner relating to said Josephine (Posey) Boston or to her claim to citizenship in the Creek Nation.

George Tiger also states that after the Supreme Court of the nation declared what was known as the Alien Act unconstitutional he, as acting chairman of the Colbert Commission, notified Mrs. Boston, who, he states, had already presented her evidence to that Commission, to appear and receive a certificate of admission. The records of the Supreme Court of the Creek Nation show that said court never rendered a decision that the Alien Act was unconstitutional, but that, on the contrary, in response to a communication from the chairman of the Colbert Commission, it rendered an opinion that said Alien Act was not unconstitutional. The Colbert Commission kept during its existence a complete record of its proceedings. The record contains copies of all

Applications for Enrollment of Creek Newborn
Act of 1905   Volume X

applications made to said commission, of the testimony offered in support of same, and of the judgments rendered in the cases heard by it. This record, which is in the possession of this office, has been carefully examined and it appears therefrom that no application was received, no testimony taken ad no judgment rendered in the case of Josephine (Posey) Boston.

It appears, then, from the weight of the evidence in the case that the applicant, Josephine (Posey) Boston, is not identical with the Joseph Bosey whose name appears upon the 1890 roll, that she has never been enrolled as a citizen of the Creek Nation, nor has she ever been admitted to citizenship in said nation by the Creek tribal authorities, the Commission to the Five Civilized Tribes or the United States Court in Indian Territory.

If further appears from the evidence in the case that the applicants, Ella Boston, Don Boston and Lizzie Perkins are the children and that Muggy Perkins is the Grandchild of said Josephine (Posey) Boston; and that no claim is made that said children and grandchild, or any of them, have any right to citizenship in the Creek Nation except such as they may derive by reason of being descendants of said Josephine (Posey) Boston; that said Muggy Perkins was born subsequent to May 25, 1902 and that he is not the child of a citizen of the Creek Nation whose enrollment has been approved by the Secretary of the Interior prior to March 3, 1905; and that none of the applicants are full blood Creek Indians.

It is, therefore, ordered and adjudged that there is no authority of law for the enrollment of said Josephine (Posey) Boston, Ella Boston, Don Boston, Lizzie Perkins and Muggy Perkins, or any of them, as citizens by blood of the Creek Nation blood of the Creek Nation, and the application for their enrollment as such is accordingly denied.

Tams Bixby   Commissioner.

Muskogee, Indian Territory.
OCT 2 - 1905

NC-827.

Muskogee, Indian Territory, October 19, 1905.

Hardin Brown,
   c/o Larry Brown,
      Olive, Indian Territory.

Dear Madam:

In the matter of the application for the enrollment of your minor child, Georgia Brown, born February 13, 1903, as a citizen by blood of the Creek Nation, this office

Applications for Enrollment of Creek Newborn
Act of 1905 Volume X

requires the affidavit of the physician or midwife who attended on you when said child was born and a blank for that purpose is inclosed herewith.

If there was no physician or midwife present when said Georgia Brown was born it will be necessary for you to furnish this office with the affidavits of two disinterested persons relative to the birth of said child. Said affidavits must set forth said child's name, the date of her birth, the names of her parents, and whether or not she was living on March 4, 1905.

                Respectfully,

                                        Commissioner.

B C
Env.

United States of America ⎫
Western District Ind Terry ⎬ ss.

Personally appeared before me L. S. Holcomb a notary public Big Mosquito Who on oath states that he is 56 years of age and is acquainted with Hardin Brown wife of Larry Brown and that he was present on or about the 13th day of February 1903 when a Girl child was born to her and that said child has been named Georgia Brown and was living on the 4th day of March 1905
                                        his
                                     Big x Mosquito

Witness to mark   mark
A H *(Illegible)*
J W Warlick

Subscribed and sworn to before me this the 20th day of Nov. 1905

                                  L.S. Holcomb
                                        Notary Public

My Com. Ex June 27, 1905[sic].

United States of America ⎫
Western District Ind Terry ⎬ ss.

Personally appeared before me L. S. Holcomb a notary public Jency Mosquito Who on oath states that she is 28 years of age and that she is acquainted with Hardin Brown wife of Larry Brown and that she was present on or about the 13th day of February 1903 when a girl child was born to her and that said child has been named Georgia Brown and was living on the 4th day of March 1905
                                        his
                                     Jency x Mosquito

Witness to mark   mark
A H *(Illegible)*
J W Warlick

Applications for Enrollment of Creek Newborn
Act of 1905   Volume X

Subscribed and sworn to before me this the 20th day of Nov. 1905

                                         L.S. Holcomb
                                         Notary Public

My Com. Ex June 27, 1908.

BIRTH AFFIDAVIT.

DEPARTMENT OF THE INTERIOR.
COMMISSION TO THE FIVE CIVILIZED TRIBES.

IN RE APPLICATION FOR ENROLLMENT, as a citizen of the Creek Nation, of Georgia Brown, born on the 13 day of Feb , 1903

Name of Father: Larry Brown   a citizen of the   Creek   Nation.
Name of Mother: Hardin Brown   a citizen of the   Creek   Nation.

                        Postoffice   Olive I.T.

AFFIDAVIT OF MOTHER.

UNITED STATES OF AMERICA, Indian Territory,
    Western   **DISTRICT.**

       I, Hardin Brown , on oath state that I am 32 years of age and a citizen by Blood, of the Creek Nation; that I am the lawful wife of Larry Brown , who is a citizen, by Blood of the Creek Nation; that a Female child was born to me on 13th day of February , 1903 , that said child has been named Georgia Brown , and is now living.

                                                          her
                                       Hardin x Brown
                                             mark

Witnesses To Mark:
   { L. C. Holcomb
     G.G. Holcomb

      Subscribed and sworn to before me this 24th day of April , 1905.

                                     L. S. Holcomb
                                     Notary Public.

Applications for Enrollment of Creek Newborn
Act of 1905   Volume X

AFFIDAVIT OF ATTENDING PHYSICIAN OR MID-WIFE.

UNITED STATES OF AMERICA, Indian Territory, ⎫
    Western   DISTRICT.   ⎬
                                           ⎭

I, Larry Brown , a *(illegible)* , on oath state that I attended on Mrs. Hardin Brown , wife of Larry Brown on the 13th day of Feb. , 1903 ; that there was born to her on said date a Female child; that said child is now living and is said to have been named Georgia Brown

                                            Larry Brown

Witnesses To Mark:
  ⎰ L. C. Holcomb
  ⎱ G.G. Holcomb

Subscribed and sworn to before me this 24$^{\underline{th}}$ day of April , 1905.

                                          L. S. Holcomb
                                              Notary Public.

NC-828.

                                    Muskogee, Indian Territory, October 19, 1905.

Lucinda Pitman[sic],
    Sapulpa, Indian Territory.

Dear Madam:

    In the matter of the application for the enrollment of your minor child, Robert Pitman, Jr., born August 8, 1902, as a citizen by blood of the Creek Nation, this office requires the affidavit of the physician or midwife who attended on you when said child was born and a blank for that purpose is inclosed herewith.

    If there was no physician or midwife present when said Robert Pitman was born it will be necessary for you to furnish this office with the affidavits of two disinterested persons relative to the birth of said child. Said affidavits must set forth said child's name, the date of his birth, the names of his parents and whether or not he was living on March 4, 1905.

                                Respectfully,
                                                       Commissioner.

B C
Env.

Applications for Enrollment of Creek Newborn
Act of 1905 Volume X

BIRTH AFFIDAVIT.

DEPARTMENT OF THE INTERIOR.
COMMISSION TO THE FIVE CIVILIZED TRIBES.

IN RE APPLICATION FOR ENROLLMENT, as a citizen of the Creek Nation, of Robert Pittman, Jr., born on the 8 day of August, 1902

Name of Father: Robert Pittman	a citizen of the Creek	Nation.
Name of Mother: Lucinda Pittman	a citizen of the Creek	Nation.

Postoffice Sapulpa I.T.

AFFIDAVIT OF MOTHER.

UNITED STATES OF AMERICA, Indian Territory,
Western DISTRICT.

I, Lucinda Pitman, on oath state that I am 37 years of age and a citizen by Birth, of the Creek Nation; that I am the lawful wife of Robert Pitman, who is a citizen, by residence of the Creek Nation; that a male child was born to me on 8" day of August, 1902, that said child has been named Robert Pitman, Jr., and is now living.   her
                                         Lucinda x Pitman
Witnesses To Mark: mark
  Clue W. Weeks
  C.A. Vaughn

Subscribed and sworn to before me this 25 day of ~~August~~ October, 1905.

John W. Weeks
Notary Public.

My Commission Expires July 8th. 1906.

AFFIDAVIT OF ATTENDING PHYSICIAN OR MID-WIFE.

UNITED STATES OF AMERICA, Indian Territory,
Western District DISTRICT.

I, Matilda Pitman, a Midwife, on oath state that I attended on Mrs. Lucinda Pitman, wife of Robert Pitman on the 8 day of August, 1902; that there was born to her on said date a Male child; that said child is now living and is said to have been named Robert Pitman Jr.

Matilda Pitman

Applications for Enrollment of Creek Newborn
Act of 1905   Volume X

Witnesses To Mark:
{

    Subscribed and sworn to before me this   25 day of   ~~August~~   October , 1905.

John W. Weeks
Notary Public.

My Commission Expires July 8th. 1906.

BIRTH AFFIDAVIT.

DEPARTMENT OF THE INTERIOR.
COMMISSION TO THE FIVE CIVILIZED TRIBES.

IN RE APPLICATION FOR ENROLLMENT, as a citizen of the Creek Nation, of Robert Pitman, Jr. , born on the 8 day of August , 1902

Name of Father: Robert Pitman   a citizen of the United States ~~Nation~~.
Name of Mother: Lucinda Pitman   a citizen of the   Creek   Nation.
(Hickory Ground)

                Postoffice   Sapulpa I.T.

AFFIDAVIT OF MOTHER.

Child Present

UNITED STATES OF AMERICA, Indian Territory, }
    Western   DISTRICT.

    I, Lucinda Pitman , on oath state that I am 33   years of age and a citizen by blood , of the   Creek   Nation; that I am the lawful wife of Robert Pitman , who is a citizen, by ----- of the United Stated ~~Nation~~; that a male child was born to me on 8 day of August, 1902 , that said child has been named Robert Pitman Jr , and was living March 4, 1905.

her
Lucinda x Pitman
mark

Witnesses To Mark:
{ David Shelby
  Jesse McDermott
    Subscribed and sworn to before me this 25 day of April , 1905.

(Seal)   Edw C Griesel
Notary Public.

Applications for Enrollment of Creek Newborn
Act of 1905   Volume X

father
AFFIDAVIT OF ~~ATTENDING PHYSICIAN OR MID-WIFE~~.

UNITED STATES OF AMERICA, Indian Territory, ⎫
    Western   DISTRICT.   ⎬

I, Robert Pitman, ~~a~~——, on oath state that I attended on Mrs. Lucinda Pitman my wife of —— on the 8 day of August , 1902 ; that there was born to her on said date a male child; that said child was living March 4, 1905, and is said to have been named Robert Pitman Jr

                                    his
                           Robert x Pitman

Witnesses To Mark: mark
  ⎧ David Shelby
  ⎩ Jesse McDermott
Subscribed and sworn to before me this 25 day of April , 1905.

(Seal)   Edw C Griesel
                              Notary Public.

BIRTH AFFIDAVIT.

DEPARTMENT OF THE INTERIOR.
COMMISSION TO THE FIVE CIVILIZED TRIBES.

IN RE APPLICATION FOR ENROLLMENT, as a citizen of the Creek Nation, of Lula Mildred Morrison , born on the 17 day of August , 1902

Name of Father: Manny Morrison   a citizen of the   Creek   Nation.
  Coweta Town
Name of Mother: Julia Morrison   a citizen of the United States Nation.

                     Postoffice   Lenna, Ind. Terr.

AFFIDAVIT OF MOTHER.
                                    Child present
UNITED STATES OF AMERICA, Indian Territory, ⎫
    Western   DISTRICT.   ⎬

I, Julia Morrison , on oath state that I am 20 years of age and a citizen ~~by~~ (blank) , of the United States Nation; that I am the lawful wife of Manny Morrison , who is a citizen, by blood of the Creek Nation; that a female child was born to me

Applications for Enrollment of Creek Newborn
Act of 1905   Volume X

on 17 day of August, 1902, that said child has been named Lula Mildred Morrison, and was living March 4, 1905.

Julia Morrison

Witnesses To Mark:
{

Subscribed and sworn to before me this 4 day of April, 1905.

Drennan C Skaggs
Notary Public.

AFFIDAVIT OF ATTENDING PHYSICIAN OR MID-WIFE.

UNITED STATES OF AMERICA, Indian Territory, ⎫
       Western   DISTRICT.   ⎬
                                             ⎭

I, W P Jones, a Witness, on oath state that I attended on Mrs. Julia Morrison, wife of Manny Morrison on the 17 day of August, 1902; that there was born to her on said date a female child; that said child was living March 4, 1905, and is said to have been named Lula Mildred Morrison

W. P. Jones

Witnesses To Mark:
{   My Commission Expires July 20, 1907.

Subscribed and sworn to before me 6ᵗʰ day of April, 1905.

Henry A McDaniel
Notary Public.

BIRTH AFFIDAVIT.

DEPARTMENT OF THE INTERIOR.
COMMISSION TO THE FIVE CIVILIZED TRIBES.

IN RE APPLICATION FOR ENROLLMENT, as a citizen of the Creek Nation, of Stan Watie Morrison, born on the 24 day of November, 1904

Name of Father: Manny Morrison   a citizen of the   Creek   Nation.
  Coweta Town
Name of Mother: Julia Morrison   a citizen of the United States Nation.

Postoffice   Lenna, Ind. Terr.

Applications for Enrollment of Creek Newborn
Act of 1905   Volume X

Child present
AFFIDAVIT OF MOTHER.

UNITED STATES OF AMERICA, Indian Territory, }
Western   DISTRICT.

I, Julia Morrison , on oath state that I am 20 years of age and a citizen ~~by~~ *(blank)* , of the United States Nation; that I am the lawful wife of Manny Morrison , who is a citizen, by blood of the Creek Nation; that a male child was born to me on 24 day of November , 1904 , that said child has been named Stan Watie Morrison , and was living March 4, 1905.

                                        Julia Morrison

Witnesses To Mark:
{

Subscribed and sworn to before me this 4 day of April , 1905.

                                        Drennan C Skaggs
                                        Notary Public.

AFFIDAVIT OF ATTENDING PHYSICIAN OR MID-WIFE.

UNITED STATES OF AMERICA, Indian Territory, }
Western   DISTRICT.

I, Susie McDaniel , a Witness , on oath state that I attended on Mrs. Julia Morrison , wife of Manny Morrison on the 24 day of November , 1904 ; that there was born to her on said date a male child; that said child was living March 4, 1905, and is said to have been named Stan Watie Morrison

                                        Susie McDaniel

Witnesses To Mark:
{ My Commission Expires July 20, 1907.

Subscribed and sworn to before me 6th day of April, 1905.

                                        Henry A McDaniel
                                        Notary Public.

Applications for Enrollment of Creek Newborn
Act of 1905   Volume X

NC-829.

Muskogee, Indian Territory, October 19, 1905.

Julia Morrison,
Lenna, Indian Territory.

Dear Madam:

In the matter of the application for the enrollment of your minor children, Lula Mildred Morrison, born August 17, 1902, and Stan Watie Morrison, born November 24, 1904, as citizens by blood of the Creek Nation, this office requires evidence of your marriage to Manny Morrison, the father of said children.

Such evidence may consist of either the original or a certified copy of your marriage license and certificate.

Respectfully,

Commissioner.

NC-829

Muskogee, Indian Territory, November 20, 1905.

Julia Morrison,
Lenna, Indian Territory.

Dear Madam:

There is herewith returned you[sic] marriage license. A copy thereof has been made and filed in the matter of the application for the enrollment of your minor children, Lula Mildred, and Stan Watie Morrison, as citizens by blood of the Creek Nation.

Respectfully,

Acting Commissioner.

JYM-20

:::::   :::::
:::::   :::::
:::::   MARRIAGE LICENSE   :::::

NC-829   No. 115

UNITED STATES OF AMERICA,
   Indian Territory,   ss.
   Northern W̶e̶s̶t̶e̶r̶n̶----------District.

TO ANY PERSON AUTHORIZED BY LAW TO SOLEMNIZE MARRIAGE--GREETING:

Applications for Enrollment of Creek Newborn
Act of 1905   Volume X

You are hereby commanded to Solemnize the Rite and Publish the Banns of Matrimony between Mr. Maurice M. Morrison of Burney, in the Indian Territory, aged 21 years, and Miss Julia F. McDaniels, of Burney, in the Indian Territory, aged 17 years, according to law, and do you officially sign and return this License to the parties therein named.

Witness my hand and official seal ~~at Muskogee, Indian Territory~~, this 13" day of July, A. D. 1901.

CHAS. A. DAVIDSON,
Clerk of the U. S. Court.

By P. M. Ford,
  Deputy.
(seal)

CERTIFICATE OF MARRIAGE.

United States of America,
  Indian Territory,   ss.
Northern ~~Western~~ District.

I, W. P. Jones, a Minister of the Gospel, do hereby certify that on the 21 day of July, A. D. 1901 did duly and according to law as commanded in the foregoing License, solemnize the Rite and Publish the Banns of Matrimony between the parties therein named.

Witness my hand this 21" day of July, A. D. 1901.

My credentials are recorded in the office of the clerk of the United States Court, Indian Territory, Northern ~~Western~~ District, Book B, Page 264.

(signed)   W. P. JONES,
a Minister of the Gospel.

Filed and duly recorded, this 24 day of July, 1901, Book L, page 27.
Chas. A. Davidson, Clerk U. S. Court.

CERTIFICATE OF TRUE COPY.

United States of America,
  Indian Territory,   ss.
  Western District.

I, R. P. Harrison, Clerk of the United States Court in the Western District, Indian Territory, do hereby certify that the instrument hereto attached is a full, true and correct copy of a Marriage License as the same appears from the records of my office.

Witness my hand and seal of said Court at Muskogee, in said Territory, this 14" day of Nov. A. D. 1905.

R. P. Harrison,
Clerk and Ex-Officio Recorder.

By John Harlan,
  Deputy Clerk.

Applications for Enrollment of Creek Newborn
Act of 1905   Volume X

(SEAL)   Book L, page 27.

                                  :   I, J. Y. Miller, a stenographer to the
INDIAN TERRITORY, Western District.   :   Commissioner to the Five Civilized
                                  :   Tribes, do hereby certify that the
above and foregoing is a true and complete copy of its original.

                                       JY Miller

Sworn to and subscribed before me
this the 18th day of November,
1905.

                                  J McDermott
                                  Notary Public.

                                                       HGH
                                                       EG.

REFER IN REPLY TO THE FOLLOWING:	**DEPARTMENT OF THE INTERIOR,**
NC-830.	**COMMISSIONER TO THE FIVE CIVILIZED TRIBES.**

                             Muskogee, Indian Territory, October 19, 1905.

Casey Cumsey,
      c/o Lewis Cumsey,
            Mounds, Indian Territory.

Dear Madam:
      In the matter of the application for the enrollment of your minor children, Lena Cumsey, born April 23, 1902, and Annie Cumsey, born May 2, 1904, as citizens by blood of the Creek Nation, this office requires the affidavits of the midwife or physician who attended on you at the birth of said children and blanks for that purpose are inclosed herewith.

      If there was no physician or midwife in attendance when said children were born it will be necessary for you to furnish this office with the affidavits of two disinterested witnesses relative to the birth of said children. Said affidavits must set forth the names of said children, the dates of their birth, the names of their parents and whether or not they were living on March 4, 1905.

                             Respectfully,
                               Tams Bixby   Commissioner.

2 B C
Env.

Applications for Enrollment of Creek Newborn
Act of 1905   Volume X

NC-830

Muskogee, Indian Territory, December 15, 1905.

Casey Cumsey,
    Care of Lewis Cumsey,
        Mounds, Indian Territory.

Dear Madam:

    In the matter of the application for the enrollment of your minor children, Lena Cumsey, born April 23, 1902, and Annie Cumsey, born May 2, 1904, as citizens by blood of the Creek Nation, this Office requires the affidavit of the midwife or physician in attendance at the birth of each of said children. Blanks for that purpose are herewith enclosed. If there was no midwife or physician in attendance at the birth of these children, it will be necessary for you to obtain the affidavits of two disinterested persons relative to said children's birth, and blanks for that purpose are herewith enclosed.

    This matter should receive your immediate attention.

                Respectfully,

                                Commissioner.

2 B A
2 Dis

BIRTH AFFIDAVIT.

DEPARTMENT OF THE INTERIOR.
COMMISSION TO THE FIVE CIVILIZED TRIBES.

    IN RE APPLICATION FOR ENROLLMENT, as a citizen of the Creek Nation, of Lena Cumsey, born on the 23 day of April, 1902

Name of Father: Lewis Cumsey   a citizen of the   Creek   Nation.
Tulwarthlocco Town
Name of Mother: Cassie   "   nee Tiger   a citizen of the   Creek   Nation.
Euchee Town
                        Postoffice   Mounds, Ind. Ter

Applications for Enrollment of Creek Newborn
Act of 1905   Volume X

AFFIDAVIT OF MOTHER.   (Child present)

UNITED STATES OF AMERICA, Indian Territory,
    Western   DISTRICT.

I, Cassie Cumsey nee Tiger , on oath state that I am 29 years of age and a citizen by blood , of the Creek Nation; that I am the lawful wife of Lewis Cumsey , who is a citizen, by blood of the Creek Nation; that a female child was born to me on 23 day of April , 1902 , that said child has been named Lena Cumsey , and was living March 4, 1905.

                                        Casey Cumsey

Witnesses To Mark:
{

Subscribed and sworn to before me this 25" day of April , 1905.

(Seal)   J McDermott
                                        Notary Public.

                    Father
AFFIDAVIT OF ~~ATTENDING PHYSICIAN OR MID-WIFE~~.

UNITED STATES OF AMERICA, Indian Territory,
    Western   DISTRICT.

I, Lewis Cumsey , ~~a (blank)~~ , on oath state that I attended on ~~Mrs~~. my wife ~~of~~ when on the 23 day of April , 1902 ; that there was born to her on said date a female child; that said child was living March 4, 1905, and is said to have been named *(blank)*

                                        Lewis Cumsey

Witnesses To Mark:
{

Subscribed and sworn to before me this 25" day of April , 1905.

(Seal)   J McDermott
                                        Notary Public.

Western   District
Indian Territory   SS

We, the undersigned, on oath state that we are personally acquainted with Casey Cumsey   wife of   Lewis Cumsey   and that on or about the 23rd. day of April , 1902, a   female   child was born to them and has been named   Lena Cumsey, (is now living)   ; that said child was living March 4, 1905.

Applications for Enrollment of Creek Newborn
Act of 1905   Volume X

We further state that we have no interest in the above case.

(Illegible)
her
Lucy x Davis
mark

Witness to mark:
 Timmie Fife
 Sapulpa I.T.
 James Sapulpa
 Sapulpa I.T.

Subscribed and sworn to before
me this 26th day of Dec. 1905.

James J. Mars
Notary Public.

Western   District
Indian Territory   SS

We, the undersigned, on oath state that we are personally acquainted with Casey Cumsey   wife of   Lewis Cumsey   and that on or about the   2nd. day of May , 1904, a   female   child was born to them and has been named   Annie Cumsey, (is now living) ; that said child was living March 4, 1905.

We further state that we have no interest in the above case.

(Illegible)
her
Lucy x Davis
mark

Witness to mark:
 Timmie Fife
 Sapulpa I.T.
 James Sapulpa
 Sapulpa I.T.

Subscribed and sworn to before
me this 26th day of Dec. 1905.

James J. Mars
Notary Public.

Applications for Enrollment of Creek Newborn
Act of 1905 Volume X

BIRTH AFFIDAVIT.

DEPARTMENT OF THE INTERIOR.
COMMISSION TO THE FIVE CIVILIZED TRIBES.

IN RE APPLICATION FOR ENROLLMENT, as a citizen of the Creek Nation, of Annie Cumsey, born on the 2 day of May , 1904

Name of Father: Lewis Cumsey   a citizen of the   Creek   Nation. Tulwarthlocco Town
Name of Mother: Cassie Cumsey nee Tiger   a citizen of the   Creek   Nation. Euchee Town
                            Postoffice   Mounds, I.T.

AFFIDAVIT OF MOTHER.
(Child present)

UNITED STATES OF AMERICA, Indian Territory,
     Western   DISTRICT.

I, Cassie Cumsey nee Tiger , on oath state that I am 29 years of age and a citizen by blood , of the Creek Nation; that I am the lawful wife of Lewis Cumsey , who is a citizen, by blood of the Creek Nation; that a female child was born to me on 2 day of May , 1904 , that said child has been named Annie Cumsey , and was living March 4, 1905.

                                        Casey Cumsey
Witnesses To Mark:
{

Subscribed and sworn to before me this 25" day of April , 1905.

     (Seal)   J McDermott
                                          Notary Public.

Father
AFFIDAVIT OF ~~ATTENDING PHYSICIAN OR MID-WIFE~~.

UNITED STATES OF AMERICA, Indian Territory,
     Western   DISTRICT.

I, Lewis Cumsey , ~~a (blank)~~ , on oath state that I attended on ~~Mrs.~~ my ~~wife of~~ when on the 2 day of May , 1904 ; that there was born to her on said date a female child; that said child was living March 4, 1905, and is said to have been named Annie Cumsey

                                        Lewis Cumsey
Witnesses To Mark:
{

Applications for Enrollment of Creek Newborn
Act of 1905   Volume X

Subscribed and sworn to before me this 25" day of April, 1905.

(Seal) J McDermott
Notary Public.

NC-831.

Muskogee, Indian Territory, October 19, 1905.

Anna Mantooth,
Coweta, Indian Territory.

Dear Madam:

In the matter of the application for the enrollment of your minor child, Isabella Mantooth, born July 29, 1902, as a citizen by blood of the Creek Nation, this office is unable to identify you upon the final roll of citizens by blood of the Creek Nation. It is necessary that you be so identified before the rights of said child can be finally determined.

You are, therefore, requested to state the name under which you are finally enrolled, the names of your parents and other members of your family, the Creek Indian town to which you belong and your final roll number as the same appears upon your allotment certificate and deeds.

Respectfully,

Commissioner.

BIRTH AFFIDAVIT.
DEPARTMENT OF THE INTERIOR.
COMMISSION TO THE FIVE CIVILIZED TRIBES.

IN RE APPLICATION FOR ENROLLMENT, as a citizen of the Creek Nation, of Isabella Mantooth, born on the 29th day of July, 1902

Name of Father: James H Mantooth   a citizen ~~of the (blank) Nation~~. Intermarried
Name of Mother: Anna Mantooth   a citizen of the Creek Nation.

Postoffice   Coweta I.T.

Applications for Enrollment of Creek Newborn
Act of 1905   Volume X

AFFIDAVIT OF MOTHER.

UNITED STATES OF AMERICA, Indian Territory, ⎫
   Western   DISTRICT. ⎭

    I, Anna Mantooth , on oath state that I am fourty one years of age and a citizen by blood , of the Creek Nation; that I am the lawful wife of James H. Mantooth , who is an intermarried citizen, by *(blank)* of the *(blank)* Nation; that a female child was born to me on 29th day of July , 1902 , that said child has been named Isabella Mantooth , and was living March 4, 1905.

                                            Anna Mantooth

Witnesses To Mark:
⎰
⎱

    Subscribed and sworn to before me this 8th day of April , 1905.

                                            B.J. Beavers
                                                Notary Public.

My commission expires Dec 19, 1908.

AFFIDAVIT OF ATTENDING PHYSICIAN OR MID-WIFE.

UNITED STATES OF AMERICA, Indian Territory, ⎫
   Western   DISTRICT. ⎭

    I, Rose Childers , a midwife , on oath state that I attended on Mrs. Anna Mantooth , wife of James H Mantooth on the 29th day of July , 1902 ; that there was born to her on said date a female child; that said child was living March 4, 1905, and is said to have been named Isabella Mantooth

                                                her
                                       Rose x Childers

Witnesses To Mark: mark
⎰ Joe Fennel
⎱ Aluca Hocking

    Subscribed and sworn to before me 10th day of April, 1905.

                                         Beth J. Beavers
                                            Notary Public.

My commission expires Dec 19- 1908.

Applications for Enrollment of Creek Newborn
Act of 1905   Volume X

Affidavit.

Indian Territory, :
                        ss.
Western District. :

  I, Annie Mantooth, being first duly sworn according to law deposes and says that I am a resident of Coweta, Indian Territory and a citizen of the Creek Nation by blood; that I was enrolled under the name of Annie Mantooth that the names of my parents were Josephine Thompson, my father has been dead for many years; *(BJB N.P. 10/23/05 written margin next to this insertion)* that my name before this was Annie Payne. I am a member of the Cheyaha Town and on the rolls as a member of said Town; that my name is on the Creek Indian Roll, No. 1029, all of which I verily believe to be true of my own personal knowledge.

              Annie Mantooth

Subscribed and sworn to before me this 23rd day of October, 1905.
and I further certify that the above correction was made this day

              B.J. Beavers
My commission expires Dec. 19, 1908.

                       COPY.
Refer in reply to the following:
Land: 52309-1906.
       DEPARTMENT OF THE INTERIOR,
         OFFICE OF INDIAN AFFAIRS,
           WASHINGTON, July 3, 1906.

The Honorable,
  The Secretary of the Interior.

Sir:

  I have the honor to invite your attention to the enclosed letter of June 15, 1906, from Tams Bixby, Commissioner to the Five Civilized Tribes, who says that on April 12, 1905, there was filed with this office an affidavit in connection with an application for the enrollment of Silas Jefferson, minor child of Manuel and Jane Jefferson, as a citizen by blood of the Creek Nation; that the records of his office show that the parents of the child were identified as Manuel and Jane Jefferson, whose names appear on the approved schedule of citizens by blood of the Creek Nation opposite numbers 1165 and 1166 respectively, and that the applicant, Silas Jefferson, was listed for enrollment on New Creek Indian care no. 832, and that his name was placed on the schedule of citizens by

Applications for Enrollment of Creek Newborn
Act of 1905 Volume X

blood of the Creek Nation, approved by the Department on November 27, 1905, opposite No. 796.

Mr. Bixby reports that it appears from the transcript of proceedings had in this matter on March 2, 1906, a copy of which is enclosed, and from the records of his office, that the former identification of the parents of Silas Jefferson was incorrect, that the father of the applicant is identified as the Manuel Jefferson whose name appears on Creek Indian card field No. 1404 opposite Roll No. 4457, and that Jane Jefferson, the mother of the applicant, is identified as the Jane Jefferson whose name appears on Creek freedman card, field No. 114, opposite roll No. 423.

In view of the facts as above set forth, the Commissioner recommends that the name of Silas Jefferson be stricken from the partial list of new-born citizens of the Creek Nation, approved June 2, in order that his name may be placed on the new-born Creek freedman schedule now under preparation in his office. In view of the conditions as outlined by the Commissioner I concur in his recommendation.

Very respectfully,
C.F. Larrabee,
Acting Commissioner.

EBH-Y.

JF Jr.
LLB.LRS.

I.T.D. 11908-1906. DEPARTMENT OF THE INTERIOR,
WASHINGTON, July 14, 1906.

Commissioner to the Five Civilized Tribes,
Muskogee, Indian Territory.

Sir:

On June 15, 1906, you forwarded the testimony of Jane Jefferson taken March 2, 1906, at Muskogee, Ind. T.

It appears that on April 12, 1905, there was filed with the Commission to the Five Civilized Tribes an affidavit in the matter of the application for enrollment of Silas Jefferson, minor child of Manuel and Jane Jefferson, as a citizen by blood of the Creek Nation.

Your records show that the parents of said child were identified as the Manuel and Jane Jefferson whose names appear upon approved schedule of citizens by blood of the Creek Nation, opposite Nos. 1165 and 1166, respectively, and that the applicant, Silas Jefferson, was listed for enrollment on new Creek Indian care No. 842, and that his name was placed upon the schedule of citizens by blood of the Creek Nation, opposite No. 796, approved by the Secretary of the Interior November 27, 1905.

Applications for Enrollment of Creek Newborn
Act of 1905   Volume X

From the testimony transmitted it appears that the former identification of the parents of Silas Jefferson was incorrect; that the father of said applicant is identified as the Manuel Jefferson whose name appears on Creek Indian card file no. 1404, opposite roll No. 4457, and that Jane Jefferson is identified as the Jane Jefferson whose name appears on Creek Freedman card file No. 114, opposite Roll No. 423.

You therefore recommend that the name of Silas Jefferson be stricken from the partial list of new-born citizens of the Creek Nation, opposite roll No. 796, approved November 27, 1905, in order that his name may be placed upon a new-born Creek freedman schedule now in preparation in your office.

Reporting July 3, 1906, the Indian Office concurs in your recommendation. A copy of its letter is inclosed.

I have this day canceled the name of Silas Jefferson from the approved roll in this office. The Commissioner of Indian Affairs has been authorized to make said cancellation in that office, and you are authorized to cancel the roll in your possession accordingly.

                    Respectfully,
                    Jesse E. Wilson,
                    Assistant Secretary.

1 inclosure[sic].

                    HGH
                    EG

REFER IN REPLY TO THE FOLLOWING:
NC-833.

DEPARTMENT OF THE INTERIOR,
COMMISSIONER TO THE FIVE CIVILIZED TRIBES.

Muskogee, Indian Territory, October 19, 1905.

Hannah Frank,
    c/o Noah Frank,
        Sapulpa, Indian Territory.

Dear Madam:

In the matter of the application for the enrollment of your minor child Vera Frank, born September 9, 1903, as a citizen by blood of the Creek Nation, the words "that said child was living March 4, 1905", in the affidavit of the physician who attended at the birth of said child, have been scratched out.

Applications for Enrollment of Creek Newborn
Act of 1905   Volume X

It is necessary, in order that the rights of said child may be determined, that you furnish this office with the affidavit of the physician who attended at the birth of said child showing that the said Vera Frank was living March 4, 1905.

In the event that you are unable to secure the affidavit of said physician it will be necessary for you to furnish this office with the affidavits of two disinterested witnesses relative to the birth of said child. Said affidavits to set forth said child's name, the date of her birth, the names of her parents and whether or not she was living on March 4, 1905.

This office requires evidence of marriage between you and Noah Frank, the father of said child. Such evidence may consist of either the original or a certified copy of your marriage license and certificate.

Respectfully,
Tams Bixby   Commissioner.

B C
Env.

833

W. P. ROOT,
Attorney at Law,
Sapulpa, Ind. Ter.

Oct 24th, 1905.

Hon Tams Bixby, Commissioner.
Muskogee, Ind. Ty

Dear Sir:
Inclosed find application of Vera Frank for Allotment with affidavits a requested. I also inclose[sic] the Marriage Certificate of her Parents, which please return to Mrs. Hannah Frank, at Sapulpa, I. T.

Yours Truly,
(signed) HANNAH FRANK,
by W.P. Root.

Muskogee, Indian Territory, October 27, 1905.

Hannah Frank,
Care W. P. Root,
Sapulpa, Indian Territory.

Dear Madam:
There is herewith enclosed your marriage license and certificate, a copy of which has been made for the files of this office.

Applications for Enrollment of Creek Newborn
Act of 1905   Volume X

Respectfully,

Commissioner.

AG-15

NC-833   (Copy)

x----------------------------------x
: MARRIAGE-LICENSE :
x----------------------------------x

UNITED STATES OF AMERICA,
    Indian Territory,   ss.   No. 209
    Western District.

    Y o u   a r e   h e r e by   c o m m a n d e d   to solemnize the Rite and Publish the Banns of Matrimony between MR. NOAH FRANK of Red Fork, in the Indian Territory, aged 19 years, and MISS HANNAH TINGLEY of Red Fork, in the Indian Territory, aged 19 years, according to law, and do you officially sign and return this LICENSE to the parties therein named.

    Witness my hand and Official Seal, at Muskogee, Indian Territory, this 24" day of September, A.D. 1902.

                        (signed)   R. P. HARRISON,
    (SEAL)   Clerk of the U. S. Court.

By A.Z. English,
        Deputy.

CERTIFICATE OF MARRIAGE.

United States of America,
    Indian Territory,   ss.
    Western District.

I, A. M. Land, a Minister of the Gospel, do hereby certify that on the 7 day of September, A.D. 1902, did duly and according to law as commanded in the foregoing License, solemnize the Rite and Publish the Banns of Matrimony between the parties therein named.
    Witness my hand this the 8 day of September, A.D. 1902.
    My credentials are recorded in the Office of the Clerk of the United States Court, Indian Territory, Western District, Book C, Page 166.

                        (signed)   REV. A. M. LAND,
                                       A Minister of the Gospel.

Applications for Enrollment of Creek Newborn
Act of 1905   Volume X

Certificate of Record.

United States of America,
    Indian Territory,   ss.
    Western District.

    I, Robert P. Harrison, Clerk of the United States Court in the Western District, Indian Territory, do hereby certify that the instrument hereto attached was filed for record in my office the 19 day of Sept., 1902, at 5 P. M., and duly recorded in Book N, Marriage Record, Page 228.
    Witness my hand and seal of said Court at Muskogee, in said Territory, this 23 day of Sept., A.D. 1902.

                                      R. P. HARRISON, Clerk
(SEAL)

By R. A. Bayne, Deputy.

                        Western Dist. Ind. Ter.
                              FILED
                            SEP 19, 1902
                          R.P HARRISON,
                        Clerk, U.S. Courts.

INDIAN TERRITORY, Western District.
    I, J. Y. Miller, a stenographer to the Commission to the Five Civilized Tribes, do hereby certify that the above and foregoing is a true and complete copy of its original as found in the files of the aforesaid Commissioner, in Muskogee, Indian Territory.

                                      JY Miller

Sworn to and subscribed before me
   this the 26th day of October,
   1905.   J McDermott
                                        Notary Public.

United States of America   )
Western District of the   ) ss
Indian Territory.   )   AFFIDAVIT.

Noah Frank, being first duly sworn on his oath states that he is a Citizen of the Creek Nation, by blood, that, he is a duly enrolled Citizen of said Nation, and has heretofore selected his Allotment, of the Lands of the Creek Nation Indian Territory, that he is the Lawful Husband of Hannah Frank, and was married to her be[sic] A M Land, a Minister of the Gospel, on the 7th day of September 1902, in the Western District Indian Territory,

Applications for Enrollment of Creek Newborn
Act of 1905 Volume X

and that said Certificate of Marriage is duly recorded with the Clerk of the United States Court at Muskogee, Ind- Ty,;

That on the 9th day of September 1903, a Female Child was born to his Wife, that he is the Father of said Child and that she has been Named Vera Frank, and was Living on the 4th day of March 1905, and is still Living.

Affiant further States that Dr. H. O. Lyford, was the attending Physician at the time of Birth of said Child, and that your Affiant was present at said time.

Noah Frank

Subscribed and sworn to before me this the 23rd, day of Oct- 1905.

My Commission expires Oct- 21st 1906.   W^m P Root
Notary Public.

Post Office Address of Affiant is
Sapulpa, Indian Territory.

BIRTH AFFIDAVIT.

DEPARTMENT OF THE INTERIOR.
COMMISSION TO THE FIVE CIVILIZED TRIBES.

IN RE APPLICATION FOR ENROLLMENT, as a citizen of the Creek Nation[sic] Nation, of Vera Frank , born on the 9th day of September , 1903

Name of Father: Noah Frank   a citizen of the   Creek   Nation.
Name of Mother: Hannah Frank   (A Non-Citizen)/////////////   Nation.

Postoffice   Sapulpa, Indian Territory.

AFFIDAVIT OF MOTHER.

UNITED STATES OF AMERICA, Indian Territory, ⎫
     Western   DISTRICT.   ⎭

I, Hannah Frank , on oath state that I am Twenty years of age and a citizen by *(blank)* , of the *(blank)* Nation; that I am the lawful wife of Noah Frank , who is a citizen, by Blood of the Creek Nation; that a Female child was born to me on 9th day of September , 1903 , that said child has been named Vera Frank , and is now living.

Hannah Frank

Applications for Enrollment of Creek Newborn
Act of 1905 Volume X

Witnesses To Mark:
- Noah Frank
- Everett A Kern

Subscribed and sworn to before me this 23d day of October, 1905.

My Commission expires Oct- 21st 1906. W^m P Root
Notary Public.

AFFIDAVIT OF ATTENDING PHYSICIAN OR MID-WIFE.

UNITED STATES OF AMERICA, Indian Territory,
Western   DISTRICT.

I, H.O. Lyford a regular Practising[sic] Physician , on oath state that I attended on Mrs. Hannah Frank , wife of Noah Frank on the 9th day of September , 1903 ; that there was born to her on said date a Female child; that said child is now living and is said to have been named Vera Frank

H.O. Lyford

Witnesses To Mark:

Subscribed and sworn to before me this 23d day of October, 1905.

My Commission expires Oct- 21st 1906. W^m P Root
Notary Public.

BIRTH AFFIDAVIT.

DEPARTMENT OF THE INTERIOR.
COMMISSION TO THE FIVE CIVILIZED TRIBES.

IN RE APPLICATION FOR ENROLLMENT, as a citizen of the Creek Nation, of Vera Frank , born on the 9 day of Sept, 1903

Name of Father: Noah Frank   a citizen of the Creek   Nation.
 (Hitchita)
Name of Mother: Hannah Frank   a citizen of the U.S.   Nation.

Postoffice   Sapulpa, I.T.

Applications for Enrollment of Creek Newborn
Act of 1905   Volume X

AFFIDAVIT OF MOTHER.

UNITED STATES OF AMERICA, Indian Territory, }
   Western   DISTRICT.

    I, Hannah Frank , on oath state that I am 20 years of age and a citizen by *(blank)* , of the U S Nation; that I am the lawful wife of Noah Frank , who is a citizen, by blood of the Creek Nation; that a female child was born to me on 9 day of September , 1903 , that said child has been named Vera Frank , and was living March 4, 1905.

                                    Hannah Frank

Witnesses To Mark:
{

    Subscribed and sworn to before me this 24th day of April , 1905.

(Seal)   Edw C Griesel
                                      Notary Public.

AFFIDAVIT OF ATTENDING PHYSICIAN OR MID-WIFE.

UNITED STATES OF AMERICA, Indian Territory, }
   Western   DISTRICT.

    I, H.O. Lyford , a Physician , on oath state that I attended on Mrs. Hannah Frank , wife of Noah Frank on the 9 day of Sept , 1903 ; that there was born to her on said date a female child; that said child is now living and is said to have been named Vera Frank

                                    H.O. Lyford

Witnesses To Mark:
{

    Subscribed and sworn to before me this 24 day of April , 1905.

(Seal)   J McDermott
                                      Notary Public.

Applications for Enrollment of Creek Newborn
Act of 1905   Volume X

DEPARTMENT OF THE INTERIOR,
COMMISSIONER TO THE FIVE CIVILIZED TRIBES.
Muskogee, Indian Territory, June 28, 1906.

N.C. 834.

In the matter of the application for the enrollment of Fannie Nero as a citizen by blood of the Creek Nation.

GOVERNOR NERO, being duly sworn, testified as follows:

Q What is your name? A Governor Nero.
Q What is your age? A Thirty some odd.
Q What is your post office address? A Eufaula.
Q To what Creek Indian town do you belong? A Tuskegee.
Q What is the name of your father? A William Nero.
Q What is the name of your mother? A Nancy.
Q How much Creek Indian blood do you claim to have? A About 1/16.
Q What is the rest of your blood? A Colored.

Witness is identified as Governor Nero on Creek Indian card No. 7026.

Q Have you a child named Fannie Nero? A Yes
Q Is she living? A Yes, sir.
Q How old is she? A About going on five.
Q Aren't you mistaken about that, when was she born? A 1902.
Q What month? A July 8th.
Q If she was born in 1902 she would be going on four wouldn't she? A Yes, sir.
Q Why did you say five? A I said four of five.
Q What is the name of the midwife in attendance at the birth of the child? A Nancy Nero.
Q What is the name of the mother of the child? A Mary Nero.
Q Is she your wife? A Yes
Q When were you married to her? A It has been a good while.
Q How many years? A About eight.
Q What was Mary's name before her marriage? A Sarwanoka.
Q Do you know to what Creek Indian town she belonged? A Eufaula Canadian.
Q What was the name of her father? A Mitchell.
Q What was the name of her mother? A I didn't know her mother, Fannie, I believe; she has been dead a long time.

Witness presents original memorandum of selection of land in the Creek Nation issued to Mary Sarwanoka, opposite Creek Indian roll No. 8709 to land in section 35, township 14, range 8, 160 acres.

You should furnish this office with the original or a certified copy of your marriage license and certificate to show the change in the name of your wife from Sarwanoka to Nero.

Applications for Enrollment of Creek Newborn
Act of 1905 Volume X

Q What is the name of the other children you want to enroll? A Lucy and Sammie.

I, Anna Garrigues, on oath state that the above and foregoing is a true and correct transcript of my stenographic notes as taken in said cause on said date.

Anna Garrigues

Subscribed and sworn to before me this 2 day of July 1906.

Edward Merrick
Notary Public.

BIRTH AFFIDAVIT.

DEPARTMENT OF THE INTERIOR.
COMMISSION TO THE FIVE CIVILIZED TRIBES.

IN RE APPLICATION FOR ENROLLMENT, as a citizen of the Creek Nation, of Fannie Nero , born on the 8th. day of July , 1902
and of Eufaula Town
Name of Father: Governor Nero   a citizen of the   Creek   Nation.
Name of Mother: Mary Nero   a citizen of the   Creek   Nation.

Postoffice   Eufaula, Indian Territory

AFFIDAVIT OF MOTHER.

UNITED STATES OF AMERICA, Indian Territory, }
        Western   DISTRICT.

I, Mary Nero , on oath state that I am Twenty years of age and a citizen by blood , of the Creek Nation; that I am the lawful wife of Governor Nero , who is a citizen, by blood of the Creek Nation; that a female child was born to me on Eighth day of July , 1902 , that said child has been named Fannie Nero , and was living March 4, 1905.

her
Mary x Nero
mark

Witnesses To Mark:
{ Frank W Rushing
  Virgil Winn

Subscribed and sworn to before me this 25th. day of April , 1905.

My Commission Expires Jan. 30, 1909.   Frank W Rushing
Notary Public.

Applications for Enrollment of Creek Newborn
Act of 1905 Volume X

AFFIDAVIT OF ATTENDING PHYSICIAN OR MID-WIFE.

UNITED STATES OF AMERICA, Indian Territory, }
    Western   DISTRICT.

I, Nancy Nero , a midwife , on oath state that I attended on Mrs. Mary Nero , wife of Governor Nero on the 8th. day of July , 1902 ; that there was born to her on said date a female child; that said child was living March 4, 1905, and is said to have been named Fannie Nero

                                            her
                                   Nancy x Nero

Witnesses To Mark: mark
  { Frank W Rushing
    Virgil Winn

My Commission Expires Jan. 30, 1909.

Subscribed and sworn to before me this 25th. day of April , 1905.

                                      Frank W Rushing
                                        Notary Public.

NC-834.

                            Muskogee, Indian Territory, October 19, 1905.

Mary Nero,
    c/o Governor Nero,
        Eufaula, Indian Territory.

Dear Madam:

    In the matter of the application for the enrollment of your minor child, Fannie Nero, born July 8, 1902, as a citizen by blood of the Creek Nation, this office is unable to identify you upon the final roll of citizens by blood of the Creek Nation. It is necessary that you be so identified before the rights of your said child can be finally determined.

    You are therefore requested to state the name under which you are finally enrolled, the names of your parents and other members of your family, the Creek Indian town to which you belong and your final roll number as the same appears upon your allotment certificate and deeds.

                            Respectfully,
                                            Commissioner.

Applications for Enrollment of Creek Newborn
Act of 1905 Volume X

Muskogee, Indian Territory, June 27, 1906.

Mary Nero,
    Care Governor Nero,
        Eufaula, Indian Territory.

Dear Madam:

    In the matter of the application for the enrollment of your minor child, Fannie Nero, born July 8, 1902, as a citizen by blood of the Creek Nation, this office is unable to identify you upon the final roll of citizens by blood of the Creek Nation. It is necessary that you be so identified before the rights of your said child can be finally determined.

    You are therefore requested to state the name under which you are finally enrolled, the names of your parents and other members of your family, the Creek Indian town to which you belong and your final roll number as the same appears upon your allotment certificate and deeds.

                Respectfully,

                            Commissioner.

                            JWH

N C 834

        Muskogee, Indian Territory, March 1, 1907.

Mary Nero,
    % Governor Nero,
        Eufaula, Indian Territory.

Dear Madam :--

    You are hereby advised that on February 15, 1907, the Secretary of the Interior approved the enrollment of your minor child, FannieNero, as a citizen by blood of the Creek Nation, and that the name of said child appears upon the roll of New Born citizens by blood of the Creek Nation, enrolled under the Act of Congress approved March 3, 1905, as number 1174.

    This child is now entitled to allotment and application therefor should be made without delay at the Creek Land Office, Muskogee, Indian Territory.

                Respectfully,

                            Commissioner.

Applications for Enrollment of Creek Newborn
Act of 1905   Volume X

BA 2229 B.

DEPARTMENT OF THE INTERIOR,
COMMISSIONER TO THE FIVE CIVILIZED TRIBES.
MUSKOGEE, IND. TER. May 9, 1905.

In the matter of the application for the enrollment of Billie Scott as a citizen by blood of the Creek Nation.

Maleskey Scott, being duly sworn, testified as follows, through official interpreter, Jesse McDermott.

By the Commission:
Q What is your name? A Maleskey Scott.
Q What is your age? A About 30.
Q What is your post office address? A Okmulgee.
Q Are you a citizen of the Creek Nation? A I am a Seminole.
Q Have you got your land in the Seminole Nation? A Yes sir.
Q You have a child named Billie Scott? A Yes sir.
Q You are making application for him now? A Yes sir.
Q Who is the father of Billie Scott? A James Scott.
Q Are you lawfully married to James Scott? A Yes sir.
Q When was Billie Scott born? A 17th day of February.
Q This year? A Yes sir.
Q This is the child here, (Pointing to child)? A Yes sir.
Q If it should be found that he is entitled to enrollment in both the Seminole and Creek Nations, in which Nation do you elect to have your child Billie Scott enrolled and receive his allotment of land? A In the Creek Nation.

Lona Merrick being, duly sworn, states that the above and foregoing is a true and correct transcript of her stenographic notes taken in said cause on said date.

Lona Merrick

Subscribed and sworn to before me this 10th day of May, 1905.

Edw C Griesel
Notary Public.

Applications for Enrollment of Creek Newborn
Act of 1905   Volume X

BIRTH AFFIDAVIT.

DEPARTMENT OF THE INTERIOR.
COMMISSION TO THE FIVE CIVILIZED TRIBES.

IN RE APPLICATION FOR ENROLLMENT, as a citizen of the Creek Nation, of Billie Scott, born on the 17 day of February, 1905

Name of Father: James Scott　　　　a citizen of the　Creek　Nation.
Name of Mother: Maleskey Scott　　　a citizen of the　Creek　Nation.

　　　　　　　　　　　Postoffice　　Okmulgee IT

AFFIDAVIT OF MOTHER.

UNITED STATES OF AMERICA, Indian Territory, }
　　Western　　　　DISTRICT.

I, Maleskey Scott, on oath state that I am about 30 years of age and a citizen by Blood, of the Creek[sic] Nation; that I am the lawful wife of James Scott, who is a citizen, by Blood of the Creek Nation; that a male child was born to me on 17" day of February, 1905, that said child has been named Billie Scott, and is now ~~living~~.
　　　　　　　　　　　　　　　　　　　　　　　　　　　　Deceased.

　　　　　　　　　　　　　　　　　　　her
　　　　　　　　　　　　　　　Maleskey x Scott
Witnesses To Mark:　　　　　　　　mark
　{ W.W. Morton
　　Nathan Benson

Subscribed and sworn to before me this 31 day of October, 1905.

My Com Exp July 23-06　　　　　W^m P Morton
　　　　　　　　　　　　　　　　　　Notary Public.

AFFIDAVIT OF ATTENDING PHYSICIAN OR MID-WIFE.

UNITED STATES OF AMERICA, Indian Territory, }
　　Western　　　　DISTRICT.

I, Nicey Scott, a midwife, on oath state that I attended on Mrs. James[sic] Maleskey Scott, wife of James Scott on the 17" day of February, 1905; that there was born to her on said date a male child; that said child is now ~~living~~ Deceased and is said to have been named Billie Scott
　　　　　　　　　　　　　　　　　her
　　　　　　　　　　　　　　Nicey x Scott
Witnesses To Mark:　　　　　　　mark

Applications for Enrollment of Creek Newborn
Act of 1905   Volume X

{ W.W. Morton
{ Nathan Benson

    Subscribed and sworn to before me this 31 day of October, 1905.

My Com Exp July 23-06   W^m P Morton
                                                       Notary Public.

BIRTH AFFIDAVIT.

DEPARTMENT OF THE INTERIOR.
COMMISSION TO THE FIVE CIVILIZED TRIBES.

    IN RE APPLICATION FOR ENROLLMENT, as a citizen of the Creek Nation, of Billie Scott, born on the 17th day of Feby, 1905

Name of Father: James Scott   a citizen of the   Creek   Nation.
Cussehta
Name of Mother: Maleskey Scott   a citizen of the   Seminole   Nation.

                          Postoffice   Okmulgee, Indian Territory

---

                          AFFIDAVIT OF MOTHER.
                                      Child Brought in
UNITED STATES OF AMERICA, Indian Territory, }   May 9-05
      Western   **DISTRICT.**   Gr.

    I, Maleskey Scott, on oath state that I am about 29 years of age and a citizen by blood, of the Seminole Nation; that I am the lawful wife of James Scott, who is a citizen, by blood of the Creek Nation; that a male child was born to me on 17th day of Feby, 1905, that said child has been named Billie Scott, and is now living.

                                                    her
                                        Maleskey x Scott
Witnesses To Mark: mark
  { LL Sessions
  { A. A. Viersen

    Subscribed and sworn to before me this 25th day of April, 1905.

                                        M. F. *(Illegible)*
                                              Notary Public.

Applications for Enrollment of Creek Newborn
Act of 1905   Volume X

AFFIDAVIT OF ATTENDING PHYSICIAN OR MID-WIFE.

UNITED STATES OF AMERICA, Indian Territory,
Western   DISTRICT.

I, James Scott, husband of Maleskey Scott , on oath state that I attended on Mrs. Maleskey Scott , wife of myself on the 17th day of Feby , 1905 ; that there was born to her on said date a male child; that said child is now living and is said to have been named Billie Scott

     Sig.   James Scott
Witnesses To ~~Mark~~:
 { LL Sessions
   A. A. Viersen

Subscribed and sworn to before me this 25th day of April , 1905.

          M. F. *(Illegible)*
           Notary Public.
Commission Expires Oct 9th 1907

            J.D.

Muskogee, Indian Territory, April 28, 1905.

James Scott,
 Okmulgee, Indian Territory.

Dear Sir:

  The Commission is in receipt of an affidavit executed by you and your wife, Maleskey Scott, relating to the birth of your minor child, Billie Scott. Said affidavit has been filed with the Commission and is considered as an application for the enrollment of Billie Scott as a citizen by blood of the Creek Nation.

  It appears from said affidavit that your wife, Maleskey Scott, the mother of said child, is a citizen of the Seminole Nation. You are hereby notified that it will be necessary for you to appear before the Commission at its office, in Muskogee, Indian Territory, for the purpose of electing in which Nation you desire said child to be enrolled and receive his allotment of land.

      Respectfully,
         Chairman.
Register.

Applications for Enrollment of Creek Newborn
Act of 1905 Volume X

NC. 835.

Muskogee, Indian Territory, July 15, 1905.

Chief Clerk,
    Seminole Enrollment Division,
        Muskogee, Indian Territory.

Dear Sir:

    April 27, 1905, application was made to the Commission to the Five Civilized Tribes for the enrollment of Billie Scott, born February 17, 1905, as a citizen by blood of the Creek Nation. It is stated in said application that the father of said child is James Scott, a citizen of the Creek Nation, and that the mother is Maleskey Scott, a citizen of the Seminole Nation.

    You are requested to inform the Creek Enrollment Division as to whether application has been made for the enrollment of said Billie Scott as a citizen of the Seminole Nation, and if so, what disposition has been made of the same.

                Respectfully,
                          Commissioner.

W.F.

DEPARTMENT OF THE INTERIOR.
COMMISSION TO THE FIVE CIVILIZED TRIBES.

Muskogee, Indian Territory, July 19, 1905.

Chief Clerk,
    Creek Enrollment Division.

Dear Sir:

    Receipt is acknowledged of your letter of July 15, 1905, (NC-835) stating that application was made to the Commission to the Five Civilized Tribes for the enrollment of Billie Scott, born February 17, 1905, child of James Scott, a citizen of the Creek Nation, and Maleskey Scott, a citizen of the Seminole Nation, as a citizen by blood of the Creek Nation and requesting to be informed as to whether application was made for the enrollment of said child as a citizen of the Seminole Nation.

    In reply to your letter you are advised that it does not appear from an examination of the records of this office that any application was made for the enrollment of Billie Scott as a citizen of the Seminole Nation.

                Respectfully,
                    Tams Bixby Commissioner.

Applications for Enrollment of Creek Newborn
Act of 1905   Volume X

NC-835.

Muskogee, Indian Territory, October 19, 1905.

Maleskey Scott,
    c/o James Scott,
        Okmulgee, Indian Territory.

Dear Madam:

    In the matter of the application for the enrollment of your minor child, Billie Scott, born February 17, 1905, as a citizen by blood of the Creek Nation, this office requires the affidavit of the physician or midwife who attended on you at the birth of said child and a blank for that purpose is inclosed herewith.

    In the event that there was no attending physician or midwife when said child was born it will be necessary for you to furnish this office with the affidavits of two disinterested persons relative to the birth of said Billie Scott. Said affidavits to set forth said child's name, the date of his birth, the names of his parents and whether or not he was living on March 4, 1905.

        Respectfully,

                Commissioner.

B C
Env.

NC 835

Muskogee, Indian Territory, November 13, 1906

Chief Clerk,
    Seminole Enrollment Division,
        General Office.

Dear Sir:

    You are hereby advised that the name of Billie Scott born February 17, 1905 to James Scott, a citizen by blood of the Creek Nation and Maleskey Scott, an alleged citizen of the Seminole Nation, is contained in schedule of minor citizens by blood of the Creek Nation, approved by the Secretary of the Interior the Interior, January 4, 1905, opposite Roll number 974.

        Respectfully,

                Commissioner.

Applications for Enrollment of Creek Newborn
Act of 1905 Volume X

DEPARTMENT OF THE INTERIOR,
COMMISSIONER TO THE FIVE CIVILIZED TRIBES.
May 1st, 1905, Sapulpa, I.T.

In the matter of the application for the enrollment of Lucinda Simms, as a citizen by blood of the Creek Nation.

Ko-ten-nay being duly sworn by E.C. Griesel, a Notary Public, testified as follows, through interpreter, Noah Gregory.

By Commission.
Q What is your name? A Ko-ten-nay.
Q How old are you? A About 60.
Q What is your post office address? A Beggs.
Q Are you a citizen of the Creek Nation? A Yes sir.
Q To what town do you belong? A Euchee.
Q Did you know a child named Lucinda Simms? A Yes.
Q Who is the father of that child? A Maxey Simms.
Q Who is the mother? A Eliza Simms.
Q Both of the parents are living are they? A Yes sir.
Q About how old is that child? A Born on the 27th day of December, 1904.
Q This is the child (Pointing to the child)? A Yes sir.
Q How near do you live to these people? A About a half a mile.
Q Are you related to them in anyway? A Not very close kin.
Q[sic]

E.C. Criesel[sic], being duly sworn, on his oath, states that the above and foregoing is true and correct transcript of his stenographic notes as taken in said cause on said date.

Edw C Griesel

Subscribed and sworn to before me this 5 day of May, 1905.

Zera E Parrish
Notary Public.

AFFIDAVIT OF DISINTERESTED WITNESSES.

United States of America)
Indian Territory   ) SS
Western District   )

We, the unersigned[sic], on oath state that we are personally acquainted with Louisa Simms, wife of Maxcey[sic] Simms and that there was born to her on or about the 27 day of Dec. 1904, a female child; that said child was living March 4, 1905, and is said to have been named Lucinda Simms.

Applications for Enrollment of Creek Newborn
Act of 1905 Volume X

We further state that we have no interest in this case.

                        J. S. Aldridge
                        (Name Illegible)

(2) Witnesses to mark:

_____

_____

Subscribed and sworn to before me this 13 day of Nov. 1905.

                    (Illegible) Barker

My Com Ex 7/14-1906.   Notary Public.

BIRTH AFFIDAVIT.

DEPARTMENT OF THE INTERIOR.
COMMISSION TO THE FIVE CIVILIZED TRIBES.

IN RE APPLICATION FOR ENROLLMENT, as a citizen of the Creek Nation, of Lucinda Simms, born on the 27 day of December, 1904

Name of Father: Maxcy Simms   a citizen of the Creek Nation.
Name of Mother: Louisa Simms   a citizen of the Creek Nation.

                  Postoffice   Beggs, I. T.

AFFIDAVIT OF MOTHER.

UNITED STATES OF AMERICA, Indian Territory,
    Western   DISTRICT.

I, Louisa Simms, on oath state that I am 20 years of age and a citizen by blood, of the Creek Nation; that I am the lawful wife of Maxcy Simms, who is a citizen, by blood of the Creek Nation; that a female child was born to me on 27 day of Dec., 1904, that said child has been named Lucinda Simms, and was living March 4, 1905.

                          Louisa Simms

Witnesses To Mark:

Subscribed and sworn to before me this 21st. day of April, 1905.

                        N. ?. Barker
                          Notary Public.

My commission expires July 14, 1906.

Applications for Enrollment of Creek Newborn
Act of 1905 Volume X

BIRTH AFFIDAVIT.

See former app   Testimony taken 6/1/05

DEPARTMENT OF THE INTERIOR.
COMMISSION TO THE FIVE CIVILIZED TRIBES.

IN RE APPLICATION FOR ENROLLMENT, as a citizen of the Creek Nation, of Lucinda Simms, born on the 27 day of December, 1904

Name of Father: Maxey[sic] Simms   a citizen of the   Creek   Nation.
Tulwarthlocco
Name of Mother: Louisa   "   a citizen of the   "   Nation.
(Euchee)

Postoffice   Beggs

AFFIDAVIT OF MOTHER.

Child Present

UNITED STATES OF AMERICA, Indian Territory, }
   Western   DISTRICT.   }

I, Louisa Simms, on oath state that I am 20 years of age and a citizen by blood, of the Creek Nation; that I am the lawful wife of Maxcy Simms, who is a citizen, by blood of the Creek Nation; that a female child was born to me on 27 day of December, 1904, that said child has been named Lucinda Simms, and was living March 4, 1905.

Louisa Simms

Witnesses To Mark:
{

Subscribed and sworn to before me this 1 day of May, 1905.

(Seal)   Edw C Griesel
                                    Notary Public.

AFFIDAVIT OF ATTENDING PHYSICIAN OR MID-WIFE.

UNITED STATES OF AMERICA, Indian Territory, }
   Western   DISTRICT.   }

I, Maxcy Simms, a (blank), on oath state that I attended on Mrs. Louisa Simms my wife of (blank) on the 27 day of Dec, 1904; that there was born to her on said date a female child; that said child was living March 4, 1905, and is said to have been named Lucinda Simms

Maxcy Simms

Applications for Enrollment of Creek Newborn
Act of 1905   Volume X

Witnesses To Mark:
{

Subscribed and sworn to before me this 1 day of May, 1905.

(Seal)   Edw C Griesel
                                       Notary Public.

BIRTH AFFIDAVIT.

DEPARTMENT OF THE INTERIOR.
COMMISSION TO THE FIVE CIVILIZED TRIBES.

IN RE APPLICATION FOR ENROLLMENT, as a citizen of the Creek Nation, of Lucindy Sims, born on the 27th day of December, 1904

Name of Father: Maxie Sims   a citizen of the Creek Nation.
Name of Mother: Louisa Sims   a citizen of the Creek Nation.

                        Postoffice   Beggs I.T.

AFFIDAVIT OF MOTHER.

UNITED STATES OF AMERICA, Indian Territory, }
     Western   DISTRICT.

      I, Louisa Sims, on oath state that I am 20 years of age and a citizen by blood, of the Creek Nation; that I am the lawful wife of Maxie Sims, who is a citizen, by blood of the Creek Nation; that a female child was born to me on 27 day of December, 1904, that said child has been named Lucindy Sims, and was living March 4, 1905.

                                   Louisa Sims

Witnesses To Mark:
{

Subscribed and sworn to before me 21st day of April, 1905.

                               Richard J Hill
                                 Notary Public.

My commission expires March $25^{\underline{th}}$ 1909

Applications for Enrollment of Creek Newborn
Act of 1905   Volume X

AFFIDAVIT OF ATTENDING PHYSICIAN OR MID-WIFE.

UNITED STATES OF AMERICA, Indian Territory,
    Western   DISTRICT.

    I, Maxie Sims , a Acting Midwife , on oath state that I attended on Mrs. Louisa Sims , wife of Maxie Sims (Myself) on the 27th day of December , 1904 ; that there was born to her on said date a female child; that said child was living March 4, 1905, and ~~is said to have~~ has been named Lucindy Sims

                                       Maxie Sims

Witnesses To Mark:

    Subscribed and sworn to before me 21st day of April , 1905.

                                       Richard J Hill
                                              Notary Public.
My commission expires March 25th 1909

                          Muskogee, Indian Territory, October 5, 1905.

Maxey Simms,
    Beggs, Indian Territory.

Dear Sir:

    In the matter of the application for the enrollment of your minor child, Lucinda Simms, as a citizen by blood of the Creek Nation, this office is unable to identify your wife, Louisa Simms on its roll of Creek citizens.

    You are requested to state her maiden name, the names of her parents, the Creek Indian Town to which she belongs, and, if possible, the roll number which appears on her deeds to land in the Creek Nation.

                                Respectfully,
                                                 Commissioner.

Applications for Enrollment of Creek Newborn
Act of 1905   Volume X

NC-836.

Muskogee, Indian Territory, October 19, 1905.

Louisa Simms,
 c/o Maxey Simms,
  Beggs, Indian Territory.

Dear Madam:

 In the matter of the application for the enrollment of your minor child, Lucinda Simms, born December 27, 1904, as a citizen by blood of the Creek Nation, this office is unable to identify you upon the final roll of citizens by blood of the Creek Nation. It is necessary that you be so identified before the rights of said child can be finally determined.

 You are, therefore, requested to state the name under which you have been finally enrolled, the names of your parents and other members of your family, the Creek Indian town to which you belong and your final roll number as the same appears upon your allotment certificate and deeds.

      Respectfully,

          Commissioner.

(The letter below typed as given.)

NC-836   (copy)

      BEGGS, IND. TER. 10/25, 1905.

Commission to the five civilized Tribes,
  Muskogee, I. T.

Dear Sir:

 Replying to the first & second will state that my wife Louisa Simms' parents are as follows Capanny Snow yarla cowera Snow Louisa Snow Wesley Snow &Hattie Snow, one her sisters is omitted in this, not knowing whether it shows on the Record By the name of Snow because she is married her name may go by Pepper so I omitted her. But Louisa Simms, her maiden name would show as Louisa Snow. The number of her certificate is No. 10707 I will also request the Commission how long will it be before it would be ready to file for Lucinda Simms And, I further request the Commission if the deeds of Maxcy Simms Bunner Simms Wesley Willies and Rogee Willies and Louisa Snow's are ready to be deliver. Please send me the plate of Township 16 Range 10 east and T. S. 16 R 11 E showing the vcant land as it is impossible for any of us to find out which is vcant and which is not, and also will ask the Commission if they would hold or not fear all the land will be taken before we could file

       Yours truly
        (signed)   MAXCY SIMMS
       By Louisa Snow Simms

Applications for Enrollment of Creek Newborn
Act of 1905 Volume X

N.C. 836

Muskogee, Indian Territory, November 2, 1905.

Maxey Sims,
    Beggs, Indian Territory.

Dear Sir:

    Receipt is acknowledged of your letter of October 25, 1905, containing information which enables this office to identify your wife, Louisa Sims, on the approved roll of citizens by blood of the Creek Nation.

    You are advised that before the right to enrollment of your child, Lucinda Sims, can be determined, it will be necessary for you to furnish this office with the affidavit of one disinterested witness, a blank for which is herewith enclosed.

                    Respectfully,

                                      Commissioner.

1 Dis.

(The letter below typed as given.)

N C 836

Beggs Ind. Ter Nov. 13, 1905

Commission to the Five Civilized tribes
    Muskogee I. T.

Dear Sir,

    I had over looked the letter and got two witness, But I have witness who are not interested in this case whatever. But they know the time and that the child was liveing March fourth, Please let us know if we could come to file and if both of us or Just one of us need come

                                        (Signed) Maxey Simms.

Applications for Enrollment of Creek Newborn
Act of 1905 Volume X

NC-837.

Muskogee, Indian Territory, October 19, 1905.

Millie Fulsom,
    c/o Tom Fulsom,
        Kellyville, Indian Territory.

Dear Madam:

    In the matter of the application for the enrollment of your minor child, Rhoda Fulsom, born March 2, 1904, as a citizen by blood of the Creek Nation, you are advised that this office requires the affidavit of the physician or midwife who attended at the birth of said child and a blank for that purpose is inclosed herewith.

    If there was no physician or midwife in attendance when said child was born it will be necessary for you to furnish this office with the affidavits of two disinterested witnesses relative to the birth of said child. Said affidavits must set forth said child's name, the date of her birth, the names of her parents and whether or not she was living on March 4, 1905.

                      Respectfully,

                                  Commissioner.

B C
Env.

BIRTH AFFIDAVIT.

DEPARTMENT OF THE INTERIOR.
COMMISSION TO THE FIVE CIVILIZED TRIBES.

    IN RE APPLICATION FOR ENROLLMENT, as a citizen of the Creek Nation, of Rhoda Fulsom, born on the 2 day of March, 1904

Name of Father: Tom Fulsom (Euchee)	a citizen of the Creek	Nation.
Name of Mother: Millie Fulsom (Euchee)	a citizen of the "	Nation.

                      Postoffice   Kellyville

                  AFFIDAVIT OF MOTHER.   Child Present

UNITED STATES OF AMERICA, Indian Territory, ⎫
    Western   DISTRICT. ⎭

    I, Millie Fulsom, on oath state that I am 30 years of age and a citizen by blood, of the Creek Nation; that I am the lawful wife of Tom Fulsom, who is a citizen, by

Applications for Enrollment of Creek Newborn
Act of 1905   Volume X

blood of the Creek Nation; that a female child was born to me on 2 day of March, 1904, that said child has been named Rhoda Fulsom, and was living March 4, 1905.

                                                Her
                                     Millie x Fulsom

Witnesses To Mark: mark
  { David Shelby
    Jesse McDermott

Subscribed and sworn to before me this 24 day of April, 1905.

                                        Edw C Griesel
                                        Notary Public.

            AFFIDAVIT OF ATTENDING ~~PHYSICIAN OR MID-WIFE~~. No one else present
                                   Father

UNITED STATES OF AMERICA, Indian Territory, }
    Western   **DISTRICT.**

I, Tom Fulsom, a ~~Mid wife~~, on oath state that I attended on Mrs. Millie Fulsom my, wife ~~of Tom Fulsom~~ on the 2 day of March, 1904; that there was born to her on said date a female child; that said child was living March 4, 1905, and is said to have been named Rhoda Fulsom
                                       His
                                   Tom x Fulsom
                                      mark

Witnesses To Mark:
  { David Shelby
    Jesse McDermott

Subscribed and sworn to before me this 24 day of April, 1905.

                                      Edw C Griesel
                                        Notary Public.

BIRTH AFFIDAVIT.
                          DEPARTMENT OF THE INTERIOR.
           COMMISSION TO THE FIVE CIVILIZED TRIBES.

    IN RE APPLICATION FOR ENROLLMENT, as a citizen of the Creek Nation, of Rhoda Fulsom, born on the 1st day of March, 1904

Name of Father: Thomas Fulsom   a citizen of the Creek   Nation.
Name of Mother: Millie Fulsom   a citizen of the Creek   Nation.

                    Postoffice   Sapulpa, Ind. Ter.

Applications for Enrollment of Creek Newborn
Act of 1905 Volume X

AFFIDAVIT OF ~~MOTHER~~. Ac<u>quaintance</u>

UNITED STATES OF AMERICA, Indian Territory, }
Western DISTRICT.

I, Wydie Co-tan-ny , on oath state that I am about 35 years of age and a citizen by blood , of the Creek Nation; that I am ~~the lawful wife of~~ acquainted with Millie Fulsom , who is a citizen, by blood of the Creek Nation; that a female child was born to ~~me~~ her on 1st day of March , 1904 , that said child has been named Rhoda Fulsom , and is now living.

                                                               her
                                      Wydie x Co-tan-ny
Witnesses To Mark: mark
{ James J. Mars
{ S.W. Brown

Subscribed and sworn to before me this 23rd day of October , 1905.

                                      James J Mars
                                      Notary Public.

BIRTH AFFIDAVIT.

DEPARTMENT OF THE INTERIOR.
COMMISSION TO THE FIVE CIVILIZED TRIBES.

IN RE APPLICATION FOR ENROLLMENT, as a citizen of the Creek Nation, of Rhoda Fulsom , born on the 1st day of March , 1904

Name of Father: Thomas Fulsom	a citizen of the Creek	Nation.
Name of Mother: Millie Fulsom	a citizen of the Creek	Nation.

                             Postoffice   Sapulpa, Ind. Ter.

AFFIDAVIT OF MOTHER.

UNITED STATES OF AMERICA, Indian Territory, }
Western DISTRICT.

I, Millie Fulsom , on oath state that I am 32 or 33 years of age and a citizen by blood , of the Creek Nation; that I am the lawful wife of Thomas Fulsom , who is a citizen, by blood of the Creek Nation; that a female child was born to me on 1st day of March , 1904 , that said child has been named Rhoda Fulsom , and is now living.

Applications for Enrollment of Creek Newborn
Act of 1905   Volume X

                                                  her
                                      Millie x Fulsom
Witnesses To Mark: mark
 { James J. Mars
  S.W. Brown

Subscribed and sworn to before me this 23rd day of October, 1905.

                                          James J Mars
                                          Notary Public.

AFFIDAVIT OF ATTENDING PHYSICIAN OR MID-WIFE.

UNITED STATES OF AMERICA, Indian Territory, }
    Western   DISTRICT.

                                                  know that
I, Co-tan-ny , a Creek citizen , on oath state that I ~~attended on Mrs~~. Mrs Thomas Fulsom , wife of Thomas Fulsom on the 1st day of March, 1904 ; that there was born to her on said date a female child; that said child is now living and is said to have been named Rhoda Fulsom
                                         his
                                    Co-tan-ny x
Witnesses To Mark: mark
 { James J. Mars
  S.W. Brown
Subscribed and sworn to before me this 23rd day of October, 1905.

    My commission expires May 7, 1907.   James J Mars
                                              Notary Public.

NC-836.

                                  Muskogee, Indian Territory, October 19, 1905.

Mary Tate,
      c/o John Washington Tate,
          Sapulpa, Indian Territory.

Dear Madam:

      In the matter of the application for the enrollment of your minor child, Flora Ada Tate, born July 26, 1903, as a citizen by blood of the Creek Nation, the words "that said child was living March 4, 1905" in the affidavit of the physician, who attended at the

Applications for Enrollment of Creek Newborn
Act of 1905 Volume X

birth of said child, have been erased. It is necessary, in order that the rights of said child may be determined, that you furnish this office with the affidavit of the physician, who attended at the birth of said child, showing that the said Flora Ada Tate was living March 4, 1905.

In the event that you are unable to secure the affidavit of said physician it will be necessary for you to furnish this office with the affidavits of two disinterested witnesses relative to the birth of said child. Said affidavits to set forth said child's name, the date of her birth, the names of her parents and whether or not she was living on March 4, 1905.

This matter should receive your immediate attention.

Respectfully,

Commissioner.

B C
Env

BIRTH AFFIDAVIT.

DEPARTMENT OF THE INTERIOR
COMMISSION TO THE FIVE CIVILIZED TRIBES.

In Re Application for Enrollment, as a citizen of the Creek Nation, of Annie May Tate, born on the 9 day of Sept , 1901

Name of Father: J. W. Tate   a citizen of the ——————Nation.
Name of Mother: Mary P Tate   a citizen of the Creek Nation.
(Ketchepatche)

Postoffice   Sapulpa, I. T.

Affidavit of Mother   Child Brought in
5/24/05 - Gr

UNITED STATES OF AMERICA, INDIAN TERRITORY,
     Western   DISTRICT.

I, Mary Tate , on oath state that I am 39 in Aug 1905 years of age and a citizen by blood , of the Creek Nation; that I am the lawful wife of J. W. Tate , who is a non citizen, by (blank) of the (blank) Nation; that a female child was born to me on 9 day of September , 1901 , that said child has been named Annie May Tate , and was living March 4, 1905.

                                      her
                               Mary x Tate

WITNESSES TO MARK: MARK
    { D.A. McDougal
      Angie Pettigrew

Applications for Enrollment of Creek Newborn
Act of 1905   Volume X

Subscribed and sworn to before me this   12 day of Apr , 1905.

E. S. (Illegible)
Notary Public.

𝕬𝖋𝖋𝖎𝖉𝖆𝖛𝖎𝖙 𝖔𝖋 𝕬𝖙𝖙𝖊𝖓𝖉𝖎𝖓𝖌 𝕻𝖍𝖞𝖘𝖎𝖈𝖎𝖆𝖓 𝖔𝖗 𝕸𝖎𝖉-𝖂𝖎𝖋𝖊

UNITED STATES OF AMERICA, INDIAN TERRITORY,⎫
   Western   DISTRICT.⎭

    I, Angie Pettigrew , a midwife's assistant , on oath state that I attended on Mrs. Mary Tate , wife of J. W. Tate on the 9$^{\underline{th}}$ day of Sept. , 1901 ; that there was born to her on said date a female child; that said child was living March 4, 1905, and is said to have been named   Annie May Tate

Angie Pettigrew

WITNESSES TO MARK:
{

Subscribed and sworn to before me this   12 day of Apr , 1905.

E. S. (Illegible)
Notary Public.

BIRTH AFFIDAVIT.

DEPARTMENT OF THE INTERIOR.
COMMISSION TO THE FIVE CIVILIZED TRIBES.

    IN RE APPLICATION FOR ENROLLMENT, as a citizen of the Creek Nation, of Flora Ada Tate, born on the 26 day of July , 1903

Name of Father: John W. Tate   a citizen of the not a citizen   Nation.
Name of Mother: Mary Tate   a citizen of the   Creek   Nation.

Postoffice   Sapulpa, Ind. Ter.

AFFIDAVIT OF MOTHER.

UNITED STATES OF AMERICA, Indian Territory,⎫
   Western   DISTRICT.⎭

    I,   Mary Tate , on oath state that I am 39 years of age and a citizen by blood , of the Creek   Nation; that I am the lawful wife of   John W. Tate, a non-citizen , ~~who is a citizen, by~~ *(blank)* of the Creek Nation; that a Female child was born to me on 26 day of July , 1903 , that said child has been named Flora Ada Tate , and is now living.

Applications for Enrollment of Creek Newborn
Act of 1905 Volume X

                                        her
Witnesses To Mark: Mary x Tate
{ R. B. Thompson   mark
  J J Query

Subscribed and sworn to before me this 26 day of October, 1905.

                                    R. C. Kinnaird
                                    Notary Public.

AFFIDAVIT OF ATTENDING PHYSICIAN OR MID-WIFE.

UNITED STATES OF AMERICA, Indian Territory,
    Western   DISTRICT.

I, H. O. Lyford, a Physician, on oath state that I attended on Mrs. Mary Tate, wife of John W. Tate on the 26 day of July, 1903; that there was born to her on said date a female child; that said child is now living and is said to have been named Flora Ada Tate

                                 H. O. Lyford
Witnesses To Mark:
{

Subscribed and sworn to before me this 28 day of April, 1905.

                                    Notary Public.

BIRTH AFFIDAVIT.

DEPARTMENT OF THE INTERIOR.
COMMISSION TO THE FIVE CIVILIZED TRIBES.

IN RE APPLICATION FOR ENROLLMENT, as a citizen of the Creek Nation, of Flora Ada Tate, born on the 26 day of July, 1903

Name of Father: John Washington Tate   a citizen of the   U. S.   Nation.
Name of Mother: Mary Tate   a citizen of the   Creek   Nation.
(Ketchapatacha)
                            Postoffice   Sapulpa

Applications for Enrollment of Creek Newborn
Act of 1905   Volume X

AFFIDAVIT OF MOTHER.   Child Present

UNITED STATES OF AMERICA, Indian Territory, }
Western   DISTRICT.

I, Mary Tate , on oath state that I am 39 years of age and a citizen by blood , of the Creek Nation; that I am the lawful wife of John Washington Tate , who is a citizen, by *(blank)* of the U. S. Nation; that a female child was born to me on 26 day of July , 1903 , that said child has been named Flora Ada Tate , and was living March 4, 1905.

                                              Her
Witnesses To Mark: Mary x Tate
  { David Shelby   mark
    Jesse McDermott

Subscribed and sworn to before me this 24 day of April , 1905.

(Seal)   Edw C Griesel
                                              Notary Public.

AFFIDAVIT OF ATTENDING PHYSICIAN OR MID-WIFE.

UNITED STATES OF AMERICA, Indian Territory, }
Western   DISTRICT.

I, H. O. Lyford , a Physician , on oath state that I attended on Mrs. Mary Tate , wife of Jon W. Tate on the 26 day of July , 1903 ; that there was born to her on said date a female child; that said child was living March 4, 1905, and is said to have been named Flora Ada Tate

                                            H. O. Lyford

Witnesses To Mark:

{

Subscribed and sworn to before me this 24 day of April , 1905.

(Seal)   Edw C Griesel
                                              Notary Public.

Applications for Enrollment of Creek Newborn
Act of 1905 Volume X

NC-839.

Muskogee, Indian Territory, October 19, 1905.

Mary Peeper,
    c/o Frank Peeper,
        Kellyville, Indian Territory.

Dear Madam:

    In the matter of the application for the enrollment of your minor child, Viney May Peeper, born December 23, 1904, as a citizen by blood of the Creek Nation, rthis office requires the affidavit of the physician or midwife who attended at the birth of said child and a blank for that purpose is inclosed herewith.

    In the event that no physician or midwife attended on you when said child was born it will be necessary for you to furnish this office with the affidavits of two disinterested persons relative to the birth of said child. Said affidavits must set forth said child's name, the date of her birth, the names of her parents and whether or not she was living on March 4, 1905.

                Respectfully,

                            Commissioner.

B C
Env.

BIRTH AFFIDAVIT.

DEPARTMENT OF THE INTERIOR.
COMMISSION TO THE FIVE CIVILIZED TRIBES.

    IN RE APPLICATION FOR ENROLLMENT, as a citizen of the Creek Nation, of Viney May Peeper , born on the 23 day of Dec , 1904

Name of Father: Frank Peeper   a citizen of the U.S.A.   Nation.
Name of Mother: Mary Peeper   a citizen of the   Creek   Nation.

                      Postoffice   Kellyville I.T.

AFFIDAVIT OF MOTHER.

UNITED STATES OF AMERICA, Indian Territory, ⎫
    Western   DISTRICT. ⎬

    I, Mary Peeper , on oath state that I am about 30 years of age and a citizen by Blood , of the Creek Nation; that I am the lawful wife of Frank Peeper , who is a citizen, by birth of the U.S.A. Nation; that a female child was born to me on 23

Applications for Enrollment of Creek Newborn
Act of 1905   Volume X

day of December, 1904, that said child has been named Viney May Peeper, and is now living.

Mary Peeper

Witnesses To Mark:
{ W.W. Holder
  T.J. Taggart

Subscribed and sworn to before me this 26 day of Oct, 1905.

My Commission   W.W. Holder
Expires Sept 8, 1906   Notary Public.

AFFIDAVIT OF ATTENDING PHYSICIAN OR MID-WIFE.

UNITED STATES OF AMERICA, Indian Territory,
    Western   DISTRICT.

I, Ca-Pon-na Snow, a Indian Dr., on oath state that I attended on Mrs. Frank Peeper, wife of Frank Peeper on the 23 day of Dec, 1904; that there was born to her on said date a female child; that said child is now living and is said to have been named Viney May Peeper

Mary
His
x   Ca-Pon-na Snow
mark

Witnesses To Mark:
{ W.W. Holder
  T.J. Taggart

Subscribed and sworn to before me this 26 day of Oct, 1905.

W.W. Holder
Notary Public.

BIRTH AFFIDAVIT.

DEPARTMENT OF THE INTERIOR.
COMMISSION TO THE FIVE CIVILIZED TRIBES.

IN RE APPLICATION FOR ENROLLMENT, as a citizen of the Creek Nation, of Viney May Peepar, born on the 23 day of Dec, 1904

Name of Father: Frank Peepar   a citizen of the   U.S.   ~~Nation~~.
Name of Mother: Mary "   a citizen of the   Creek   Nation.
(Euchee Town)

Postoffice   Kellyville I.T.

Applications for Enrollment of Creek Newborn
Act of 1905   Volume X

AFFIDAVIT OF MOTHER.   Child present.

UNITED STATES OF AMERICA, Indian Territory, ⎱
    Western   DISTRICT. ⎰

      I, Mary Peepar , on oath state that I am 25 years of age and a citizen by blood , of the Creek   Nation; that I am the lawful wife of Frank Peepar , who is not a citizen, by *(blank)* of the Creek   Nation; that a female   child was born to me on 23   day of Dec , 1904 , that said child has been named Viney May Peepar , and was living March 4, 1905.

Mary Peepar

Witnesses To Mark:
⎰
⎱

      Subscribed and sworn to before me this 24" day of April , 1905.

(Seal)   J McDermott
                                             Notary Public.

Father
AFFIDAVIT OF <s>ATTENDING PHYSICIAN OR MID-WIFE</s>.

UNITED STATES OF AMERICA, Indian Territory, ⎱
    Western   DISTRICT. ⎰

      I, Frank Peepar , <s>a</s> *(blank)* , on oath state that I attended on <s>Mrs</s>.   my   , wife of   when   on the 23 day of Dec , 1904 ; that there was born to her on said date a *(blank)* child; that said child was living March 4, 1905, and is said to have been named Viney May Peepar

Frank Peepar

Witnesses To Mark:
⎰
⎱

      Subscribed and sworn to before me this 24" day of April , 1905.

(Seal)   J McDermott
                                             Notary Public.

Applications for Enrollment of Creek Newborn
Act of 1905   Volume X

BIRTH AFFIDAVIT.

DEPARTMENT OF THE INTERIOR,
COMMISSIONER TO THE FIVE CIVILIZED TRIBES.

IN RE APPLICATION FOR ENROLLMENT, as a citizen of the Creek------------------ Nation, of   Arlie S. Blank,----------------, born on the 20th. day of September-----------, 1901
(Here insert name of child.)

Name of Father: John C.W. Bland-----------------   a citizen of the United States Nation.
Name of Mother: Sue A. Bland--------------------   a citizen of the Creek----------Nation.

Postoffice   Red-Fork, Indian Territory.

AFFIDAVIT OF MOTHER.

UNITED STATES OF AMERICA, Indian Territory,
Western Judicial   District.

I, Sue A. Bland----------------- , on oath state that I am 38------ years of age and a citizen by blood------ , of the Creek--------------- Nation; that I am the lawful wife of John C.W. Bland------------- , who is a citizen, by *(blank)* of the *(blank)* Nation; that a female------- child was born to me on 20th. day of September , 1901 , that said child has been named Arlie S. Bland------------------ , and was living March 4, 1905.

Sue A Bland

Witness to Mark:

Subscribed and sworn to before me this 24   day of   April , 1905.

W. S. McCluskey
My Commission Expires April 28th 1907.   Notary Public.

AFFIDAVIT OF ATTENDING PHYSICIAN OR MID-WIFE.

UNITED STATES OF AMERICA, Indian Territory,
Western Judicial ------------ District.

I,   Rhoda Cash---------------- , a citizen of Sapulpa, I.T.   , on oath state that I attended on Mrs. Sue A. Bland---------- , wife of John C:W. Bland-------------------- on the 20th.---- day of September , 1901 ; that there was born to her on said date a female--child; that said child was living March 4, 1905, and is said to have been named Arlie S. Bland-------------------
her
Rhoda x Cash
mark

Applications for Enrollment of Creek Newborn
Act of 1905 Volume X

Witness to Mark:
(Illegible) Cash }
FL Mars }

Subscribed and sworn to before me this 24th day of April A.D. , 1905.

         F.L. Mars
            Notary Public.
My Commission expires July 11, 1906.

BIRTH AFFIDAVIT.

DEPARTMENT OF THE INTERIOR,
COMMISSIONER TO THE FIVE CIVILIZED TRIBES.

IN RE APPLICATION FOR ENROLLMENT, as a citizen of the Creek-------------- Nation, of Davis M. Blank,---------------, born on the 1st. day of March-----, 1905
(Here insert name of child.)

Name of Father: John C.W. Bland---------------- a citizen of the United States---Nation.
Name of Mother: Sue A. Bland-------------------- a citizen of the Creek-----------Nation.

     Postoffice Red-Fork, Indian Territory.

AFFIDAVIT OF MOTHER.

UNITED STATES OF AMERICA, Indian Territory, }
 Western Judicial -----   District. }

  I, Sue A. Bland----------------, on oath state that I am 38------ years of age and a citizen by blood------, of the Creek---------------------Nation; that I am the lawful wife of John C.W. Bland-------------, who is a citizen, by ---------- of the ---------- Nation; that a male------- child was born to me on 1st.----- day of March--------, 1905, that said child has been named Davis M. Bland------------------, and was living March 4, 1905.

          Sue A Bland

Witness to Mark:
----------------------------------}
----------------------------------}

Subscribed and sworn to before me this 24 day of April , 1905.

         W. S. McCluskey
My Commission Expires April 28th 1907.   Notary Public.

Applications for Enrollment of Creek Newborn
Act of 1905 Volume X

AFFIDAVIT OF ATTENDING PHYSICIAN OR MID-WIFE.

UNITED STATES OF AMERICA, Indian Territory,
Western Judicial ------------ District.

    I, Carrie Daugherty------------, a citizen of Red Fork, I.T., on oath state that I attended on Mrs. Sue A. Bland----------, wife of John C.W. Bland-------------------- on the 1st---- day of March, 1905; that there was born to her on said date a male-- child; that said child was living March 4, 1905, and is said to have been named Davis M. Bland---

                                            Carrie Daugherty

Witness to Mark:

    Subscribed and sworn to before me this 24 day of April, 1905.

                                        W. S. McCluskey
My Commission Expires April 28th 1907.   Notary Public.

BIRTH AFFIDAVIT.

DEPARTMENT OF THE INTERIOR.
COMMISSION TO THE FIVE CIVILIZED TRIBES.

    IN RE APPLICATION FOR ENROLLMENT, as a citizen of the Creek Nation, of Ada Littlehead, born on the 27 day of ~~June~~ May, 1903.

Name of Father: Willie Littlehead   a citizen of the   Creek   Nation.
(Euchee)
Name of Mother: Nannie   "   a citizen of the   Creek   Nation.
(Euchee)

                              Postoffice   Kellyville

                          AFFIDAVIT OF MOTHER.   Child Present

UNITED STATES OF AMERICA, Indian Territory,
    Western   DISTRICT.

    I, Nannie Littlehead, on oath state that I am 29 years of age and a citizen by blood, of the Creek Nation; that I am the lawful wife of Willie Littlehead, who is a citizen, by blood of the Creek Nation; that a female child was born to me on 27 day of ~~June~~ May, 1903, that said child has been named Ada Littlehead, and was living March 4, 1905.

321

Applications for Enrollment of Creek Newborn
Act of 1905 Volume X

Her
Nannie x Littlehead
mark

Witnesses To Mark:
  { David Shelby
    Jesse McDermott

Subscribed and sworn to before me this 24 day of April, 1905.

Edw C Griesel
Notary Public.

AFFIDAVIT OF ATTENDING PHYSICIAN OR MID-WIFE.

UNITED STATES OF AMERICA, Indian Territory, }
    Western   DISTRICT.

I, Po-kan-ney-wee Littlehead, a Mid wife, on oath state that I attended on Mrs. Nannie Littlehead, wife of Willie Littlehead on the 27 day of ~~June~~ May, 1903; that there was born to her on said date a female child; that said child was living March 4, 1905, and is said to have been named Ada Littlehead

her
Po-kan-ney-wee x Littlehead
mark

Witnesses To Mark:
  { David Shelby
    Jesse McDermott

Subscribed and sworn to before me this 24 day of April, 1905.

Edw C Griesel
Notary Public.

OCP

REFER IN REPLY TO THE FOLLOWING:

**DEPARTMENT OF THE INTERIOR,
COMMISSIONER TO THE FIVE CIVILIZED TRIBES.**

Muskogee, Indian Territory, November 10, 1906.

Rebecca Harry,
    Care of Wheaton Harry,
        Sapulpa, Indian Territory.

Dear Madam:--

Applications for Enrollment of Creek Newborn
Act of 1905 Volume X

Receipt is acknowledged of your letter of October ?, 1906, in which you request that certain land be reserved from allotment pending the enrollment of your minor child, Lizzie Harry.

You are advised that this office does not deem it advisable to reserve from allotment any land in the Creek Nation for persons who may have pending applications for enrollment. However, if you will furnish this office with a detailed description of said land, giving the section, township and range, it will be noted on the plats of this office as claimed by you, and should any other person make application for it, you will be duly notified.

                        Respectfully,
                        Tams Bixby
                                  Commissioner.

JP.

BIRTH AFFIDAVIT.

DEPARTMENT OF THE INTERIOR.
COMMISSION TO THE FIVE CIVILIZED TRIBES.

Twin of Liza

    IN RE APPLICATION FOR ENROLLMENT, as a citizen of the Creek Nation, of Susie Harry, born on the 5 day of Feb, 1902

Name of Father: John Harry   a citizen of the Creek Nation.
(Tuskegee)
Name of Mother: Mary Harry   a citizen of the Creek Nation.
(Tuskegee)

                        Postoffice   Keystone, Oklahoma

                      AFFIDAVIT OF MOTHER.   Child Present

UNITED STATES OF AMERICA, Indian Territory,
    Western   **DISTRICT.**

    I, Mary Harry, on oath state that I am 30 years of age and a citizen by blood, of the Creek Nation; that I am the lawful wife of John Harry, who is a citizen, by blood of the Creek Nation; that a female child was born to me on 5 day of Feb, 1902, that said child has been named Susie Harry, and was living March 4, 1905.

                                    Mary Harry

Witnesses To Mark:

Applications for Enrollment of Creek Newborn
Act of 1905   Volume X

Subscribed and sworn to before me this 24 day of April , 1905.

(Seal)   Edw C Griesel
                                              Notary Public.

AFFIDAVIT OF ATTENDING PHYSICIAN OR MID-WIFE.

UNITED STATES OF AMERICA, Indian Territory, ⎫
      Western   DISTRICT.   ⎬
                                                ⎭

I, Annie Staley , a Mid Wife , on oath state that I attended on Mrs. Mary Harry, wife of John Harry on the 5 day of Feb , 1902 ; that there was born to her on said date a female child; that said child was living March 4, 1905, and is said to have been named Susie Harry

                                            Her
                                     Annie x Staley
Witnesses To Mark: mark
   ⎰ David Shelby
   ⎱ Jesse McDermott

Subscribed and sworn to before me this 24 day of April , 1905.

(Seal)   Edw C Griesel
                                              Notary Public.

BIRTH AFFIDAVIT.

DEPARTMENT OF THE INTERIOR.
COMMISSION TO THE FIVE CIVILIZED TRIBES.

Twin of Susie

IN RE APPLICATION FOR ENROLLMENT, as a citizen of the Creek Nation, of Liza Harry, born on the 5 day of Feb , 1902

Name of Father: John Harry   a citizen of the   Creek   Nation.
(Tuskegee)
Name of Mother: Mary Harry   a citizen of the   Creek   Nation.
(Tuskegee)

                    Postoffice   Keystone, Okla

AFFIDAVIT OF MOTHER.   Child Present

UNITED STATES OF AMERICA, Indian Territory, ⎫
      Western   DISTRICT.   ⎬
                                                ⎭

I, Mary Harry , on oath state that I am 30 years of age and a citizen by blood , of the Creek   Nation; that I am the lawful wife of John Harry , who is a citizen, by blood of the Creek   Nation; that a female child was born to me on 5 day of Feb , 1902 , that said child has been named Liza Harry , and was living March 4, 1905.

Applications for Enrollment of Creek Newborn
Act of 1905   Volume X

Mary Harry

Witnesses To Mark:
{

Subscribed and sworn to before me this 24 day of April, 1905.

Edw C Griesel
Notary Public.

AFFIDAVIT OF ATTENDING PHYSICIAN OR MID-WIFE.

UNITED STATES OF AMERICA, Indian Territory,
    Western   DISTRICT.

I, Annie Staley, a Mid wife, on oath state that I attended on Mrs. Mary Harry, wife of John Harry on the 5 day of Feb, 1902; that there was born to her on said date a *(blank)* child; that said child was living March 4, 1905, and is said to have been named Liza Harry

                              Her
                       Annie x Staley

Witnesses To Mark: mark
{ David Shelby
  Jesse McDermott

Subscribed and sworn to before me this 24 day of April, 1905.

Edw C Griesel
Notary Public.

BIRTH AFFIDAVIT.

DEPARTMENT OF THE INTERIOR.
COMMISSION TO THE FIVE CIVILIZED TRIBES.

IN RE APPLICATION FOR ENROLLMENT, as a citizen of the Creek Nation, of Bunch Harry, born on the 12th day of July, 1904

Name of Father: John Harry   a citizen of the Creek Nation.
                Tuskegee
Name of Mother: Mary Harry   a citizen of the Creek Nation.
                Tuskegee
                       Postoffice   Keystone, Okla

Applications for Enrollment of Creek Newborn
Act of 1905   Volume X

AFFIDAVIT OF MOTHER.   Child Present

UNITED STATES OF AMERICA, Indian Territory, ⎱
   Western   DISTRICT. ⎰

    I, Mary Harry , on oath state that I am 30 years of age and a citizen by blood , of the Creek Nation; that I am the lawful wife of John Harry , who is a citizen, by blood of the Creek Nation; that a male child was born to me on 12th day of July , 1904 , that said child has been named Bunch Harry , and was living March 4, 1905.

                                      Mary Harry

Witnesses To Mark:
{

    Subscribed and sworn to before me this 24 day of April , 1905.

(Seal)   ~~Mary Harry~~
                                       Edw C Griesel
                                           Notary Public.

AFFIDAVIT OF ATTENDING PHYSICIAN OR MID-WIFE.

UNITED STATES OF AMERICA, Indian Territory, ⎱
   Western   DISTRICT. ⎰

    I, Annie Staley , a mid wife , on oath state that I attended on Mrs. Mary Harry, wife of John Harry on the 12th day of July , 1904 ; that there was born to her on said date a male child; that said child was living March 4, 1905, and is said to have been named Bunch Harry

                                     her
                                 Annie x Staley
Witnesses To Mark: mark
  { David Shelby
    Jesse McDermott

    Subscribed and sworn to before me this 24th day of April , 1905.

(Seal)   Edw C Griesel
                                         Notary Public.

Index

ADAMS
  Andrew 221,222
  Annie 219,220,221,222
  Ethel 219,220,222
  Lewis 212,214,215,218,219, 220,221,222
ALBERTY
  Elnora 78
ALDRIDGE
  J S 302
ALEXANDER
  Austin 13,14,15,17
  L 52,53
  Mary 14,15,17
  Rosa 12,13,14,15,17,51
ANDERSON
  Nevada 178
  William L 178
  Wm L 178
ASBUREY
  Mary 6
AUNT MARY 179

BARKER
  (Illegible) 302
  N ? 302
BARNETT
  Clifford Marion 243,244,245,248, 249
  Clifton 247,248
  Geo S 246
  George 243,244,247,248,249
  Hattie 243,244,247,248,249
BAYNE
  R A 287
BEALL
  Wm O 88,125
BEAR
  Hannah 144
  Joe 148,149,152,153
  Lena 123
  Lola 145,146,154
  March 147,148,149,150,151,152
  Marche 149,150,154
  Margie 154,155
  Morgie 145,146

  Nettie 145,146,147,148,149,150, 151,152,154
  Roley 147,148,149,150,151,154
BEARD
  Dr 181
  G W 184
BEAVER
  Daniel 12
  Heliswa 123
  Kaska 123
BEAVERS
  B J 281,282
  Beth J 281
BEDFORD
  Edwin G 140
BEHEN
  Cheyargee 185
  Sefiye 185
BELL
  Sarah 33
BENSON
  Nathan 296,297
BENTLEY
  Farnes E 173
  James E 169,170,172
BENTON
  Robert 67,68,70
BERRYHILL
  Elnora 76,77,80
  Elnore 77
  Ione 76,77,80
  James 76,77,78,80
  Lizzie 86,89,90
  Tobe 90
BERRYHILLE
  Elnora 79,80
  Ione 79,80
  James 79
BIG MOSQUITO 265
BIGPOND
  Nancy 186
BIRD
  Millisie 188,190
BIXBY 59
  Commissioner 57
  Mr 283

Tams 10,35,54,61,74,77,87,103, 110,111,121,124,130,132,134,155,159, 167,168,176,185,204,230,243,255, 275,282,285,323
BLAND
  Arlie S 319
  Davis M 320,321
  John C W 319,320,321
  Sue A 319,320,321
BOSEY
  Joseph 262,263,264
BOSTON
  Don 262,264
  Ell 262
  Ella 264
  Josephine (Posey) 262,263,264
  Mrs 262,263
BOWMAN
  Dollie 66
BRIGHT
  John 82
BROOK
  Jeanetta 118
  Jeannette A 123
  John 123
BROWN
  Annie 31,32
  Belle 56,57
  Delpha May 56,57
  Ella 192
  George 31
  Georgia 264,265,266,267
  Hardin 264,265,266,267
  Henry 31,32
  Larry 264,265,266,267
  Lizzie 31
  S W 310,311
  Thomas 31
BRUNER
  Bertha 27,28
  Betty 27,28,29
  Daniel 27,28,29
  John 29
  Lucy 29,169,170,171,172,173
  Maggie 28,29
BUCK
  John 32

Rosa 32
Rose 32
BUFORD
  Charles 226,227
BURGESS
  Fannie 138

CAIN
  W A 80
CALL
  Charles 66
  John M 66
  Pearl 66
CARLOS
  C C Don 183
CARSON
  M D 57
CASH
  (Illegible) 320
  Rhoda 319
CAT
  Matilda 209
CESARPE 56
CHAMBERLAIN
  Maggie 210
CHAMBLEN
  Sarah 215,216,220,221
  Sarak 212
CHAMBLIN
  Anna 218
  Sarah 213,216
CHILDERS
  Rose 281
CHISHOLM
  Jennie 99
CHOFULOP 44
CHOSILEE 119
CHOTKA 162,165
CHOTKY 117,119,122,124
  William 117,119,120,121,122,123, 124,125,126
CLINTON
  Ella 190,191,192
  Rachel 190,191
  Willis E 191
  Willis R 190
CLOWRY

Robert C 59
COMSTOCK
   Fred 213,214,216,219
COOK
   W C 189,190
COSARPE 57
CO-TAN-NY 311
   Wydie 310
COTSILEE 117
COTS-IL-EE 122
COUNTERMAN
   R M 140
CRABTREE
   Bessie 33
   Braxton 33,34
   Lynn 33
   Malinda 33,34,35
   Melinda 34
   Melindy 35,39,40
   Willie 33
CRAIG
   Lula 135
   Mr 248
CRAWFORD
   Emma 58
CRIESEL
   E C 301
CROME
   William 193,194
   Wm 193,194
CUMSEY
   Annie 275,276,278,279
   Casey 275,276,277,278
   Cassie 277,279
   Lena 275,276,277
   Lewis 275,276,278,279

DAN
   Will 171
DAUGHERTY
   Carrie 321
DAVIDSON
   Charles A 78,224
   Chas A 78,218,224,225,274
DAVIS
   Benjamin 33,34,35,36,37,38,39,40, 41,42,43

Emma 106
Jeff 106
John 33
Lucy 278
Malida 38
Malinda 33,35,36,37,41,42
Mattie 33,34,38,40,41,42
Melinda 34,37
Melindy 35,36,37,39,40,41,43
Millie 150
Samuel 33,34,35,36,37,39,42,43
DAWS
   Mr 223
DAY
   Beatrice 126,127
   Robert 126,127
   Robert, Jr 127,128
   Robert, Sr 127,128
   Vinita 126,127,128
DEARSAW
   David 210,211,212,214,215,217
   Lila 211,212,217
   Maggie 211,212,214,215
   Willie 214,215,217
DEARSHAW
   David 210,217
   Lila 217
   Maggie 217
   Willie 217
DEERE
   John 86,87,88,89,90,91
   Lizzie 86,87,88,89,90,91
   Lucy ... 119,120,121,122,123,124,126
   Wiley 90
   Willey 86,87,88,89,91
   Willy 88
DERISAW 217
   David 210,215,216,218
   Davie 216
   Deavid 213
   Lila 213,216
   Maggie 213,215,216
   Willie 215,216
DOAK
   Mattie 58
DODSON
   J S 211

DONOVAN
  Irwin 238
DOTSON
  Louis 25
DOYLE
  Bedia 7,8,9
  Cecil 30
  Cecil Lee 30,31
  Dell 30,31
  H, Jr 8
  Leo 7,8,9
  Mabel 8
  Sam 7,8,9
  Sebron J 30,31
DRESBACK
  Nellie 12,14,28
  Ralph 11,12,13,14,15,28,29,51,52
DUNN
  Tupper 45,48,49,50,188,189,190
DUNSON
  Lucy 187,189,190
  Lucy Hale 188,189
  Luna E 187,188,189,190
  Raymand 187,188,189,190

ELLIE 94
ELLIS
  Cora 93,96,97,101,102
  Dick 93,95
  Emma 133,135
  Hannah 138
  James 138,139
ENGLISH
  A Z 286
ESCOE
  Charles J 227,230,231,234
  Charlie 229
  Charlie J 227,228,229,230,231,
    232,233
  Chas J 227
  Dora 229,230,231,232,233,234
  Ferdinand 227,230,231,233
  Ferdinand De Soto 229,230
  Ferdinand DeSoto 227,228,233
  Leo Bennet 228
  Leo Bennett 227,228,229,230,231,
    232,233,234

Mr 228
EVERT
  L H 146
EWING
  P P 155,159,165

FEARS
  W T 6
FENNEL
  Joe 281
FIELD
  George 70
FIFE
  Timmie 278
FISHER
  Andrew 206
  Aubrey 1,3
  Carrie 1,3
  Mrs S W 1
  Sam 1,2,3
  Samuel W 1,2
  Sarah C 3
FLEETWOOD
  Solome 32
FLYNN
  Tom 62
FORD
  P M 78,274
FOSTER
  Abe W 169,170,171,172,173,174
  Abraham 173,174,175
  Lucy 169,171,172,173,174,175
  Sallie 169,170,171,172,173
  Susie Mills 169,170,171,172,173,
    174
FOWLER
  J W 108,115,116,117,136,137,138
  Leulah C 108
FRANCIS
  Amos 235,236,240
  Annie 235,236,238,239,240,241
  Elizabeth 235,236,237,240
  Freeland 237,238,239,241
  Lizzie 237
  William 236,238,239,240
FRANK
  Hannah 284,285,287,288,289,290

Noah ...284,285,286,287,288,289,290
Vera 284,285,288,289,290
FULSOM
  Millie 308,309,310,311
  Mrs Thomas 311
  Rhoda 308,309,310,311
  Thomas 309,310,311
  Tom 308,309
FURMAN
  Chas R 85

GAMBLER
  John 73
GANO
  Katy 123
  Nicey 123
GARRIGUES
  Anna 2,32,99,100,202,203, 205,237,292
GIBBONS
  Marha 2
GIERKES
  Wm F A 198,199,200,212,214,215, 220,221,222
GIVENS
  Choctaw 67,69,71,75,80,81,84
  Kizzie 73
GOAT
  John 93
GOBBLER 92
GOBLER 94
GOODEN
  Bessie 201,202
  Jim 201,203
  John 146
  Louisa 175
  Mary 201,203
  Nancy 201,202,206,207,208
GRAYSON
  G W 117,118,119,121,122
  Gertrude 160,161
  Hannah 18,21,25,26
  Hattie 160,161
  Julia 56,57
  Pete 160,161
GREEN
  Hozen 69,70

GREGORY
  Carrie 260,261
  Fletcher Raymond 260,261
  Noah 248,260,301
  Noah W 248
  Nosh 261
GRIESEL 192
  E C 65,92,93,133,139,142,144, 148,149,152,261,301
  Edw C.......... 16,17,45,60,93,120,133, 134,135,136,139,144,145,147,148,151, 161,186,187,224,229,250,251,252, 253,260,269,270,290,295,301,303,304, 309,315,322,324,325,326
  Edward C 248

HAINS
  H G 33,34,37,38,89,205,239
  Henry G 32,37,41,44,100,237
HALE
  Lucy 187
HALL
  Elder D D 79
HAMILTON
  Ed 61,62,63,64,65
  Fannie 63,64
  Louis..........................61,62,63,64,65
HARHOLA
  Jefferson 82
HARJO
  Chito 207
  Ithas 56,57
  Mahalay 52
  Mahaley 53,55,58,59
  Ophelia 52,53
  Ophila..........52,53,54,55,56,57,58,59
  Ophla 52
  Sampson 52,56,57
  Samuel 59
  Simon 52,53,54,55,58,59
  Tulmochus 46
HAR-KO-THE-WAY 92
HARLAN
  John 274
HARLEY
  Jennie 129,130,131,132
  Joseph 129,130,131,132

Index

Sampson 129,130,131,132
Samson 129
HARPER
    Jennie.. 99
HARRIS
    E B 191,192
HARRISON
    R P 169,170,172,173,274,286,287
    Robert P 287
HARRY
    Bunch 325,326
    Jackson 198,199,200
    Jessie 197,198
    John 323,324,325,326
    Liza 324,325
    Lizzie 323
    Mary 323,324,325,326
    Rebecca 322,323
    Rosanna 197,198,199,200
    Susie 323,324
    Wheaton 322,323
    William 197
    Wilson 199,200
HARY
    Jessie 206
    Rosanna 206
    William 206
HAWKINS
    Fannie 61,62,63,64,65
    H S 203
    Louis 62,63,64
    Sarah 59,60
HAYNES
    Martha 107
HENGST
    Charles A 257
    Charles Augustus 257
    Emma J 255,256,257
    Joseph A 255,256
    William C 255,256,257
HENSHAW
    F A 139
HILL
    Richard 201,203
    Richard J 206,304,305
    Selie 72
    Solie 81,83

HITCHCOCK
    E A 56
HOCKING
    Aluca 281
HODJOE
    William 100
HOLCOMB
    G G 266,267
    L C 266,267
    L S 265,266,267
HOLDER
    W W 181,182,317
HOMAHTA
    Chepe 123
    Folle 123
HOPE
    Beaden 106,107,108,109
    Emma 106,107,108,109
    Robert 106,107,108,109
    Willie 106
HUGHES
    George 185
INGRAM
    Janetta 113,114
    Jeanetta 110,111,112
    Jennatte 114
    Sarah 110,111,113
    Sudie 112,113,114
    Thomas 110,111,112,113
    Thomas J 113,114
JACK
    Eddie 63,64
JACOB
    Eli 20
    Millie 20
JACOBS
    Silla 146
JANWAY
    Preston 114
JEFFERSON
    Jane 282,283,284
    John J, Jr 249
    Manuel 282,283,284
    Silas 282,283,284
JOHNSON

Index

Ahullie 45
Elijah T 85
Floyd Ila 85
Indie 45
Lorena 85
Louana 56
Louanna 57
Mandoche 45
Onate 123
Susanna 123
Wiley 45
JONES
  B B 178,179,180
  W P 271,274

KELLEY
  John 119,120
  Mrs 120
  Mrs John 117
  Susanna 11
KELLY
  Amy 123
  John 118
  Rosella 50,51
  Susanna 11,14,50,51
  Wesley 50,51
KERN
  Everett A 289
KERNALS
  Temiye 263
KING
  Elizabeth 115,116
  Henry Lee 116
  John B 115
  Nancy E 115,116,117
  W L 115
KINNAIRD
  R C 314
KNIGHT
  David 144
  Dvid 145
  Hannah 144,145
  Wiley 144,145
KO-TEN-NAY 301

LAFALLIER
  Louis A 56,57

LAND
  A M 286,287
  Rev A M 286
LARNEY
  Cella 149
LARRABEE
  C F 58,283
LEADER
  Absalom 194,196,197
  Absolom 195
  Edward 194,195,196
  Elwood 195
  Joshua 194,195,196,197
  Mahala 194,195,196,197
LEWIS
  Lizzie 231
LIEBER
  J G 33
LIKOWSKI
  Senora 137
LITCHLYTER
  Emma 249
LITTLEHEA
  Po-kan-ney-wee 322
LITTLEHEAD
  Ada 321,322
  Nannie 321,322
  Willie 321,322
LIVINGSTON
  ? W 146
LODIE 162
LONDON
  Ellen 176,178,179,180
LOVE
  Dorcas 231,232,234
LOVETT
  R W 180
LUCAS
  J B 85,86
LYFORD
  Dr H O 288
  H O 289,290,314,315

MCCLANAHAN
  J B 149
MCCLUSKEY
  W S 319,320,321

MCCOMB
William 237
MCCOMBS
Sarah 37,41
William 37
Wm 37
MCCOY
Peggy 56,57
MCDANIEL
Henry A 271,272
Susie 272
MCDANIELS
Julia F 274
MCDERMOTT
J 2,4,14,20,24,47,64,89,100,118,
142,143,144,145,147,148,149,150,151,
152,153,160,161,162,165,186,187,
202,211,240,261,275,277,279,280,287,
290,318
Jesse 43,46,59,60,62,63,64,65,142,
144,145,147,148,149,151,152,160,162,
163,186,187,201,239,250,252,260,
269,270,295,309,315,322,324,325
Jessie 167
MCDOUGAL
D A 312
MCFARLAND
James 4,6,7
Jim 5
Yanch 6,7
Yancy 4,5
MCGILBRA
Jennie 131
Lewis 6
MCGIRT
Lena 56,57
MCGUIRE
William O 2
MCINTOSH
Amos 136,137,138
Ben 170,171
Ellen 176,179,180
Ellen London 178
Elllen London 178
George 56,57
Jihn Granville 177
John 114

John Granville .. 176,177,178,179,180
Julia 56,57
L G 6,67,68,69,70,72,73,82,83,84
Louine 136,137,138
Louise 108
Malissa Christa 136,137
Malissa Christy 136
Mary 114
Maudy Van 137,138
William R 176,177,178,179,180
Wm R 176,179
MACKAY
Bessie Adella 104,105
Cherokee 104,105
George 104,105
MCLEAN
J H 234,235
MCNAC
Alice 142
Caroline 142,143,144
MCNACK
Caroline 198,199,200
Rosey 206
MCNULTY
Cherokee 104,105
MANN
Hannah 133,138,139
J F 133,139
MANTOOTH
Anna 280,281
Annie 282
Isabella 280,281
James H 280,281
MARCH
Estella 192,193,194
William K 192,193,194
Willie H 192,193,194
MARS
F L 257,258,320
James J 256,278,310,311
MARSHALL
Nettie 147,150
MARTHLOCHEE
Fus-hut-che 119
MASSEY
L K 67,68,69,70
MATOY

Maud.................................. 127,128
MAY
   Alfred 170,172
MERITT
   E B... 104
MERRICK
   Edward 34,52,53,91,238,239,292
   Lona...............34,37,38,90,91,239,295
MEWIKE................................ 56
MEWILE................................ 57
MILAN
   A M 30,31
MILLER
   Edgar 18,22,23
   J Y 14,23,24,46,181,211,224,
   228,229,236,275,287
   Mrs N J 80
   Nancy J 80
MILLIEON
   Joseph 194
   Joseph, MD 194
MILLS
   Susie 169,172,174,175
MILLSAP
   Sarah C 226
MILLSAPS
   Naomi 225
MINGO
   Joe 262,263
MITCHELL............................. 156
   Fannie 155,156,157,158,159
   Mahlahsee.............................. 123
   Nancy 157
MONTGOMERY
   A R 225
MOORE
   Cora 53
MORRIS
   Sylvester 210
MORRISON
   Julia 270,271,272,273
   Lula Mildred................... 270,271,273
   Manny 270,271,272,273
   Maurice M 274
   Stan Watie 271,272,273
MORROW
   J B....................... 3,105,231,232,233

Mat H 261
MORTON
   F H 170,172
   W W 296,297
   Wm P................................. 296,297
MOSQUITO
   Jency...................................... 265
MOSS
   F L 163
MOTT
   M L................................. 33,54,125
MRS
   James Maleskey Scott 296
MUKES
   Ada 143,144
   Alice 142,143
   Hattie... 142
   Thomas 142,143

NERO
   Fannie.....................291,292,293,294
   Governor 25,291,292,293,294
   Lucy 292
   Mary 291,292,293,294
   Nancy 291,293
   Sammie...................................... 292
   William..................................... 291
NEUHARD
   C J 51

OSHEA
   Bob 191
OVERSTREET
   John W 183

PA HO SEY AHOLA
   Josie.. 165
PAHO
   Bennie 165
   Josie.. 165
PAHO SEY AHOLA
   Soatka....................................... 165
PAHOSEYAHOLA
   Bennie 162,163,165,167,168
   Josie.......................162,166,167,168
   Soatka....................162,166,167,168
PANTHER

J F 32,33,66,67,196,197
PARKER 181
PARRISH
   Zera E 90,93,181,228,236,239,301
PAYNE
   Annie 282
PEEPAR
   Frank 317,318
   Mary 317,318
   Viney May 317,318
PEEPER
   Frank 316,317
   Mary 316,317
   Mrs Frank 317
   Viney May 316,317
PEMBERTON
   Naana 224
   Naomi 223,226
   Reacy Adeline 223,226
   William T 223,225,226
PENSE
   Malissa 191
PEPPER 306
PERKINS
   Lizzie 262,264
   Muggy 262,264
PERRYMAN
   Hattie 160,161
   Legus 263
   Susanna 160
PETERS
   Isom 28,29,195
PETTIGREW
   Angie 312,313
PHILLIPS
   Jos W 210,211
   Joseph W 211
   Tecumseh 34
   Wisey 34
PIGEON
   Nancy 28,29
PITMAN
   Lucinda 267,268,269,270
   Matilda 268
   Robert 267,268,269,270
   Robert, Jr 267,268,269,270
PITTMAN

   Lucinda 268
   Robert 268
   Robert, Jr 268
PLUMMER
   W A 234,235
PORTER
   J M 219
POSEY
   Alex 4,26,36,39,40,41,44,71,84,
   102,106,107,110,112,119,123,125,131,
   132,158,164
   Eliza Allen 263
   James 263
   John M 263
   Joseph 262
   Josephine 262
   Nancy 40
   T B 263
   Walter 263
POWELL
   Hester 56,57
   Murtle 56
   Myrtle 57
PRUETT
   Hattie 245
PUBERTON
   William 224
PUTT
   E H 63,64

QUERY
   J J 314

RED
   D J 251,252,253,254,255,258,259
REEDY
   W T 183,184
REID
   Wm A 232,233
RESCOM
   Carrie 2
RICHARDSON
   Ivy 56,57
ROBBINS
   James 185
   Mack 185
   Thomas 185

Index

ROBERSON
   Lewis 170
ROBERT
   Eundel 44
   Millie 44
ROBERTS
   Cainey 45,46,48,49
   Cundal 45
   Fucinda 44
   Indie 44,45,46,48,49,50
   Indy 44,47
   Johnson 45,46
   Kendal 46
   Kendall 44,45,46,47,48,49,50
   Mandoche 45
   Mary 45,46,47,48,49,50
   Millie 45
   Wiley 45,48,49,50
   Willie 45
ROBERTSON
   John W 67,68
ROBINS
   Mack 186
   Thomas 186
ROBINSON
   Lewis 169,171,172,174
   Louis 169,172
   Susie Mills 169,172,174
ROBISON
   Lewie 171
   Lewis 174
RODGERS
   Paris 107
ROLLINS
   John W 2
ROOT
   W P 285
   Wm P 288,289
ROUTH
   A L 245
ROWELL
   J R 247
ROWLAND
   Annie 31
   M 31
RUSHING
   Frank W 292,293

SALEECHE 118
SAPULPA
   James 278
SARTY 123
SAR-WA-NO-KA 156
SARWANOKA
   Mary 291
SAR-WA-NO-KE 156
SARWANOKE
   Fannie 155
   Mitchell 155,157
SAR-WA-NO-KE
   Mitchell 155,156
SARWANOKE
   Nancy 155,157
SARWANOKEE
   Fannie 157,159
   Mitchell 157,158,159
   Nancy 157,158,159
SAULSBERRY
   Fred 173
   Raiford 173
SAYLES
   Mary 52
SCOTT
   Billie 295,296,297,298,299,300
   James 295,296,297,298,299,300
   Maleskey ... 295,296,297,298,299,300
   Nicey 296
   Setepake 123
SE-FAR-YES 186
SELF
   Jackson C 180,181,183,184
   James A 182
   Jas R 182
   John R 180,181,182,183,184
   Sarah E 181,182,183,184
SELVIDGE
   Clarence 242
   R B 242
   Susan 243
   Susie 242
SESSIONS
   L L 297,298
SHACKELFORD
   Wm R 225

Index

SHELBY
  David 250,252,260,261,269,270,
  309,315,322,324,325
SHICK
  Roy 170,171
SHOOT
  Se-far-yes 186
SIMMS
  Brunner 208
  Bunner 203,204,205,208,238,306
  Eliza 203,301
  Jesse 202,203,204,205,207,209,238
  Jessie 202,208
  Louisa 301,302,303,305,306
  Louisa Snow 306
  Lucinda 301,302,303,305,306
  Mark 203
  Mary 203,204,205,209
  Maxcey 301
  Maxcy 238,302,303,306
  Maxey 301,303,305,306,307
SIMPSON
  Catherine 141
SIMS
  Bunna 207
  Bunner 200,202,205,206
  Jesse 200,201,202,207,208
  Jessie 205,206
  Louisa 304,305,307
  Lucinda 307
  Lucindy 304,305
  Mark 200
  Mary 201,205,206
  Maxey 200,307
  Maxie 304,305
  May 207
  Sunner 208
SKAGGS
  D C 4,19,26,36,39,40,41,45,71,84,
  102,106,107,110,112,118,119,120,125,
  131,132,158,164
  Dremmam C 128
  Drennan C....3,7,9,26,36,39,40,41,44,
  71,84,108,110,111,112,113,122,123,
  127,131,132,141,158,164,242,271,272
SKY
  Motley 103

Nancy 103
SMITH
  A A 105,231,232,233
  Bennie 162,163,164,165,166,167,
  168
  Chotka 130,131,163,164,166
  Jessie 131
  Joseph 162,163,164,165,166,167
  Josiff 5
  Lawrence 56,57
  Mary 4,5,6,7
SMOCK
  J C 25
SNAKIS 207
SNAPP
  Amanda 209
  Cicero 209
  Stella 209
SNOW
  Capanny 306
  Ca-Pon-na 317
  Hattie 306
  Louisa 306
  Wesley 306
  Yarla Cowera 306
SPEER
  Lucy J 256,257
STALEY
  Annie 324,325,326
  John 250,251,252,253,254,255
  Kissie 251,254,255
  Kizzie 250,251,254,255
  Nellie 252,253,254
  Sa-Co-Ta 251
  Sa-co-ta 252
  Sa-Co-Ta 253,254,259
  Sak-co-ta ...250,252,253,254,255,260
STARR
  Annie 92,93,95,96,97,98,99,
  100,101,102,103
  Charles 96,98,99
  Charley 92
  Charlie 93,94,100,101
  Clara 93,95,96,97,98,101,102,103
  Cora 97
  Cora Ella 92
  Cora Ellis 92,96,98,99,100,102,103

Frank 95,96,98
Gertrude 92,93,95,97,99,100,101,
102,103
Gertrued 93
Henry 92,93,95,96,97,98,99,100,
101,102,103
Jesse 97
Jesse J 96,99,100,102,103
Jesse, Jr 92
Jessie 99
Mr 93
STATON
Will 206
SUTHERLAND
George 56,57

TAGGART
T J 317
TATE
Annie May 312,313
Flora Ada 311,312,313,314,315
J W 312,313
John W 313,314
John Washington 311,314,315
Jon W 315
Mary 311,312,313,314,315
Mary P 312
TECUMSEH
Austin 13,15,16
Edward 9,10,12
Effie 9,10,11
Mary 13,15,16,17
Nancy 9,10,11,12,13,15,16,17
Nero 9,10,11,12,51
Rosa 13,15,16
THOMAS
Lizzie 259
THOMPSON
Josephine 282
R B 314
THORNSBURY
Rachael 85
TIGER
Cassie 276,277,279
Chotka 118
Chotky 119,121,122,123
Daniel 59,60

George 263
Joseph 89
Lena 277
Lewis 277
Lillie 89
Lizzie 250,253,259,260
Lizzie Thomas .. 251,252,254,258,259
Lucy 118
Mahala 195
Martha 59,60
Nellie 60,64,65
Porter 258,259,260
S W 255
Sallie 81
Sarah 59,60
Stand Waity 251,253,258,259
Stanwaitie 259,260
Susan 243
Susie 242
William 118,123,125
TINGLEY
Hannah 286
TOLLESON
W A 9,31

VANDERGRIFF
Hazy Ann 58
VAUGHN
C A 268
John W 56,57
VIERSEN
A A 297,298
VORE
Tewahley 196,197
VORS
Mrs Tewahley 195

WALCOTT
Arthur 210
WALL
Mrs Cathren 256
WARLICK
J W 265
WASHINGTON
Catherine 140,141
E M 141
Edward M 140

M M 31
Sue 140,141
Taye 83
Tayo 81
WATSON
 D H 198,199,200
WATTS
 Mary 105
WEBBER
 Harrie B 246
WEEKS
 Clue W 268
 John W 268,269
WEST
 Dr G W 243
 Ella 47
 Geo W, MD 243
 Louisa 201,203
 Mary 45
WHITE
 Annie 236
 Clara 135
 Craft 132,133,135
 Emma 132,133,135
 George 68,69,70,71,72,73,74,
  75,76,83
 Hattie 247
 Laura 18,19,20,21,24,25,26,27
 Lizzie 67,68,69,71,72,73,74,75,76
 M H 24
 Mac 25
 Mack 18,19,20,21,23,26
 Mark H 24,25
 Myrtle Izona 132,133,134
 Phenia 20,22,24,25,27
 Phenie 18,19,26
 Sarah 68,69,70,71,72,73,74,75,76,
  81,82,83,84
WILLIAMS
 Dinah 236,237,239,241,242
 Mary Jane 58
WILLIES
 Rogee 306
 Wesley 306
WILSON
 Jesse E 284
 Mahala 195

Noonley 195
Simeon J 195
WINELAND
 H L 249
WINN
 Virgil 292,293
WINSTON
 J A 246
 James A 246
 Jas A 218,246
WISENER
 Annie D 173
 Ben J 173
WISNER
 Annie D 173
WITE
 Laura 26
 Mac 26
 Phenia 26

YAHOLA
 Chotka 163
 Jefferson 80,82,83,84
 Joseph 163
 Sampson 82,83,84
 Sarah 70,83,84
YARHALAR
 Sarah 71,75,83
YARHOLA
 Jefferson 81
 Sarah 74
YOAKUM
 Martin M 57
YOUNG
 Myra 96
 N S 218
 Sam 178

ZEVELY
 Forest 181

www.ingramcontent.com/pod-product-compliance
Lightning Source LLC
Chambersburg PA
CBHW020243030426
42336CB00010B/589